BUT

HE NEVER HIT ME

BUT

HE NEVER HIT ME

The Devastating Cost of
Non-Physical Abuse to Girls and Women

Dr. Jill A. Murray

iUniverse, Inc.

New York Lincoln Shanghai

But He Never Hit Me
The Devastating Cost of Non-Physical Abuse to Girls and Women

iUniverse books may be ordered through booksellers or by contacting:

iUniverse
2021 Pine Lake Road, Suite 100
Lincoln, NE 68512
www.iuniverse.com
1-800-Authors (1-800-288-4677)

The information, ideas, and suggestions in this book are not intended as a substitute for professional advice. Before following any suggestions contained in this book, consult your physician or mental health professional. Neither the author nor the publisher shall be liable or responsible for any loss or damage allegedly arising as a consequence of your use or application of any information or suggestions in this book.

ISBN-13: 978-0-595-41139-9 (pbk)
ISBN-13: 978-0-595-85497-4 (ebk)
ISBN-10: 0-595-41139-8 (pbk)
ISBN-10: 0-595-85497-4 (ebk)

Printed in the United States of America

To Frank
I'm everything I am because you loved me.
(From the song "Because You Loved Me," by Dianne Warren)

Contents

Preface xiii

Introduction xix

Part I   *WHAT IS IT? WHY NONPHYSICAL ABUSE IS SO INSIDIOUS*

CHAPTER 1   Some Universal Truths and Why They Are So
Important to You 5

CHAPTER 2   What Is Nonphysical Abuse? 17

CHAPTER 3   Who Are Nonphysical Abusers? 36

CHAPTER 4   How This Whole Mess Began: Your Original
Abusers and What They Told You 48

Part II   *BUT WHAT IF HE'S RIGHT? UNDERSTANDING YOURSELF AND YOUR RELATIONSHIPS*

CHAPTER 5   A Slippery Slope: The Many Faces of Nonphysical
Abuse 71

CHAPTER 6   Victims? 83

CHAPTER 7   How Your Abusive Relationship Affects the Way
You Feel, Think, Act, and React 90

CHAPTER 8   Does He Really Love You, and, For That Matter,
Do You Really Love Him? 97

CHAPTER 9   Are You a People-Pleaser, Martyr, Codependent,
             Drama-and-Chaos Junkie? 103

CHAPTER 10   Could Low Self-Esteem Have Anything to Do
             with This Mess? 116

Part III   WHAT ARE THE COSTS? DO YOU HAVE TO
             GIVE UP ON YOURSELF IF YOU GIVE UP ON
             HIM?

CHAPTER 11   Overwhelming Feelings of Grief, Loss, Anger,
             Guilt, Shame, and Fear That Keep You Stuck 129

CHAPTER 12   What You're Feeling Is Normal 145

CHAPTER 13   Why Can't He Just Change? 151

CHAPTER 14   Resolving Unfinished Business with Your Family
             of Origin so That You Can Move On 158

Part IV   WHAT ARE THE STEPS TO GET OUT?
             MAKING DECISIONS AND TAKING A STAND

CHAPTER 15   You Have Rights! 173

CHAPTER 16   Should You Stay or Leave? 179

CHAPTER 17   Actions to Take before You Leave 192

CHAPTER 18   What He'll Do If You Leave 208

Part V   GETTING BETTER—CHANGING YOUR
             LIFE! MOVING FORWARD INTO YOUR
             NONABUSIVE LIFE

CHAPTER 19   Who Are You Really, and What Do You Want?
             Getting to Know Yourself Again 219

CHAPTER 20   Changing Your Abusive Relationship Patterns 232

CHAPTER 21   Becoming Your Own Good Parent 245

CHAPTER 22   The Temptation to Go Back to Him If You Are
Broke or Feel Lonely and Scared 253

CHAPTER 23   Are You Self-Abusive? 263

Part VI   *MOVING FORWARD HOW TO BUILD NEW*
RELATIONSHIPS IN YOUR NEW LIFE

CHAPTER 24   Are You an Abusive Parent? 277

CHAPTER 25   Looking for Nonabusive Men ... and Women 287

CHAPTER 26   Dealing with Your "Ex" in Your New Life 301

CHAPTER 27   Off You Go! 308

Resource Guide 313

About the Author 321

Acknowledgments

First and foremost, I'd like to thank all the wonderful women who have shared their stories and their lives with me. You are all so strong and courageous. I know that life holds amazing and remarkable secrets for you to discover.

To my agents, Arielle Ford and Brian Hilliard: You are two of the kindest people I have the pleasure of knowing. I learn so much from the two of you. Thank you for all that you've meant to me. I hope our association will continue and grow even stronger.

To the staff and residents of Laura's House Domestic Violence Shelter: Thank you for sharing yourselves with me and for the courage, dedication, and faith that inspire me every day. I owe so much to all of you.

To superior court judge Pamela Iles: I am humbled to be your friend. You are my hero and role model. Your dedication to those in pain amazes me on a daily basis. Thank you for all that you are.

To my "sister," Myra Gordon: You're the best friend any woman could have. I feel honored just to walk in your shadow.

To Dr. Paul Fick: You will always be the person who started this wonderful journey for me. You taught me to be a therapist and opened every door to my publishing career. You are unfailingly generous, funny, warm, and wise. I will always be in your debt. Thank you.

To Aunt Cathi and Uncle Bob: I hope you know how much we all love you both. What amazing friends and neighbors you are. I couldn't do half of what I do, or do it half as well, without your love and support.

To my husband, Dr. Frank Murray III: I will never stop thanking you for taking this little, brokenhearted person and helping to make me who I am today. I would never be where I am without you, Frank. You have shown me that true love can and does heal a lifetime of pain.

To my children, Jennifer and Michael: OK, I won't get mushy this time. Please know how much I love you. I have complete pride in the two of you. You will always be my greatest accomplishments and what I am most proud of. You are lovely and compassionate people. I am proud to know you.

Preface

The Devastating Costs of an Abusive Relationship

I should have gotten out sooner. If I had one piece of information to pass on to other women, that would be it. I don't know how else to say it. This last relationship nearly killed me emotionally, spiritually, financially, and even physically. In the end, the costs were much too great for the small benefits I got from it.

I was with a man for five years who seemed to have it all together. He was great at his job, great with his kids, great with other people. In the beginning, he was great with me, too.

I thought I was a good girlfriend. I thought I was giving him everything he asked for and lots of things he never had to ask for. I'd bring in and pick up his dry cleaning because I knew he was so busy. His house was so disorganized you couldn't find anything, so sometimes, if he was away for the day with his kids, I'd come in and surprise him by cleaning out closets or organizing his garage for him. There were tons of things he had taken from his marriage that he hadn't done anything with for the last six years, so I helped him with them. I'd make him dinners and give him massages. I didn't think of myself as his little slave; I was just treating him in the same kind and considerate manner that I'd have liked to be treated.

Now, keep in mind that I had an executive-level job. I was making almost a hundred thousand dollars per year. I had my own home, car, and great handbags! I could take trips and didn't have a lot of financial worries. I had a master's degree and good friends. I was no dumb bunny on any level. I was a single girl making my way in a man's world and doing OK with it. My guy was successful in his professional career, as well, and owned his own home and stuff. His two kids lived with their mom five miles from his house, so they saw each other as much as they all wanted, which was a few times a week.

I had always struggled with a weight issue. I was usually twenty to thirty pounds overweight. I came from a heavy family and learned bad habits early on. I'm tall, so the weight never looked as bad as it would have on a smaller person. Plus, it never held me back in terms of popularity in school or my career. I didn't look like a skinny Minnie but certainly didn't look fat, either. My current boyfriend and I always had a very pleasing and dynamic sex life, and he never made any comments about my body. Admittedly, I had put on maybe another ten or fifteen pounds during our relationship, just because I was playing wife so much and making him gourmet meals a few times a week and not getting as much exercise as I used to.

You can probably imagine my surprise when I started bringing up the idea of marriage and asking what his intentions for our relationship were, and he told me that my weight not only bothered him, but he was worried about my health because of it and couldn't think about a future with me while my weight was so high.

This took me by surprise and shocked me. I wasn't prepared for this. I tried to get him to quantify what he meant by losing weight: was it a number on the scale, a dress size, a fitness level, or what? He couldn't tell me but said that he'd know it when he saw it. I was totally confused by that. Like everyone else, I had lost weight and gained it back again a hundred times. Why was he judging me on my appearance all of a sudden?

I decided I was willing to lose the weight, because I didn't want to lose him. I was frustrated and felt horrible about myself. I also began eating better because I wanted to feel better. I also started exercising with a friend. In two weeks, I lost eight pounds.

When I told him this, instead of being proud of me, he said, "How much more do you have to lose? About forty pounds?"

I said, "I don't know, master, you never gave me a number. Are you saying you wanted me to lose about fifty pounds? I'd look like a stick then." He dropped the subject.

I continued talking to him about my feelings, and while he seemed to care, he was more focused on the weight. He also told me that he had been planning to propose to me a couple of years ago, but then I put on another five pounds or so, and he didn't ask. I asked him why he was so focused on my weight and not my character or the ways I'd been there for him during the last five years. He told me he loved me but couldn't get past the weight. You'd think I weighed 400 pounds! I was forty pounds over what I thought I should ideally be, and that was all. Losing that would be difficult, but it was definitely doable. I told him I could lose that by the time I had to fit into a wedding dress if he gave me a ring and a date. He grinned and side-stepped the question.

This got me thinking a lot and ultimately made me pretty mad. I started discussing some of these things with him because I really did love him. I felt trapped, not knowing what to do.

Then entered Dr. Jill Murray into my life.

She and I began working together because I had gotten to the point where I was unhappy with myself. I was no spring chicken, and I'd never been married before or had kids. At that point, I was in my late thirties and didn't know where the relationship was headed. I sort of drifted along with him and his wishes.

Dr. Jill asked me to think about whether I was in an unhealthy relationship, and I remember telling her, "WELL, HE NEVER HIT ME." She told me about all the different types of nonphysical abuses that occur to women that they're not even aware of. I was shocked at how many abuses I was exposed to in this relationship. He really seemed so sweet and kind.

Dr. Jill told me that I was always trying to prove my worthiness to him and show him that I was good marriage material. I was giving him a sneak preview of what he'd be signing up for if he actually popped the question. I didn't realize it at the beginning, but I think she was right. He always seemed to be very appreciative of what I did for him. I loved him, and I really cared for his kids, so I wanted to do these things for all of them. Dr. Jill would ask me why I didn't question that I wasn't getting any of these sorts of things in return and why it was OK with me to constantly give, give, give without any expectations of reciprocal behavior. I think she had a point.

Dr. Jill told me that I needed to lose weight for myself, if it seemed like it was a self-esteem or health problem. She also questioned whether my boyfriend feared commitment and what would happen if I lost the weight and then he said, "Well, I've seen you lose weight before, and you've gained it back. How do I know you're not going to do this again?" She thought he was putting all sorts of false roadblocks up and asked me to think about why I was good enough to have sex with but not marry. She asked me to consider what I wanted for myself and why he was allowed to make demands and have expectations of me with all his weird behaviors, but I wasn't allowed to make demands that he change some of his.

It was then that I began to realize how many times I had left his house or just been with him and felt lonely or frustrated and drove through a fast-food place to ease the pain. I had actually put on quite a bit of weight in this relationship because I was unhappy with him! While this was a revelation, it also scared me to death. What did this mean? What was I going to do?

We talked about all the different ways he held all the cards in the relationship and what the costs were to me because of being with him. I looked at everything I had sacrificed: (1) my relationship with my family, because they were angry that I had stayed with someone for that long who wasn't marrying me; (2) my relationships with my friends, because they were getting far less of my time as I obsessively took care of him; (3) aspects of my career, because I had been offered a job promotion to move to another state but didn't want to do that so that I could be with my boyfriend; (4) positive feelings I once had for myself; (5) my spiritual connection, because I stopped going to church when he wanted to spend Sunday mornings together and didn't have the kids; (6) probably my chance to have children, because now I was nearly forty years old. There was probably a lot more, but I'm still trying to sort through all of it.

To be honest, I'm still in the process of making a lot of decisions about what I want to do now. He's a smart guy and seems salvageable; I just don't know how hard I want to work on this anymore. Dr. Jill thinks my energies would be better spent working that hard on myself. That's still a difficult concept for me after five years of focusing on him and his needs, so she and I are now working on why I prefer to do that instead.

That's tough.

"HE NEVER HIT ME." That just sounds so weird to me now. As I said, I should have gotten out sooner. After five years, it's really hard now. I have so much of my life and my self-esteem tied up with him and also my relationship with his children. If I had left when he didn't commit to me after a year or so, my life would be so much easier than it is now.

—Kerrie, age forty

How could I only be seventeen and be on my third creepy relationship? I don't understand it myself. I wish I understood how to tell if a guy was going to be a creep later in the relationship, because they all start out really nice. About a month into the relationship, my mom gets on my case, because she tells me the guy isn't any good. This starts a big deal and a whole lot of anger between us. I hate her and don't believe what she's saying. Once, I ran away from home and lived with him and his family. So far, she's been right about the guys, and I hate that. I don't want her to be right, and I try to prove to her that she's wrong about them. Now, she's said the same thing about my new boyfriend.

The thing is, I really like having a boyfriend. It makes me feel better about myself. I like feeling that I belong to someone, and I like knowing that I have a date and someone to talk to.

I know I probably have sex with the guys too soon. I always tell myself that I'm going to wait longer than a few dates, but then I don't. I get scared about losing them, and they tell me they really care about me. It feels good to make them happy that way, and it makes me also feel very connected to them. My mother always tells me that guys don't connect that way like girls do. Could that be true? It's hard for me to believe. I don't like myself after I have sex with a guy and then he acts like he doesn't know me.

I don't see my friends when I have a boyfriend. Either my boyfriends want me to spend all my time with them, or I just choose to do that. My friends get mad at me and feel like they are second best. When I break up with a guy, I try to get back with my friends, and they are really mad at me and say things like, "Well, I guess now that you don't have a boyfriend, we're good enough for you again." I can't blame them for being mad.

My boyfriends usually end up telling me that my clothes and hair aren't quite right, and they have suggestions about how they want to see me look. They get jealous when I talk to other guys and definitely don't want me to hang out with them. I start fighting more with my mom, and my grades go down, because I feel so stressed so much of the time and can't concentrate.

It's hard for me to see these things when I'm with them, because most of the time it's really a good relationship. I know some girls with bad boyfriends get hit or knocked around, and my boyfriends HAVE NEVER HIT ME or anything like that.

I'm worried that if I keep getting involved with creepy boyfriends, my self-esteem will go even lower, and by the time I'm ready to get married, I'll end up with one of these types of guys as my husband. That really scares me. I don't know how to change this pattern and make better choices in a boyfriend.

—Laurel, age seventeen

Being in an abusive relationship is devastating on so many levels. You know this firsthand, don't you? When you really think about it, this may not be your first unhealthy relationship. If you've spent more than a month in this type of relationship, the devastation has already begun. That feeling just continues to multiply with each subsequent abusive man you bring into your life and into your heart.

The subtitle of this book is *The Devastating Cost of Nonphysical Abuse to Teenage Girls and Women.* In the course of this book we will discuss the many and varied ways you have suffered by your involvement with unhealthy, unrewarding relationships. For now, let me share with you some of the costs I personally experienced while in my first marriage:

- My health

- My self-esteem

- The professional life I wanted to create

- My children's well-being and sense of security

- My feeling of optimism and hopefulness

- My relationship with my higher power

- My relationship with my family

- My relationships with my friends

- My finances

- My feelings of powerfulness

- My ability to control my life, thoughts, and feelings

- My sense of trust in my own decisions

• Some of the better years of my life

• My ability to believe in myself

• My ability to concentrate and focus

• A lot of sleep

Throughout this book you will be developing your own list of what your relationship has cost you, and you will undoubtedly add to it as you become more aware.

In the course of reading this book you will see that no one is completely immune to abusive relationships. Many smart, productive, successful women of all ages as well as educational, religious, economic, and social backgrounds can and do become involved in emotionally abusive relationships. Abuse does not discriminate; it is an equal-opportunity offender.

At the beginning of this chapter, Kerrie mentioned that she should have gotten out of her relationship sooner. Maybe that's true. She certainly has her own list of costs, and there's a portion of her life—and yours—that she won't be able to get back again. Perhaps that's a good thing. If you are able to take those memories and learn something from the relationship, perhaps it won't be for nothing. We all resent the time we lost in an unhealthy relationship, time we can't make up. All we have is now—and the terrific opportunity to make better and healthier choices.

How many times have you said to yourself "I'll get out of this relationship when——"? Perhaps today is the day when you decide the costs are too devastating and that you deserve more. Maybe not. Today you may want knowledge about who you are, what your rights are, and whether or not you have options. Knowledge is never a bad thing. Remember: when you've lost yourself, the cost is then far too great.

I hope you gain personal wisdom and power through reading the rest of this book.

Introduction

Janice sat across from me on the leather couch in my office. Her long, shiny hair was pulled back in the current, semimessy fashion. You know the hairstyle I'm talking about; Cameron Diaz and Gwyneth Paltrow have perfected that sexy, bed-head 'do to a T.

Janice looked as though she could be a glamorous celebrity, one who was playing the gorgeous, accomplished, has-it-all, brains-and-beauty, wouldn't-you-just-hate-her-if-she-weren't-so-sweet wife of the dashingly handsome millionaire. Well, yes, Janice appeared to be the gal for the part, except that if you looked a little closer at our heroine, you'd see that she was also emotionally beaten down, depressed, confused, and lonely. She wasn't allowed to spend a dime of "his" money without his doling it out to her like a child. She had lost all her former friends, she had desperately wanted a child for the last eight years (but he didn't, so they didn't), and she couldn't remember who she used to be.

Janice had it all … and she had nothing at all.

At the age of thirty-six, Janice lived in the best neighborhood, volunteered on the best charitable committees, didn't have to work, and had designer clothes and lots of "bling." She drove a new Jaguar every two years and had a housekeeper three days a week, even though she and her husband were the only ones living in their enormous home. No kids, no pets, infrequent dinner parties.

Janice became my patient because her husband told her she must be crazy and needed immediate psychological help. How could she possibly be tired when she didn't "do anything"? Why was she depressed when he gave her everything under the sun and then some? How could she be lonely when she spent her days with other women planning fundraisers for the local animal shelter, children's home, or gardening society? Yes, he decided, the only answer must be that she was completely nuts and was ungrateful for all he gave her, and she'd better fix it right away.

Would he come to therapy with her, she once inquired? He laughed and told her that now he was convinced she was crazy; he was happy as a clam, and if he was happy, surely he didn't need help. The only thing making him unhappy these days—he told her several times a week—was that he had to beg her for sex.

She wasn't the carefree, sexy, young thing she once was, which really ticked him off. He told her she was turning into a hag with no zest for life. He said she had become a real bore.

"You know, there are plenty of women at my office just waiting to get a piece of me. You should see how they flirt with me. I'm telling you, these bitches are just shameless," he'd tell her, gloating and preening. "They wear those short skirts you used to wear, and the high heels. Sure, it's probably not appropriate dress for the office, but damned if I'm going to tell them! These young girls are hot. You can practically see the sex oozing out of their pores when they look at me."

Then, inevitably, he'd see the hurt expression on Janice's face, and he'd quickly add, "Oh, babe, I'd probably never go for them, even though they want me bad. I'm just telling you that there are other fish in the sea, and if you were the smart girl you used to be, you'd make sure I didn't decide to stick my pole in the water." Then, he'd laugh salaciously and squeeze her breasts and buttocks. "Whadaya say, cowgirl? Wanna take a turn riding the bucking bronco, or should I head out to the fillies at the office steno pool?" he'd say, badly mixing his metaphors.

Janice hated when he sounded like a jerk and tried to make her feel insecure. It was all a moot point anyway, because she knew for a fact that he had been cheating on her for about four years with a variety of young women; some were barely out of high school, and some were college coeds. She figured all of them were too young and impressionable to know any better.

As I got to know Janice better, her privileged but miserable life became clearer and clearer. Brett, her husband, insulted her every move, was insanely jealous if she chatted politely with the men in his firm, doled out every dollar she had and wanted an accounting of how and where she spent it, made ten to twenty calls to her cell phone each day to see where she was and what she was doing. He gave her advice on her hairstyles, makeup, and clothing and went with her to buy them, and he bought all of her jewelry as "gifts" so that she didn't have a say in what was chosen. He kept her from seeing her family members, and he frequently called her "stupid," "lazy," "crazy," "ridiculous," "whore," "bitch," and a host of other horrible—and untrue—names. Though she had once been a devout member of the Catholic Church, he ridiculed her religious beliefs to the point that she felt like he had spies watching her if she went to Mass during the week while he was at work. He seemed to know when she went to confession (wanting to know exactly what and why she had to confess), and in which pew she knelt to pray.

Janice felt like a caged animal. But she didn't leave her husband, because so many times he was sweet and wonderful; she still loved him for those times, wishing there could be more of them, feeling it was all her fault that there weren't. Everybody loved him; that was very nearly a fact. He was charming, outgoing, generous, smart, and funny. How and why would she ever leave a man like that? That would prove that she was crazy, wouldn't it? I mean, she had every need taken care of, didn't she?

I listened to Janice and her quandary for three sessions and then said to her very quietly, "You are in an abusive relationship."

Janice looked dumbfounded. She looked as if she had misheard me. She asked me why I would make such a ridiculous statement. I repeated back to her all of the emotionally, verbally, psychologically, financially, and spiritually unkind behaviors he displayed toward her. She sat still and was quiet for what seemed like hours but was really only minutes. And then she said it:

"BUT HE'S NEVER HIT ME. I couldn't be in an abusive relationship. He's never laid a hand on me. You're all wrong about Brett. It's me. I'm the one with the problem. No matter what I do, I can't make him happy, and I'm not happy with myself, either. He's not an abuser. You must be crazy yourself to think that. Maybe I've given you the wrong impression about him. He's really a wonderful man. I'm just not doing enough. He has a very stressful job and gives me everything I could ask for. It's me; can't you see that? He's never hit me!"

To tell you the truth, I was relieved to see that Janice still had this much passion and conviction in her voice. Her husband hadn't taken that completely away from her. That boded well for a good prognosis.

So began our weekly sessions for the next five months. I worked with Janice on recognizing that not all abuse is physical. As a matter of fact, most abuse is *not* physical. I helped her look honestly at the unhealthy behaviors in her marriage and the ways in which she was discounting—and therefore complying with—them. I helped her see her value as a person, a woman, and a wife, and then decide what she wanted for herself. We talked about her childhood, her mom and dad's marriage, and what she was told about herself when she was young. Janice did a tremendous amount of work on herself.

Did she leave Brett? Well, let's save that answer for later in the book, because I'd like you to determine for yourself, based on what you learn while reading this book, what you think she did. Given your new knowledge, I'd like you to decide what you would have done if you were Janice. As you know from your own situation, there are a lot of variables in a relationship, and nothing is as easy or clearcut as it seems to others, is it?

Janice was lucky; she had many options from which to choose. So do you. You can read, think, choose how you act and react to any situation. You have free will and can choose your own destiny. What? You mean it doesn't feel that way to you? Well, let me tell you, when I told wealthy, beautiful, intelligent Janice the same thing, she looked at me as if I were an alien and then laughed.

"You must have me confused with someone else. I don't have any choices at all," she once told me. Now, if that girl doesn't have choices, who does, right?

You, that's who. You have every single option available to Cameron Diaz, Gwyneth Paltrow, Catherine Zeta-Jones, Celine Dion, Nicole Kidman, and me. (Tricky how I insinuated myself into that group, wasn't it!)

I understand where you are mentally and emotionally right now, because I lived in the same state for many, many years. As a child I was sexually abused for several years and was left alone by my mother to raise myself and my little brother. I was the keeper of the responsibility for her well-being and emotional safety from a very young age until I left home at eighteen. I felt intensely lonely and frightened almost all of the time, and then I married a wonderful guy way too young, had two amazing children—twins—and found out that neither myself nor my husband knew a thing about being married. I re-experienced the loneliness and neglect I had endured when I was a child and didn't see the obvious and longstanding unacceptable behavior on his part. While I was funny, smart, popular, and very happily involved (well, OK, overinvolved) in my children's lives as a stay-at-home mom, I was more miserable and desperate than I can even express. How did my life become this catastrophic mess that felt completely out of my control? How did I go from a college student who felt I had the world by the tail to a pathetic woman pretending to be happy when I was barely eighty-three pounds, chronically ill, and crying in my closet so my children wouldn't hear me?

Probably pretty much the same way you did. I was unhappy, but hey, my relationship wasn't abusive or anything! HE NEVER HIT ME. He never even came close to hitting me. If anything, I probably came closer to hitting him out of frustration and desperation, although, of course, I never did.

This book is all of our stories, isn't it? We are all in this together and will share our strength as we go through this.

Today, I am so happy. I can't even believe this is my life. I'm married to my second husband. Though far from perfect, he is the world's most wonderful man and the perfect person for me. My children have graduated from college and are terrific people in their own right. I am successful both personally and professionally, and I have fabulous, non-narcissistic, and generous friends who care about their world, me, and themselves. My life has become so much easier.

How did this miraculous transformation take place? Ah, well, that is what I am going to share with you in this book. Actually, once you make a commitment to yourself and your emotional health, it's quite simple. By the time you finish reading this book, you will have the knowledge and tools to make crucial and life-altering changes for yourself. You will know where you came from, where you are, why you got caught up in an abusive relationship, where you want to go, and how to get there.

"BUT HE NEVER HIT ME." I've heard those words uttered by hundreds—maybe even thousands—of women as proof that they are not in unhealthy, destructive relationships, proof that they are crazy for being unhappy or disenchanted. And every time I hear that phrase, I am sickened. Let me be the first to tell you, you deserve so much more from your relationship than simply being able to say your partner does not hit you.

Throughout this book you will find stories of women's lives as told in their own words. Because this book's content is pertinent to women of all ages, the tales I've included are authored by women from different stages of life—from very young womanhood on up. Please don't be put off by the age of the story-teller and assume that, because she is not in your age group, her story has little or no meaning for you. You will soon see that this is not true.

As a woman in your forties, for example, you may read the story of a sixteen-year-old and say to yourself, "I was experiencing the same things at sixteen. Maybe, if I had learned about abusive relationships when I was her age, I wouldn't be where I am now. Oh, I wish I could talk to her." Or, maybe her story will inspire you to think, "I have a daughter her age. I wonder if she's going through the same feelings as this girl." Perhaps you are a teenage woman reading the story of a woman in her thirties. Rather than immediately thinking you couldn't possibly relate to her feelings, you might ask yourself, "I wonder if she had abusive boyfriends in high school? If I don't get out of my current relationship now, is this what my future will look like?" The answer, on both accounts, is probably yes.

Truly, my desire is to have all women, regardless of age, feel a connection through these stories. There is tremendous untapped power in women's solidarity and their understanding of each other's experiences and points of view. Age need not be a divisive factor. My intention, through these stories, is to allow you to learn not only from me, but from each other.

PART I

WHAT IS IT?
WHY NONPHYSICAL ABUSE
IS SO INSIDIOUS

OK, this may sound really pathetic, but I actually don't care that my boyfriend cheats on me. It's not like sex is such a big deal, anyway. He just does his thing with me, and then either I go home, he goes home, or we watch a video. It doesn't mean a lot, so why should I care that he does it with other girls? He tells me that sex is all I'm good for, so in a way it's a compliment, don't you think? It's not like we go out and do stuff or that he introduces me to his friends or even his parents, so technically, we're not even dating. We just hook up a couple of times a week.

Yeah, sometimes I wish that I had a real boyfriend, but guys just seem to want me for sex. I guess I'm pretty good at it. I don't get anything out of it, if you know what I'm saying. It's mainly for them. Sometimes, when I think about all of it, it makes me really sad, so I try not to think about it very much. I used to cut myself when I thought about my life and guys and stuff, but the scars were getting nasty, so now I just drink or smoke some dope, and that takes care of it. I try to make sure that I use some dope before I have sex, too. It makes it better for me.

I've been called a lot of names, both by guys and by my mom. She doesn't like me very much, and I don't like her, either. She's a real nag, and she let me be abused by a couple of her boyfriends when I was younger. She says she didn't know about what they were doing, but I don't believe her.

The guys who are interested in me are creeps, I guess, but I like having guys pay attention to me. It would be nice to have a guy really care about me as a person, but to tell you the truth, I'm not sure what they would care about. I'm not that interesting or pretty, and I'm definitely not smart. A lot of guys call me stupid, and they're right. My grades are bad, and I don't care about school, so I don't do the work. I just show up to get out of the house and see my friends.

I don't have any plans after I graduate. I don't know what I want to do. I know I want to get as far away from here as possible, but that's really all. Maybe I'll find a guy who wants to get out also and will take me with him.

A few of my girlfriends have told me that all of my relationships with guys are bad and harmful. I don't know what they're talking about, because NONE OF THEM HAVE EVER HIT ME. Sometimes I get pushed or shoved, or I've had a couple of guys who like to pull my hair or call me names when we have sex, but it's no-big-deal stuff. I don't think they are bad guys. If I did, I'd leave them.

—Patti, age sixteen

If I had a dime for every time a woman said to me, "But he never hit me," my last name would be Getty, not Murray.

Popular wisdom suggests that all abuse is physical, so if a woman doesn't have a black eye or a broken arm, she doesn't consider herself abused, and neither does the outside world. In fact, physical abuse—hitting, shoving, choking, grabbing, and assaulting by any means—constitutes the vast *minority* of abuse. The vast *majority* consists of verbal, emotional, psychological, financial, and spiritual abuse. That's what you and I are going to discuss and resolve in this book.

You are going to hear me use the word *behavior* quite a bit in the coming chapters. That's because, in therapy sessions and in my everyday life, I look largely at a person's behavior to inform me who they really are. I believe very strongly that LOVE IS A BEHAVIOR. I do not mean merely words of love; we can all say anything that will get us what we want. Love, friendship, and respect are all behaviors. What I'm talking about is the way we are treated and, for that matter, the way we treat others.

If you are a mom, consider this: how would your children really know and understand that you love them if you said "I love you" without backing that statement up with loving actions? They wouldn't, right? You cannot hit or spank your children and tell them that you love them; love and violence do not go hand in hand. Then why do we, as women, so often settle for unkind, unloving behaviors from the most important people in our lives? So often we fall into the daze of thinking, "I'm sure he loves me because he tells me he does." What kind of non-sense is that? So, in this book, I am going to repeat LOVE IS A BEHAVIOR over and over again until I'm certain that you not only understand it, but are living it on a day-to-day basis. You won't believe how easy your life will become when you start conducting yourself according to this simple rule.

But I digress … In this first part of our book, we are going to talk about universal truths of life that will completely change the ways you look at your world and the ways you've allowed others to treat you. I promise you that once you "get" these ideas, your life will become 100 percent easier.

Next, we'll uncover the types of abuse you may have been living with. You will be surprised at what abuse actually looks like in real life. Then I will give you a blueprint of who a typical abuser really is. He may not look like what you were expecting. Finally, we will strip away some childhood messages that you may have received—knowingly or unknowingly—that have set you up for a future unhealthy relationship. Who knew? We will also debunk some common myths about abuse, and I will reveal some shocking statistics about nonphysical abuse you may not have been aware of until now. You will come to understand how common these types of abuse really are and how easily you can fall into their trap.

1

Some Universal Truths and Why They Are So Important to You

"Hey, Doctor Jill, what makes you think you are the guru of abuse, and why should I listen to what you have to say?"

I'm asked these questions quite often, and hey—I'd be wondering the same thing if I were you. You spent a lot of money on this book and are expecting reasonable results. No, actually you are expecting miraculous results, and you have a right to them. You're probably miserable and confused, and who am I to advise you, anyway? After all, you may have spoken to your friends and family members and have no doubt read other self-help books on how to improve your self-esteem, live your best life, stand up and be counted, and be all you can be.

But those books and that advice didn't work. Why? Well, in my opinion, the answer lies in a few different places.

1. I believe people are where they emotionally need to be at any particular time. That may sound pretty cruel, since you are not happy and haven't been for a long time. But you've consulted all those people and read all those books. Why hasn't there been a significant change in your life? Perhaps you weren't miserable enough. Maybe you thought you were ready to change your life, but truth be told, there were still obstacles in your way. Could it be that you still had lessons to learn? I believe very strongly in the Eastern philosophy that says, "*When the student is ready, the teacher will appear.*" I'm here right now; are you ready?

2. The friends and family you've talked with are not unbiased. They love you. They are in your camp. Isn't that why you spoke with them? When we need to vent, whine, and complain, we generally go to people who will give us the support and answers we want to hear. That boosts our morale and makes us feel very self-righteous. It feels great, but it doesn't do much to motivate our forward movement. But now here I am; I am unbiased, and I have not been emotionally invested in you since your childhood. Sure, I really, really want you to make some

positive changes in your life and find some true peace and contentment. But I also want you to understand why you made the choices you did. You must be emotionally, financially, spiritually, and physically ready to make change if it is to be long-lasting. I very much want to see you succeed, but I didn't change your diapers, and I wasn't your blood sister twenty-five years ago.

3. Maybe those other authors haven't really dealt with abuse issues themselves. They may be experts telling you what you should do from an intellectual perspective, but they may not understand what it's like to feel desperate, trapped, and hopeless. They may not have spent time crying in a shower so that no one would know they were crying. They may not have shut themselves in their closet so their kids wouldn't find them crying again. Maybe they don't know how fake it feels to put on the stupid smile of, *Sure, everything is great; he just has a headache ... you know, from the stress of work again.* Maybe they don't know what it's like to wish and hope and pray for change, to be so incredibly grateful when he is nice, is having a good day, says "I love you," wears a smile rather than a scowl, says the dinner was good, pays a compliment, doesn't embarrass you in front of friends, plays with the kids, or seems to be having an easy couple of days. Those things make you think, *This is so great. I knew that once he saw how wonderful our lives could be, he would change. I'm so glad I didn't listen to my inner voice that told me to leave. I knew we could make it if I just hung in there with him and was patient long enough.*

But I have done and thought these things. I've been right there where you are, in a young first marriage that crushed me emotionally. I've cried in the shower, in the closet, in the car, in the frozen-foods aisle of the market, and anywhere else a person can cry. I woke up hoping for change (for him and myself) and went to sleep praying for change. After almost twenty years of marriage and two wonderful children, I finally realized that only one of us was going to change, so I asked him to leave. That was my change.

So, what makes me think I'm qualified to write a book for you? First, there's my own very personal life experiences—some of which I will share with you—a few initials that come after my name, and several years of working with abused women and men in my private psychology practice, at a domestic violence shelter, and in presentations and conferences around the world. I have also written two other books on the subject, *But I Love Him* and *Destructive Relationships*. Despite all these credentials, however, I have to admit unselfconsciously that I'm no smarter than you and certainly don't know your life better than you. I'm just a neutral bystander who has successfully used the information I'm going to relate to change the course of my own life—but more importantly, I've shared this information with tens of thousands of other women just like us, and thankfully, they've given me so much positive feedback that I'd like to pass on this information to you.

The first thing I'd like you to do—before you go any further in this book—is to go out and buy yourself a really lovely journal to write your thoughts in while you read and grow. You can purchase it from the ninety-nine-cent store or from a high-end stationery store. It doesn't matter where you get it, but buy a journal that has large pages and is very pleasing to you. In this journal you are going to record a personal inventory of your metamorphosis.

At the conclusion of each chapter in this book you will find a journal activity entitled, "What is this costing you?" These are not easy activities; they will require you to look at yourself in a way that you may never have done. The activities will call on you to examine your "stuff," and they may bring up painful memories that you had successfully walled off until now. What you will find is that those very memories and ideas have kept you stuck. Each chapter will build on the lessons of the preceding chapter, and each subsequent activity will be based on the knowledge you learned not only in that chapter, but in all the others that came before it. Consequently, it is very important that you read the chapters in order, OK?

Now, in order to make these changes possible within yourself, it's crucial that we begin by understanding some universal truths and why they will be critical to our work together. Please do not gloss over these ideas. Write them in your journal, jot them on pieces of paper to keep in your wallet, on your mirrors, and on your refrigerator, and use them as your computer's screen saver. They are life-changing concepts, and once you really "get" them, your life will make more sense and will become 100 percent easier than it currently is. I promise you that.

UNIVERSAL TRUTH #1
LOVE IS A BEHAVIOR

Quick question: When does the man in your life say, "Oh baby, you know I love you"? When he's in a good mood? When his life is going his way? When he wants sex? After he's said or done something unkind and you've cried over it?

Second quick question: when he exhibits unkind behaviors, would you call them loving behaviors? For example, when he calls you stupid, crazy, or fat, would you call that a *loving behavior*? No excuses or rationalizations: you don't need to defend his behavior to me. Remember, I'm not your best friend or your mom. I'm just your personal book shrink. Therefore, would you say that name-calling is *loving behavior*? I didn't think so.

Another example—when he lies to you, is *that* loving behavior? When he disses your family or "encourages" you not to see certain friends, when he makes threats, when he hides money from you, when he tells you how you should dress, when he makes you feel like you're going crazy, when he won't compromise and you have to do everything his way, when he checks up on you or makes you feel small and unworthy, when he drinks too much even though you've told him how you feel about his drinking, when he gambles away your children's lunch money for the upcoming week, when he cheats on you—would you really call any of those behaviors *loving*? No? Neither would I. Now, I know I've made you cry or, at the very least, feel very sad.

This truth that LOVE IS A BEHAVIOR is so critical to your life, because very often people in unhealthy relationships prefer to look only at the good times. When you base your perception of the relationship on those moments when life is easy and carefree, you aren't able to see the bigger picture—that LOVE IS A BEHAVIOR, not a fleeting feeling. And not only is it a behavior, it is a behavior you have a right to expect every hour of every day, regardless of circumstance. Love is the way others really treat you, not what you'd like to believe about the way they treat you.

When you begin looking just at behaviors, you lose excuses that have kept you stuck. You lose denial, lies, and unhealthy wish-making. You look at reality, which is not a bad thing. Some of you have learned to look past your realities, which is how you've been able to survive your lives. While that survival mechanism may have helped you when you were a child, it is not useful now. In fact, it is downright detrimental to your emotional and physical well-being. That's why you are currently miserable and reading this book.

Others' behaviors they tell us everything we need to know about them. Yes, everyone is entitled to bad days, and yes, every couple has disagreements. The quality of your relationship is based on how you handle yourself in those times of disagreements. Do you attack your partner or the problem? My husband, Frank, whom I adore more than Reese's Peanut Butter Cups, and I disagree quite often. I can honestly tell you that no one on this earth can frustrate me more than my beloved Frank. We are so different in so many superficial ways. But I know that he would pour a really good pinot noir down the drain for me—and you'd have to know how serious he is about pinot noir to understand that kind of sacrifice! So, when he does or says something that doesn't feel kind, I say to him, "Hey, you can't pull that on me, buddy. Remember, I'm the LOVE IS A BEHAVIOR person, and that's not loving behavior." Usually he'll reel back a little and say something like, "Damn, busted again. I'm sorry." I'm tellin' you, when you really understand that love is a behavior, it not only makes your life easy, you also get to win a lot of battles!

Why didn't your mom or gal pals ever tell you that love is a behavior? Because we were all raised the same way. We were taught to listen to our heart. "Your heart will never lead you wrong." Well, at least that was the misinformation I was raised on. What this suggests is that you should allow your emotions to rule your thoughts and decisions.

But think about it for a moment: what is your heart's job? It pumps blood throughout your body, right? Now, why would you let a pump make your decisions? If your mother had said to you, "Listen to your aorta; it will never lead you wrong," what would you have thought of that advice? A little nuts, huh? The fact is, most of us are proud that we not only listen to our heart, but that we give it complete authority to make decisions for us. Actually, it is our brain's job to make decisions for us. When you give your child a time-out, do you say, "I want you to go into your room and *feel* about your behavior, young man"? When you are asked to make a big decision, do you say, "Let me give it some *feeling*"? No, you tell your child to *think* about his behavior, and you give some *thought* to a big decision. When you are in a suffocating relationship, remember that love is a *behavior*, not a feeling. Look at the behaviors of all those around you—especially yourself—and make good decisions based on that knowledge, rather than based on emotions, which may be caused by fear.

One of the most powerful questions you can ask yourself—which is an exercise we will talk about later in this book—is whether or not staying in an unhealthy relationship is loving behavior to yourself or to your children.

UNIVERSAL TRUTH #2
YOU ONLY HAVE CONTROL OVER THREE THINGS IN YOUR LIFE

Oh no, here comes the bad news. You thought you had complete control over everything and everyone, didn't you? Don't try to fool me. I used to be the Queen of Control, and I still have to remind myself each day that I only have true control over three things—the same three things you do:

1.   Your own thoughts

2.   Your own behaviors

3.   Your own reactions

Now, before you go ballistic and accuse me of being a charlatan for giving you such simplistic advice, let's examine some of the frustrations in your life.

- You can't get your man to change.

- You can't get your kids to change.

- You can't get your parents to change.

- You can't get your friends to change.

- You can't get your kids' teachers to change.

- You can't get your boss to change.

- You can't get your coworkers to change.

- You can't get your siblings to change.

- You can't get your neighbors to change.

- You can't get the school board to change.

- You can't get the world to change.

- You can't get your plumber to change.

Does that pretty much sum it up, or have I left anything out? Allrighty then, now that we've cleared that up, let's examine the list.

Here's the simple truth: you can't force any of those people or entities to change, because they do not revolve around your own thoughts, behaviors, or reactions. Don't scam me by saying that you *think* about changing all of these things all the time. That doesn't count.

Now for the good news: you have 100 percent control over the three things I've mentioned:

- *Your own thoughts:* That sounds bogus, doesn't it? How many times have you been awake at two in the morning with your brain running as fast as a Saab on the Autobahn? It seems as though your mind has a mind of its own. I know this one. Call me at two o'clock most mornings, and I'll be up planning my own life as well as the lives of everyone I know. The fact is, you can take control of the way in which you think; I will teach you some techniques for this (which I reteach myself on an ongoing basis) later in this book. No one has the right to tell you how and what to think. You alone make those choices.

- *Your own behaviors:* If there is one thing I know for certain, it's that all abuse is intentional. Your man makes a choice to treat you the way he does. You didn't think it was accidental when the word "bitch" came flying out of his mouth, did you? The way he chooses to act—and the way you choose to act—are not accidents; they are conscious choices. You have 100 percent control over your own actions.

- *Your own reactions:* This is very significant: you have a choice in every single situation. If your man treats you unfairly, you have a choice of many reactions: you can feel hurt, sad, and angry. You can feel unloved and unworthy. You can decide that he's correct. You can make excuses for him. You can deny that his behavior is a problem. You can take your anguish out on your children, friends, or pets. You can go to the cosmetics or shoe section of your nearest department store and buy your way out of your feelings. You can speak up. You can leave him.

Ready for some better news? Because you have 100 percent control over the way you think, act, and react, you have a world of choices at your pretty, little feet. You can actually make any decisions about any situation in your life. Isn't that exciting? Remember, though, that having total control of yourself means a few things:

- You also have 100 percent responsibility in your life and can't blame your choices on anyone else.

- Everyone else has control over the same three things in their lives.

- You can't get anyone—except yourself—to change.

Bummer, huh? Not if you continue to read the rest of this book and use this knowledge as an exciting challenge that will change your entire life. And, it will …

UNIVERSAL TRUTH #3
YOU HAVE FREE WILL

This may sound obvious to you. Now that you've seen the ways in which you pull strings and control virtually every aspect of your own life, let's agree that aside from the weather, taxes, and the ways in which others think, act, and react, you make your own decisions. When you find yourself whining, "But I don't have any choice," remember that you have free will and can make pretty much any decision that you wish. That leads into the next universal truth, which is ...

UNIVERSAL TRUTH #4
YOU ARE NOT A VICTIM

When you understand that love is a behavior, that you have control over the way you think, act, and react, and that you have free will, you can easily see that you cannot possibly be a victim.

"But, he makes me feel this way!"

"But, I can't leave. We have kids together!"

"But, I won't have a date for the senior prom!"

"But, I've invested all this time in him!"

"But, I was molested when I was young!"

"But, I depend on him for money!"

"But, I'm too old to start over!"

"But, I'm having a bad hair day!"

I can understand being a victim to your hair, but the rest of those excuses fly right past me. When I worked in a domestic violence shelter—and then later in my own office—I counseled many women whose main identity was as a victim. Here's my simple, honest philosophy on victims: I don't know of any successful victims in history. Do you? Perhaps you can think of heroic figures who were victimized, but what really makes them *sheros* (heroines) is that they didn't see themselves as victims. They worked hard, made difficult decisions, and overcame almost insurmountable odds, which made them powerful and strong. You see, victimhood is a very powerless, hopeless, helpless place in which to live. When you are a victim, it is impossible to succeed. A "successful victim" is an oxymoron.

Don't get me wrong: there are indeed victims in this world. Little kids who are sexually, emotionally, and physically abused are victims. Adults living in terrorist countries who do not think they can leave their relationship because they have been denied the opportunity to learn about choices are victims. Starving babies are victims. None of those situations apply to you, my girlfriend.

Now, you can tell me, "Doctor Jill, I was abused when I was just a little girl, and that's why I've made these choices." I'm sorry. I personally understand about childhood abuse. It happened to me. Yes, it definitely does impact the choices you make as a teen and then as an adult. The legacy of child abuse is very powerful. However, you now know that you have 100 percent control over how you think about that abuse, how you act in relation to the abuse, and how you react to other people who continue to abuse you to this day. So you can now make better choices in your life, even though you were tortured when you were young. The way you were treated wasn't fair or right. Similarly, as I will discuss later in this book, the fact that your man may have been abused when he was young doesn't give him the right to abuse you today. Bottom line? Your childhood abuse is not an excuse for you to be a victim.

When you refuse to see yourself as a victim, and stand up for yourself and your own worth, your life will change. I promise.

UNIVERSAL TRUTH #5
ALL ABUSE IS INTENTIONAL

Well, that sounds pretty harsh, doesn't it? Actually, that statement can also be a great comfort to you. Since you understand that your abuser has free will and that he has complete control over the way he thinks, acts, and reacts, you must also understand that he not only knows exactly what he is doing to you, he can also choose to change his abusive behavior at any moment. Notice that I said "he"—not you—can change his behavior. He has to have the desire and determination to do so. I believe in the power of change. I believe that anyone can change. If I didn't, I wouldn't be in the therapy business, which is all about individual change. I have seen almost miraculous changes occur in my patients. Sadly, I have not seen a whole lot of change in abusers, because of Universal Truth #6, which is …

UNIVERSAL TRUTH #6
WE DO EVERYTHING WE DO FOR A PAYOFF

Yes, we are not unlike little rodents used in experiments: we just want a payoff for our behavior. Even seemingly unselfish acts give a payoff. You smile at a stranger on the street, and he smiles back. It makes you happy, which is a nice payoff. You feed the parking meter of someone you don't know so that he doesn't receive a ticket. You feel like a good person, which is a nice payoff. You work late and are praised by your boss or get a raise. Good payoff. You chauffeur your kids and their teammates to and from soccer practice and hope that they appreciate it someday. Lovely future payoff. I could go on and on, but you get the idea. We do everything for a payoff, whether or not it's a payoff we can see and touch. Spiritual or emotional payoffs are valid and good payoffs.

Let's think for a moment about this concept. Why does your man abuse you? For a payoff. He gets what he wants: he feels like a big shot, it delays his own bad feelings about himself, whatever. When you stop giving him the payoff, he will stop treating you the way he used to. That's not because he will have changed, but because *you* will have changed. Perhaps you will have left, or perhaps you will still be with him. But you will be thinking, acting, and reacting to his abuse differently. You will change the payoff for him.

Now for the difficult question: what has been your payoff for staying in your abusive relationship? Everything we do is to receive a payoff, right? Then there must have been payoffs for you, as well. We will discuss this idea in greater detail later in this book. (Just a warning …)

UNIVERSAL TRUTH #7
ALL ABUSE IS ABOUT TWO THINGS: POWER AND CONTROL

Abuse doesn't involve anything other than power and control. It's not about his childhood pain. It's not about your childhood pain. Those things certainly contribute to why a person abuses or allows herself to be abused, but really, it's just about power and control. Very simple. Your man does what he does because he likes it, it works, and you let him. You give up your power and control to him, and he gets a huge, lottery-sized payoff. Who has the power and control in your relationship? If your relationship is unhealthy and abusive, but you still think that you have the power or that you and your partner share fifty-fifty power, then you are kidding yourself.

Keep in mind that he is not an abuser because his father beat him when he was nine years old, because his mother was an alcoholic, because none of his teachers liked him, because he was raised in poverty, because his bosses have been unfair to him, or because he had a hangnail yesterday. He abuses because he wants power and control. Nothing else.

UNIVERSAL TRUTH # 8
MOST PEOPLE PREFER THE CERTAINTY OF MISERY TO THE MISERY OF UNCERTAINTY

This is not my brilliant idea but that of a very smart therapist named Virginia Satir, who developed many theories about family therapy in general and the role of self-esteem in a family in particular.

This idea is so powerful that I have posted it in several prominent places in my home. I've turned to this quote many times in my life when I've felt stuck, miserable, victimized. When I was going through my divorce, I used to repeat this sentence over and over in the shower first thing every morning to center myself.

When we are miserable, it is *our* misery. While we may not enjoy the misery, it is ours. We own it, and we know what it looks like. To be honest, there is a certain comfort in the discomfort. Do you know what I mean? While your life may seem uncertain because your abuser changes the "rules" on a daily basis, the truth is that you wake up knowing what every day is going to look like. It's going to be miserable. The certainty of misery doesn't look like such a bad deal when you consider the alternative.

Now, the misery of uncertainty, that's a real bear. That's true terror. The misery of uncertainty means that you have to take a risk. You have to be responsible for your life. You have to wake up not knowing what the day is going to be or what you should do. There's very little structure in uncertainty. It's like jumping off a cliff and not knowing if you are going to land safely. At least when you have the certainty of misery, you're pretty sure you're not going to get a broken leg, right? Maybe a broken heart or a broken spirit, but nothing that leaves marks. But I digress ...

The certainty of misery keeps you stuck and gives you the illusion of safety, while the misery of uncertainty is very scary. Which path do you want to take? Today, it may be the certainty of misery. Next week or next month or next year, you may have the same response. That's OK. At some point, you may need to make a true decision to positively change your life.

This book is designed to help you do just that.

WHAT IS IT COSTING YOU?
HOW CAN YOU RELATE THE INFORMATION IN THIS CHAPTER TO YOUR OWN LIFE?

Unless you apply the information in this chapter to your life, you'll have basically accomplished nothing more than an hour of wasted time, and a headache for the effort. That is not my intention in asking you to consider these eight truths. Why don't you get your journal out and write about ideas that can help you better your life today?

• In the last week, month, or several months, what nonloving behaviors has your partner shown you? Be very specific. You are cheating if you write "He wasn't very nice when he got home last Tuesday." Think hard to identify each time you felt demeaned, unimportant, unworthy, unloved, or dishonored, and every time your stomach felt an uncomfortable glitch or your head started hurting. What happened at those times?

- What choices have you made recently that caused you to give up your thoughts, behaviors, and reactions to someone else? What could you have done instead?

- When was the last time you felt victimized or felt that you didn't have any choice in a matter? How many other times have you felt that way, and what were the circumstances? When have you felt the most small and hopeless?

- When was the last time you received a positive payoff just for being you? Did it include your partner? Was the payoff long-lasting or just temporary? Do you frequently get more feel-good payoffs from strangers or other people than from your man?

- When was the last time you felt powerful and in control of your life? Not just your career life or friend life, but your partner-relationship life? When was the last time you were in charge? When was the last time the ball was in your court?

- How do you relate to the idea that most people prefer the certainty of misery to the misery of uncertainty? Do you feel unhappy and miserable a good deal of the time? When? What keeps you from taking the risk and dealing with the uncertainty? How would that feel to you?

Take a good look at the answers you've just given, and sit for a while with the feelings they brought up. Do you feel desolate? Hopeless? Angry? Used? Fearful? Sad beyond words? All those feelings are good, helpful, and powerful tools for you to use during the remainder of our process together. As a matter of fact, write down exactly how you felt while you performed this activity. Not only is it good to accept your own rightful feelings, charting them will be amazingly powerful for you as you metamorphose. By the time you reach the end of this book, you will feel more consistently powerful, useful, hopeful, in charge, grateful, and the like. It's always helpful to remember where you came from so that you fully appreciate where you are!

I know this chapter may have been very difficult for you. You had to take a look at the myths you may have been harboring. You had to place responsibility for your life squarely on your own, underused shoulders. That takes a lot of guts. I'm proud of you.

2

What Is Nonphysical Abuse?

Jim made me feel like everything was all my fault. If I cooked better, he wouldn't have had to criticize me and tell me that he already knew what slop tasted like from his days in the service. If I had sex whenever he wanted, he wouldn't have had those five (that I knew about) affairs. If I didn't eat so much, he wouldn't have to call me a fat cow so often. If I didn't cry so much, he wouldn't have had to tell our kids their mommy was a complete mess who can't even raise them right. If I didn't buy the kids new shoes so often—like when their toes were bumping up against the end of the shoe—he could trust me with money and not have to dole it out as if I were the child, and he also wouldn't have to know where I spent every penny. If I could remember everything all the time, he wouldn't have to remind me every ten seconds that I was going crazy. If I had friends who liked him more, he wouldn't have to restrict my seeing them. If I had family members who thought he was the prince they once did (because I told them he was even when he wasn't), he'd allow them to come over to "his" home. If I could live like a "proper Christian wife," he wouldn't have to tell me that God was going to punish me in the afterlife for the life I've lived …
—**Nancy, age thirty-seven**

Ricky used to tell me to shut up, called me a bitch, always had to know where I was and who I was with. I never paid any attention to the names he called me. Teenagers talk like that now. I know parents don't get that, but it's true. It's sort of like words don't mean anything. When he wanted to know where I was and all that, he told me it was because he cared so much about me and didn't want anything to happen to me. He'd give me suggestions about what kinds of clothes looked good on me and how much makeup to wear. I thought I was so lucky, because hardly any guys notice that stuff, and he did. He wanted to spend more and more time together and was jealous when I was with my friends. That made me a little uncomfortable, but I thought it was nice that he wanted to be with me and that his jealousy meant he really loved me. I'll spare you all the boring details about why we aren't together anymore. It wasn't my decision; it was my parents' order. I hated them for it, but if I can be honest here, it took about two months of not seeing him or not talking to him—which felt really horrible—but then I started feeling so free and happy again. I was having fun with my friends and didn't have to answer to a guy. I don't think I realized how miserable I was with him until I was forced to get out.

—Kelly, age sixteen

Do you think Nancy is living in an abusive marriage? You do? Now, wait a minute—she never said anything about her husband laying a hand on her. Did you just assume, because of all the other things she said about him, that he must have hit her, as well? Well, guess what? He never struck her, pushed her, pulled her hair, or physically abused her in any way. Is she still in an abusive marriage? You betcha!

Did Kelly have an abusive boyfriend? Remember, she said he was jealous, called her names, isolated her from her friends, and told her how to dress. Did she ever say that he hit her? As far as I'm concerned, the behaviors these two women just described are more abusive than being coldcocked every once in a while.

Let's talk about what nonphysical abuse is for a moment, and you'll get a better idea of what I'm talking about. First, though, I'd like you to take a little test that the Battered Women's Task Force and various states' Coalition Against Domestic Violence have put together.

Does your partner

- threaten to hurt you or your children;

- threaten to hurt friends, family members, or pets;

- become jealous without reason;

- have sudden outbursts of anger or rage (including "road rage");

- behave in an overprotective manner;

- prevent you from seeing family or friends;

- prevent you from working or attending school;

- destroy personal property or sentimental items;

- prevent you from going where you want, when you want;

- control all finances and force you to account for what you spend;

- force you to have sex against your will;

- force you to engage in sexual acts you do not enjoy;

- deny you access to family assets like bank accounts, credit cards, or the car;

- insult you or call you derogatory names;

- humiliate you in front of your children, family members, or friends;

- use intimidation or manipulation to control you or your children;

- turn minor incidents into major arguments;

- hit, slap, punch, push, or bite you?

Did you answer yes to even one of those questions? Then you are in an abusive relationship. Notice that only the last question involved physical abuse. If I were constructing that questionnaire, I would have included many more questions, but we will discuss those shortly. Did the questions on the list surprise you? You may have experienced many or most of those behaviors as an everyday part of your relationship(s) and never realized they were abusive. Perhaps you've been involved in your current or other unhealthy relationships for so long—almost all of your life—that these behaviors just seem normal to you by now.

Whether or not you've considered them normal, I'm here to tell you that you don't deserve them. Today is the day you put a stop to them!

VIOLENCE

physical   *sexual*

COERCION AND THREATS:
Making and/or carrying out threats to do something to hurt her. Threatening to leave her, commit suicide, or report her to welfare. Making her drop charges. Making her do illegal things.

INTIMIDATION:
Making her afraid by using looks, actions, and gestures. Smashing things. Destroying her property. Abusing pets. Displaying weapons.

MALE PRIVILEGE:
Treating her like a servant: making all the big decisions, acting like the "master of the castle," being the one to define men's and women's roles.

EMOTIONAL ABUSE:
Putting her down. Making her feel bad about herself. Calling her names. Making her think she's crazy. Playing mind games. Humiliating her. Making her feel guilty.

POWER AND CONTROL

ECONOMIC ABUSE:
Preventing her from getting or keeping a job. Making her ask for money. Giving her an allowance. Taking her money. Not letting her know about or have access to family income.

ISOLATION:
Controlling what she does, who she sees and talks to, what she reads, and where she goes. Limiting her outside involvement. Using jealousy to justify actions.

USING CHILDREN:
Making her feel guilty about the children. Using the children to relay messages. Using visitation to harass her. Threatening to take the children away.

MINIMIZING, DENYING, AND BLAMING:
Making light of the abuse and not taking her concerns about it seriously. Saying the abuse didn't happen. Shifting responsibility for abusive behavior. Saying she caused it.

physical   *sexual*

VIOLENCE

Let's review the five types of nonphysical abuse so you will have a sense of the types of abuse you've been subjected to.

VERBAL ABUSE

> I don't know how many times I've been called a bitch in the last couple of years—maybe five hundred, six hundred times? Does that seem like a lot to you?
> **—Elie, age twenty**

Verbal abuse is very sneaky. Oftentimes, when a "loved one" calls a woman a name or makes a nasty remark, she lets it go because

- he's tired;

- his boss in an ogre;

- he just had a little too much too drink;

- it's only the first (second, fiftieth) time he's said it;

- his father used to call him that when he was a kid, so he doesn't know any better—it's really his dad's fault;

- everyone's entitled to one mistake;

- it's a full moon ...

Well, here's the truth: your man calls you names because

- he likes to;

- it keeps you in line;

- it keeps you on edge;

- it makes him feel more powerful;

- you let him.

If he's ever called you *bitch, whore, slut, cunt, stupid, ridiculous, fat, ugly*, or *crazy*, or if he's told you that no one would ever want you, you are being verbally abused. If he's used a loud voice to scare you, or if he's argued with you until he breaks your will and you give in to his demands, you are being verbally abused.

If he's threatened to

- end the relationship;

- do harm to himself;

- take your children away from you;

- do harm to you or your kids, family members, or pets;

- expose you or something you've done that you're ashamed of;

- spread rumors about you …

then you are being verbally abused.

EMOTIONAL ABUSE

> Joseph is the perfect boyfriend. He's tried to make me feel warm, loved, and protected. In the beginning, I didn't realize that his being jealous of every guy on earth was weird. I just thought that he really loved me. He wanted to spend all his time with me, because he couldn't bear to be apart from me. What girl wouldn't love that? He wanted to know where I was and who I spoke to, because there are so many creeps out there. He called me all the time—like twenty or thirty times a day—because he just wanted to make sure I was safe. Anyway, that's what he told me. Now I'm wondering: safe from what or whom? I'm starting to feel suffocated and wondering if he's the perfect boyfriend after all. But, I'd never tell him what I was thinking, because it would hurt him too much.
> **—Chrissy, age twenty-one**

Chrissy is not alone in wondering about her boyfriend's behavior and whether it's creepy. All she knows is that she doesn't feel good about it anymore and feels trapped. She is being emotionally abused.

Emotional abuse is—in my opinion—the most devastating kind of abuse. Like all abuse, it is completely intentional. What is its intent? To take your self-esteem and any good feelings you have about yourself and crush them into the ground, leaving you feeling emotionally raw and disabled.

Has your husband or boyfriend done any of the following to you?

- Wanted to know everything you're thinking

- Accused you of doing or thinking things you haven't actually done or thought

- Controlled who you see, how you dress, how much makeup you wear, how much bath or shower water you use, how much electricity you use, etc.

- Spied on you or had others spy on you (such as following you to school, to work, to meet a friend)

- Interrogated you

- Displayed extreme jealousy and/or distrust

- Used looks or gestures to intimidate you

- Made you feel as though you were unimportant

- Blamed you for anything that goes wrong in his life

- Used silence as a weapon

- Used withdrawal and withholding behaviors

- Neglected your feelings and opinions

- Made you feel that you're wrong a lot of the time

- Limited who you could see or for how long

- Listened in on phone conversations

- Prohibited you from having outside activities or interests

- Prohibited you from seeing or talking with your friends

- Restricted your access to the phone, car, or mail

- Directed hostile humor at you

- Made fun of you and then told you he's "just kidding"

- Told you that you're "too sensitive" or "can't take a joke" after he humiliated you

- Constantly criticized your appearance, parenting skills, housekeeping skills, cooking, sexual abilities, etc.

- Treated you like a servant

- Made all the decisions

- Made you feel badly or "wrong" about who you are as a person and a woman

- Acted like master of the castle

Do any of these behaviors sound familiar? If so, you are in an emotionally abusive relationship.

In her book, *Emotional Blackmail*, Dr. Susan Forward describes being lost in a FOG, which stands for *fear, obligation*, and *guilt*. "Blackmailers pump an engulfing FOG into their relationships, ensuring that we will feel afraid to cross them, obligated to give them their way and terribly guilty if we don't." Dr. Forward goes onto to explain—through a checklist—that you may be involved in an emotionally blackmailing experience if important people in your life

- threaten or imply that they will make your life more difficult, end the relationship, hurt themselves, or become depressed if you don't do what they want;

- want more and more, no matter how much you give, and assume you will give it to them;

- frequently ignore or discount your feelings, wants, and needs;

- make promises that are contingent on your behavior and then rarely keep them;

- label you as selfish, bad, greedy, unfeeling, or uncaring when you don't give in to them;

- give you approval and attention when you give in to them and take it away when you don't;

- use money or children as a weapon to get their way.

Answering yes to even one of the items on the checklist indicates that you are being emotionally blackmailed, which is a form of emotional abuse.

PSYCHOLOGICAL ABUSE

I thought I was going crazy on a daily basis. Gary would say that he told me something or told me to do something, and when I didn't do it—because as I now know, he never told me—he'd give me this rolling-the-eyeballs look and whistle, which meant "Looney Tunes!" He'd used that expression so often that pretty soon, he just called me Elmer Fudd (a Looney Tunes character). He thought it was just so hysterical and that he was so clever. He'd call me Elmer in front of his friends and all his family. It was humiliating. Of course, I'd always laugh right along, but he convinced me I was crazy, and I was grateful that he was willing to "help" me instead of putting me in an institution.
—**Claire, age forty-six**

Claire's husband, Gary was on a mission. His mission was to "drive her crazy," and, truth be told, he very nearly succeeded. When I met her after a presentation I gave on the subject of my second book, *Destructive Relationships*, she told me the short version of what he had been doing to her for the last thirteen years. She was almost convinced she was insane until she heard me speak about psychological abuse and the determined ways in which some men will lure their subjects slowly but surely into a world of madness. Why would a man who has promised to love and honor you do such a thing? For power and control, the goal of every abuser.

When you are being psychologically abused, you feel as though you are Alice in Wonderland; your sense of up and down, logic and illogic, right and wrong, good and bad is very confused. That is his plan for you: to keep you guessing, wondering, worrying, edgy, and confused. When he accomplishes this task, you are emotionally—and often physically—exhausted, unsure and frightened of yourself and the ways you think and feel. Then you are completely his, with no chance of escape.

This plan is very similar to the way certain animals capture another animal for food. Living in a canyon, I've had several opportunities to witness coyotes capture a rabbit, cat, or other small animal for their next meal. I'd often wondered how they accomplished this, since a rabbit or cat was certainly very agile and could jump, climb, and hide in places coyotes couldn't reach. However, at one point the neighborhood housecats started disappearing, as well as the wild bunnies. Then, I saw the area's pack of coyotes in their bloody, mind-numbing, but brilliant work.

One coyote made a small sound that let the smaller animal know he was close by. The little animal became frightened and darted off in another direction, only to be confronted by another coyote that was waiting, perhaps twenty or thirty yards away. Surprised and scared, the tiny animal then ran in yet another direction, where it found a third coyote in the distance. Whichever way the rabbit or cat went, another member of the coyote pack stared at it from many yards away. Mind you, the coyote wasn't directly threatening the other animal; it was just standing there, calmly and silently staring back. Soon, the little animal became frozen by fear and paralyzed by the knowledge that wherever it went, it was trapped. Tragically, the terrified animal would just stand there as the pack of coyotes slowly moved into the circle in which the rabbit or cat stood helplessly unable to move or escape. At that point, I turned my face away from what I imagine was a horrible scene, but I could hear the poor creature squeal and the coyotes yip and howl at their good fortune.

Human psychological abuse is not so different from what I've just described. Oftentimes, an abuser will enlist the aid of his equally abusive family or friends to drive the woman out of her mind, but very commonly it just takes one person: the person who tells you that he loves you and only wants to protect you from yourself and help you be the best person you can be—your husband or boyfriend.

Abusers have many different ways of going about this very intentional plan, but here are a few examples:

- He gives you approval and attention when you give in to him, and takes it away when you don't.

- You know that he's told you one thing, but then he swears that he hasn't said that or that he's told you something different.

- He isolates you from the important people or activities in your life (e.g., family members, friends, church functions, social activities).

- He acts abusively one day and then kindly the next, without reason or provocation.

- He wakes you up once or several times in the night so that you never have a good night's sleep.

- He fights with you to the point that you are mentally exhausted and give in to his demands or way of thinking.

- He threatens you with your—or your children's—safety or well-being, or threatens to leave you without money or a place to live.

- He has rules that you follow to a T, and then he changes those rules with the result that you never know which rules to follow.

- He constantly tells you that you are worthless, stupid, incapable, and crazy.

Make no mistake, this is a very determined plan on his part. He is using tried-and-true methods of capture and brainwashing that have worked over the centuries on intelligent, normal women and men:

- They exhaust their victim to the point that s/he cannot think clearly.

- They isolate the victim from all other influences but the captor's.

- They entice the victim to follow certain rules for a reward (food, sleep, affection, not being harmed), and when those rules are followed, they rescind the rules and make new ones.

- They act nicely at one time and abusively at others, even when the victim behaves in the same way with the same stimulus.

- They state threats to harm the victim or someone s/he loves, either directly or by implication.

- They feed propaganda into the victim's mind when s/he is so debilitated emotionally and physically that s/he will believe and follow anything the captor says.

The outcome of this type of psychological abuse can include the following:

- Learned helplessness—in this interesting phenomena, the victim is so debilitated and mentally crushed that she no longer fantasizes about leaving the relationship, but instead just tries to survive day to day and do the best she can with her current circumstances.

- Stockholm syndrome—in this situation, the victim begins to actually identify with her captor, feeling sorry for him and trying to help him. She has been so emotionally brainwashed that not only does she believe what she is told, but she also identifies closely with him as a person, with his plan and his goals. She hopes to be worthy enough to help him with his plan (which, unknown to her, is her total emotional devastation).

You may have heard these phrases bandied about in discussions of prisoners-of-war or a kidnapping. When you wonder why these people don't just walk away, even when their captors are not with them, those are the reasons. Many of your own family and friends may actually wonder why you don't leave your abusive relationship when you have a mind and two good legs. Now you understand some of the reasons ...

FINANCIAL ABUSE

When we first married, Jay was beginning medical school. It was a very rough time for us in every way because of the stress, lack of time together, and so on. One of the things that was particularly hard was the lack of money.

I had graduated from college at the same time Jay did, and instead of going to nursing school as I had planned, I had to go out and get a full-time job to support both of us. He certainly couldn't work for a few years. Even though I was disappointed that my dream of being a pediatric nurse was going to be delayed for a while, I was also proud that I was helping us as a team by making the money so that Jay could become a doctor. He kept telling me that in a few years, I could go back to school if I wanted, but by that time, I'd be a rich doctor's wife and probably wouldn't feel like it.

I went to work at the cosmetics counter of a large department store near us. It didn't have anything to do with my career goal, but it was a job I could easily get and perform well, and it marginally paid the bills, along with some financial help from his parents.

I paid for Jay's tuition and books, the rent on our tiny apartment, utilities, food, and the bus fare to and from school and work. We were too poor to afford a car. When I say that I paid for all those things, I guess I should say that the money I made paid for them, but Jay took my paycheck each week, deposited it in our checking account, and paid all the bills. He said he was just better at it than I was and didn't mind doing it.

After many, many years of effort on both our parts, Jay graduated from med school, did his internship and residency in pediatric oncology, and was invited to join a prestigious practice. I was so proud of him. He continued to work very hard and soon began making more money than either of us would have imagined.

As planned, I began going back to nursing school, but then I found that I was pregnant with our first child. In the beginning, I thought that I could continue to go to school, but Jay just laughed at me and wondered why in the world I would think I needed to do that when I was doing something so much more important: carrying our child. I thought he had a point, and since I'd planned to stay home with our daughter anyway, I thought I'd go back to school when she began day school.

After she was born, Jay started becoming very protective and demanding. He wanted to know where we were all the time, even when I'd tell him that every Tuesday we went to Gymboree, and every Thursday we had playgroup. By this time, we were living in a very nice home in a great, safe neighborhood.

Jay's practice continued to grow, and he was bringing home a mid-six-figure salary. Even with that much money, he gave me an allowance for the baby's diapers, food, and clothing. I couldn't believe I had to account for and justify her needing more diapers when he was making so much money, but I just rationalized that it was the stress he was under. When I asked for money to buy clothes or shoes for myself, he'd look in my closet and toss my clothes around, telling me I had so much, I didn't need any more. He made me feel like I was a spoiled little girl when I wanted something new for a charity or work party in which he was involved.

He'd also tell me that I was exaggerating the amount of money we had. When he first began his practice, I'd see our bankbooks, but soon I couldn't find them. I didn't sign checks or have access to our checking account or credit cards, because he couldn't find a good enough reason for me to do that. He gave me all the money he thought I needed in cash each week.

When our little girl was almost five years old, she started kindergarten, and I was looking forward to returning to nursing school. Then Jay suggested that we have another baby. When I protested, he accused me of not loving our daughter enough and not enjoying being a mother, and he said I was selfish. He had been an only child and always wished he'd had a brother or sister for company. I saw his logic and also his pain, so I agreed that we should have one more child. I was very exhausted during that pregnancy and couldn't go to school, take care of our other child, and stay awake, so I again put off going to school.

Jay became even more restrictive with money after our second child—a boy—was born, and I was beginning to feel like a bird in a golden cage.

Let me just cut to the end of the story. We now have four children, ranging in age from four to sixteen, and I have never gone back to nursing school. I'd still like to but feel like I'll be too old to work when our littlest one leaves home. Jay is very determined that I should be with the kids all the time and not go back to work, even part time. He tells me that it's embarrassing to him that he makes so much money, that he's a doctor, and it would look like he's not providing for his family if he had a wife who worked. He doesn't understand that it would really make me feel better about myself if I was working. I was proud of myself when I was helping put Jay through school, even though I wasn't working at a career I had planned.

He still gives me money each week and demands an accounting of where and how I spent it. I got tired of having to explain to my girlfriends that I couldn't have lunch with them—because Jay would call it a frivolous waste of the money he works so hard for. Eventually they got tired of me and my excuses, so they aren't really in my life anymore. My mother was in financial straits a few years ago, and I had told her that we would help her. When I asked Jay about it, he blew up and told me that my mother was irresponsible with money and never helped us when we needed it, so he wasn't throwing a dime her way now. My mother and siblings were so shocked and troubled by this that they thought it best just to stay out of our lives. I only see them very occasionally these days, and when I do, it's very tense, so I see them less and less. We have his folks and his friends, who think he's God's gift to the world.

I know I shouldn't complain. He's taking care of our family, and I don't have to worry about a roof over our heads or where our next meal is coming from. I feel selfish and self-centered and just wrong all of the time.
—Katherine, age forty-four

Katherine's story may seem eerily similar to your own, even if your partner makes minimum wage. You are suffering financial abuse if he

- puts restrictions on your employment, where you work, how much you can work;

- takes your paycheck away from you;

- gives you an allowance and/or doles out money to you at his whim rather than when you need it;

- makes you repeatedly ask/beg him for money;

- demands an accounting of every dollar you spend;

- does not allow you information about the family's finances;

- does not give you access to checking, savings, or credit card accounts;

- makes unilateral decisions about the ways in which the family money will be spent;

- leaves you alone for a number of days without any money or with inadequate funds.

Katherine once described to me times when her husband left a twenty-dollar bill on her bedside table as he left for work. She found it difficult to understand why he did it, until we discovered that it was always the morning after an evening of sex. She felt she was being treated like a common hooker and was naturally quite furious and hurt. Later in our treatment, when recalling those incidents, she laughed and said, "Gee, if I remember correctly, I was worth a whole lot more than twenty dollars! I was pretty good in those days!"

Money is a very tricky issue in many marriages. Money—along with sex and in-law problems—is the leading cause of disagreement in most relationships. It's easy to understand why when you realize that, very often, money represents power. Knowing that abuse of any sort is about power and control, you can then see how an abuser uses money—lack of, access to, decisions about—as a significant way of wielding power and control over his partner.

Making a woman ask for money—even money that she herself earns—infantilizes her, making him the "daddy" in the relationship and she his little girl, one with no power whatsoever. It is demeaning and degrading to a woman to be placed in that position. It strips her of her self-worth and dignity, not to mention her identity as a woman and equal partner in the relationship.

SPIRITUAL ABUSE

As a Christian woman, it was important to me to marry a Christian man. I always knew that I wanted children and wanted to raise them with my religious values and belief system. I don't think that my way of thinking is the only way, but it is the way I was raised, and I feel comfortable with it. I wanted someone who shared my way of thinking and would be part of a team with me, keeping the church at the center of our lives.

I met Dennis at a church singles group and thought he was really spectacular. Aside from going out and having a fun time, we spent many long hours discussing the Bible, our shared beliefs, and our plans for the future, which meshed perfectly. I knew within weeks that he was the "one," which gave me an amazing feeling of peace and contentment.

I had told Dennis that I didn't believe in sex before marriage and was a virgin when I met him at age twenty-four. I was really proud that, in the sexual, secular world, I had held to my principles, even when I was ridiculed over them or was pressured to go beyond them. Dennis seemed to appreciate that I had been saving myself for my future husband, which looked to be him. He seemed to feel honored, I would say.

After we had been going together for four months, he started pressuring me for more than a kiss goodnight. I loved him and knew that we were going to marry, so I agreed to some petting, or making out, I guess you'd say. I admit that I enjoyed it as much as he did but could also tell that he was becoming dissatisfied with that type of contact after a few of these sessions. I knew that he was sexually aroused but was determined not to say anything about it.

He began touching me under my blouses and putting his hands down my pants. He wanted me to do the same to him. None of that felt right to me, and I told him. He would pout and tell me that we were practically married, and so in God's eyes, it would be OK. I know that sounds pretty hokey and sleazy, but I fell for it.

After that, he started becoming very sexually aggressive. He frightened me with his sexual force and demands. We ended up having sex many times before we were married, and I would have to say that now I'd consider them rapes, although I did not identify them that way at the time. It was painful and degrading. He wanted me to do things that were demeaning and very disturbing. He told me that when a man and woman love each other, nothing they do sexually is wrong.

After we were married, everything quickly went downhill. I found myself giving up most of my spiritual beliefs and values for him. I did things that I never would have thought I was capable of as a religious woman.

We never went to church, and he ridiculed me when I said that I needed to go. He said that my religion was simple and foolish. Even with those thoughts, he didn't mind misconstruing Bible passages that said I should be submissive to him and obey him as my husband. It was strange that he could whip out scripture when it suited him!

One day, I saw my pastor at the gas station. He was very kind and solicitous and asked me where I'd been. He looked at me in a way that made me feel as though he knew everything about my miserable life and all the sins I'd committed. I felt like he looked straight through to my wretched soul. I broke down in sobs and told him I'd strayed so far from the church that I didn't know if I could find my way back, and if I did, I thought I'd lose my husband. He put his arm around my shaking shoulders and told me that there is always a way back and that he would help me get there if I would like. Suddenly, I felt very calm, strong, and determined.

Dennis was on a business trip and wasn't due home until two days later. I packed up a small suitcase, left everything else in my home, wrote him a note telling him that our life together was over, and went to stay at my parents' house. I visited my pastor the next day and told him almost everything that had happened since I began dating Dennis. He cried along with me.

That was the beginning of my long road back to my faith and myself. It eventually took more than two years to feel totally redeemed and be rid of Dennis and the hold he had on me. It wasn't easy. He continued to call and visit me, using scripture again to fortify his argument that I needed to return to him. If I didn't have a true and strong faith in God, my healing never could have taken place. He thought he took that from me, along with everything else he stole, but he was wrong.

—Maria, age thirty

I was raised in a religious family. I go to synagogue with my family every Friday night and volunteer to help out at Sunday school each week. It's a strong connection, and it's important to me. Being a Jew is who I am. This means that—even though it's difficult for others to understand—I don't go to a lot of places from sundown on Friday to sundown on Saturday, which is my Sabbath. I walk everywhere instead of driving, and things like that. It's meant to be a family and friend time and also a time of rest and reflection. I like that.

I went to a Jewish school until I was going into high school. I convinced my parents to let me go to a regular secular school, because I wanted to experience more of the real world before I left home for college. I met this guy my first week of school, and he paid a lot of attention to me. That was nice, because I didn't know anyone and felt really out of place. First of all, I didn't dress like a slut like most of the girls in school, and I probably walked around with a shocked expression on my face most of the time. I tried to fit in, but to tell the truth, I didn't think I wanted to fit into that kind of crowd at school. He was nice and interested in my life. He happened to be Jewish, which was great, but was not devout at all, just on the holidays. Slowly, he began pressuring me to do things with him on Friday night or on Saturday afternoons, which I wouldn't do. He criticized my religious beliefs and tried to make me feel wrong and like a freak. He thought I was an extremist and that I took my religion too far. He thought my parents had brainwashed me and that I didn't have any thoughts of my own. He definitely tried to separate me from my parents and my faith.

I talked to my parents and my rabbi about some of the things he told me, because I really began questioning what I was doing. It was a very difficult time for me. I started thinking that everything I had ever been taught was a sham.

My parents invited my guy over to the house for Shabbat dinner, and the rabbi and his family came over, too. I was a little nervous about the whole thing, but he got to see what my real life was like, and he knew it would be an uphill battle for him to go on convincing me of his side. They all talked to him about how we practiced Judaism and the ways it's different than the ways he practices, which are important. I decided that night to break up with him, which was far easier than I thought it would be.

—**Rachel, age sixteen**

I have seen many women in therapy who have stories similar to Maria and Rachel's. Their religious faith had always been a cornerstone of their lives until their abuser came along. Just as heinously, many abusive men actually use a woman's religious beliefs to trap her into a miserable life, which her higher power never would have wanted for her. Has your husband or boyfriend ever

- used scripture to fortify his abusive opinions or behaviors;

- used religious words, such as "submission" and "obey" to keep you "under his thumb";

- told you that your religion was simple or stupid;

- prevented you from practicing your faith;

- demanded—or at least strongly encouraged—that you give up your religious faith for his;

- requested that you go beyond what feels comfortable to you spiritually to accommodate his wishes or desires?

According to my friend Reverend Al Miles, author of *Domestic Violence: What Every Pastor Needs to Know* and *Violence in Families: What Every Christian Needs to Know*, "Spiritual abuse tactics used frequently against women by their perpetrating male intimate partners, and by some religious leaders, congregation members, and other individuals, is encoded in the words stay, pray, obey, OK. Abused women are constantly told that if they stay with, pray for, and obey the very men who are abusing them, then God will be pleased and everything will be OK. Tragically, as a result of this alleged 'divine' counsel, women have suffered even greater acts of atrocity from their abusive male intimate partners. And some of these women have even been murdered."

Your religious or spiritual beliefs are personal and private—between you and your higher power. No one has a right to strip you of your values and morals or to suggest that you give up those beliefs—or even bend them this one time—to satisfy his selfish wishes.

Oftentimes, women will tell me that they don't know who they are anymore, or that they don't know what they believe, or that they feel empty inside. Usually, we find that they have given up their religious beliefs—or moral/value convictions—which were previously the foundation for their lives.

A FEW WORDS ABOUT SEXUAL AND PHYSICAL ABUSE

While this book does not specifically address these two types of abuse, it is very important for you to understand them, as many of these abusive behaviors are not commonly considered abuse. Has your partner ever

- touched you in a way that made you feel "dirty" or uncomfortable;

- had sex with you in a way that you didn't want;

- had sex with you when you didn't want it and told him so;

- coerced you into oral or anal sex when refused intercourse;

- restrained you by holding your shoulders, arms, or hand too tightly;

- prevented you from leaving a room during a disagreement;

- shaken you;

- gotten "in your face" and intimidated you;

- pushed you aside, onto a bed, or against a wall;

- grabbed you by the hair;

- "play" punched or play wrestled with you to the extent that you were "accidentally" hurt?

Please keep in mind that the above list is composed of sexually and physically abusive behaviors that women often dismiss. These behaviors are nonetheless every bit as abusive as "hard-core" abuse; often they are the entryway to worse types of abuse. In fact, by abusing you in these ways, your partner is actually testing what you will tolerate so that he can continue to "up the ante" of abuse. Sexual and physical abuses never subside or decrease; they only increase until they are stopped.

WHAT HAS IT COST YOU?
HOW HAVE YOU BEEN ABUSED?

Now that you understand the five types of nonphysical abuse, write each one on a different sheet in your journal. Using the bullet points and stories in each subheading of this chapter, try to identify the ways your current partner has abused you verbally, emotionally, psychologically, financially, and spiritually. You may even find new and different behaviors not mentioned in this chapter. If other men in your life have treated you unkindly, make a separate set of lists for each of them.

Now, go back and take a look at your lists. What are the common threads in each of the lists? Have you suffered more emotional abuse than any other kind? Can you see how one type of abuse has led into or overlapped onto other types of abuse? Can you identify where you were in your life when these abuses occurred and what you were thinking at those times? Were you uncomfortable when those abuses first began? If so, how did you make it OK for yourself after that? Did the abuses begin to feel normal to you? Did you ever speak up? If not, why?

Keep these lists, and refer back to them as you go through this book. Although they may be difficult to look at now, you will find that, as you begin to understand more about yourself and the ways you can change your behavior, they will become valuable touchstones to your past and to the woman you used to be. You will be able to use this information as a reminder of what behaviors you do not deserve and will not tolerate in the future.

3

Who Are Nonphysical Abusers?

When I worked as a therapist at a domestic violence shelter, I frequently encountered women who, in group therapy situations, would exclaim, "I'm not like the rest of you, because my husband/boyfriend never hit me. I really haven't been abused like all of you. I'm just here because I'm giving him time to cool down and miss me before I go home."

These women, and you may relate to this, had been told that *abuse* referred only to physical battery, rather than to any kind of nonphysical abuse, no matter how horrible. As we discussed in the last chapter, there are many other types of abuse. The real tragedy is when women—and society in general—minimize nonphysical abuse and its destruction of souls and spirits.

I have other significant memories of my work in the shelter, in the form of the questions these women had about their abusers: *Why does he do this to me? Did I do something wrong? How can I help him? What's wrong with him? Will he ever change? When I told him that he was hurting me and the children with this behavior, he'd just laugh at me or call me crazy. Why didn't he listen to me? Can I really be that unimportant to him? Are the kids that unimportant to him?*

These are all fair and good questions, and you've probably asked them of yourself time after time. Who is a nonphysical abuser? How did he become so cruel? Abusive behavior typically begins in childhood and follows a very predictable pattern. Abusers

- have been physically and/or psychologically abused as children;

- have seen their father beat and/or severely demean their mother or sisters;

- grew up in a household in which one or both of their parents abused alcohol or used drugs.

As we will discuss later in this book, as mothers—or future mothers—one of our primary responsibilities to our children is to model the type of behaviors we would like them to take into adulthood. If we hit or spank them, we can expect them to understand that violence is an acceptable way to solve problems or get what they want. If we yell at them or use demeaning language, we can expect them to understand that insulting others and making them feel insignificant is fine. If a boy sees his father demean or intimidate his mother, he will learn that this is the way men behave toward women. Likewise, when our daughters witness this type of behavior, they understand that it is all right for a man to treat them this way later in life. You are the most important role model in your children's lives. You rule! As we will discuss later, this knowledge may play a large part in the way you view your relationship and in your decision to stay or leave.

In her book, *No Visible Wounds,* Dr. Mary Susan Miller quotes various studies in which abusers are further identified by psychopathologies and emotional behaviors:

- They have a *borderline personality disorder,* and are asocial, withdrawn, moody, and hypersensitive to interpersonal slights. He overreacts, has sudden outbursts of anger, and may have an alcohol problem. Some of the features of borderline personality disorder include fears of abandonment, up-and-down moods, categorizing people as all-good or all-bad and frequently changing their minds about those same people, attention-seeking, and having a pattern of unstable relationships.

- They may be narcissistic and antisocial. Because they are so self-focused, they decide how much to give to others—usually only when it is to their own advantage—and emotionally take from them as well.

- They have a dependent personality, are often inflexible in their attitudes, have low self-esteem, and require continual support from their wife or girlfriend.

Miller further cites another study in which the researchers identify eight groups of abusers, which I will summarize:

1. *The Jekyll and Hyde abuser:* men unable to control their impulses, who change swiftly in a Dr. Jekyll-Mr. Hyde pattern, oftentimes without warning

2. *The rule-following abuser:* men who demand strict adherence to rules without emotion and dish out punishment to those who break them. Sometimes, their rules haven't any justification

3. *The James Dean abuser:* men who are rebellious and hostile but are actually dependent and have low self-esteem

4. *The fist-banging abuser:* men who are aggressive and antisocial

5. *The PMSing abuser:* men who exhibit great and out-of-the-blue mood swings

6. *The two-faced abuser:* men who are outwardly pleasant but who are unable to handle rejection and are aggressive when they feel their wife or girlfriend has let them down

7. *The head-case abuser:* men who are very dependent, anxious, and depressed

8. *The neither here nor there abuser:* men who show only minor signs of the other seven characteristics and have no psychopathology

As you read these descriptions of abusers, how many times did you nod your head in agreement, saying aloud, "Yup, that's him"? It may be difficult for you to understand that your man is very dependent and has such low self-esteem when he appears to be exactly the opposite. Let's think about that for a moment. You're a nice person, right? You have a certain number of people around you who are your friends (if you are allowed to have friends) and family (if you are allowed to see your family) who think you are a good and worthwhile person. You are able to call those people (if you are allowed to call those people) and invite them to socialize with you, and when you do so, they may be pleased as punch. In other words, you don't have to coerce them or intimidate them into spending time with you. You don't have to control every situation.

Your abuser, however, doesn't have that knowledge about himself. He needs to control and manipulate others into doing what he wants. He may be very clever and charming in the way he goes about it, but he is manipulative nonetheless. He doesn't think that just because he's a swell guy, others would want to spend time with him. That's low self-esteem.

As you will also see later in this book, his dependence reveals itself in many ways, but the biggest way you may see it is if you decide to leave the relationship. The lengths he will go to in order to get you back under his control will be extreme. The fact is, his dependence on you is so high and debilitating, he cannot function effectively without abusing you! If you are gone, it may mean that he will have to look at his own behavior—not likely, but a possibility—and that's something he definitely doesn't want to do.

I don't remember ever doing anything right when I was a kid. I thought I did a whole bunch of stuff right, but you'd never know if from listening to my dad talk about me. Even when I worked real hard to get good grades or make a school team, I'd hear him say something like, "Rick won't ever amount to anything. I should just plan on him staying here the rest of his life. I don't think he'll stay at any job for long, and what woman would put up with him for more than a week? I don't know what I did wrong with that kid." I tried everything I could think of to win his love and approval.

When he yelled at my mom, I hated him, but you'd never know that. I'd rush to his defense and side with him against her. I was her youngest, and I always thought she probably loved me a little more than my other brother and my sister, so the pain in her eyes when I agreed with him that she couldn't do anything right was almost too much for me to take. That look of hurt and betrayal just killed me, but I kept on siding with him anyway. I was so desperate for his love and tried to make myself more like him. That didn't work, either.

One day, I heard my mother crying, and I went to her and put my arm around her shoulder. She shook it off and said to me, "What, are you trying to make me crazy now, too? You pretend like you're concerned about me one minute and then tell me how horrible I am the next? You're just like your father. Go away from me. You hurt me too much. I don't know what I did to deserve this from you." That just about killed me. What was I supposed to do? If I pleased my mother, I would push my father further away and never get him back. He was already calling me a *little puss* and a *wussy boy*, asking me when I was going to grow tits. I had to choose between them. My need for my father was almost obsessive. Hearing my mother's pain as she told me that I was like my father made me feel both ashamed and proud. I can't tell you what a weird feeling that was. I remember that I was almost eleven years old, and I think it was a real turning point in my life as a man.

After that time, I kept trying to grow closer to my dad, and I removed myself from my mom. I would deliberately try not to have any contact with her. I told myself that if she were stronger, she could stand up to him. Of course, I was afraid of what would happen to her if she did. HE NEVER HIT HER or pushed her or anything like that. He just made her cry a lot, which further infuriated him. Or maybe he liked making her cry, I don't know.

From the time I began dating, I know that I followed that pattern my father set. I'd find women who would do what I wanted, sexually, and who would give me my way on everything else. I'd become easily frustrated with them and blame them for stuff that didn't have anything to do with them. I'm really jealous, and I'd call them at least ten times a day, maybe more. I'd want to know who they were with and where they were and when they would be back. I'd accuse them of cheating on me when they weren't. All kinds of stuff that feels out of my control. I just do it.

I drink the same Scotch as my dad did and the same beer in the same quantity. I guess you could say I've turned into my father. The trouble is, it's not working in my life. I want to settle down and get married and have a family, but I find fault with every girl I'm with, or else they won't stay with me long enough to get serious. Maybe my father was right about me all along.

I've turned into my father and now have to figure out if that's what I really want. My mother died of cancer four years ago. She and my dad were still married, and he tortured her until the day she went into a coma. My therapist—Dr. Jill—thinks that was her way of tuning him out once and for all. Maybe she needed to die to get rid of him. Maybe she needed to get rid of me. I know I was a disappointment to her and am going to have to deal with that and the way I treated her.

About four months ago, I started therapy to try and figure all this out. I don't know if it will work. I still want my dad's love and approval. My sister won't have anything to do with me and tells me that the way I treated our mother and the way I still treat other women is disgusting. She's been divorced twice and now has sworn off men altogether. My brother has been in and out of rehab programs for drugs. I guess you could say that we all share the scars of our childhood. Dr. Jill points out to me how much fear I live in every day and how dependent I am, not only on my father, but also on all the women I've been with. She has told me that now I'm an adult man, and I can make different decisions, and that abuse is a learned behavior, so it can be unlearned. The clincher in this whole treatment, though, is my continual need for my father, who has still never said a nice word to me in thirty-nine years.
—**Rick, age thirty-nine**

As you can see from Rick's story, abuse is a very complicated problem. From all outward appearances, Rick looks like a self-assured, confident guy with lots of friends and lots of options. He's a good-looking man who has told me that he's heard himself described by others as a "playboy" or a "player" because he seems to have a different attractive woman on his arm each month. Now, you know the reason for that. Rick is a tortured, self-doubting, dependent, depressed, grief-stricken abuser with very low self-esteem, as are 99 percent of all abusers. Your abuser is no different than Rick, no matter how he conducts himself.

In my work with abusive men—facilitating court-mandated abuser/anger management groups as well as conducting individual therapy with them—I have observed several other characteristics that are universal to almost all abusers. I think that your identification of these behaviors and patterns will better help you understand what you have been living with. It will also help you make clear decisions on where you'd like your life to take you in the future. A nonphysically abusive man

- *wants instant gratification.* He doesn't want to work hard for the money, prestige, and material possessions he desires. He also doesn't want to do difficult and necessary emotional work to fix a problem. He wants everything NOW;

- *has poor impulse control.* An abusive man loses his temper frequently and more easily than most other men. He may throw or hit objects rather than people. He may have punched holes in bedroom walls or closets as a young man. He flies off the handle at little things that merely irritate others. He may go ballistic if he has to wait in a restaurant, or he may exhibit incredible road rage if cut off in traffic or made to wait at a traffic signal;

- *uses projection as a coping mechanism.* Projection is one of those handy-dandy little emotional-protection devices that an abuser uses to keep his untarnished image of himself. When an abusive man uses projection, he attributes his faults and misdeeds to others, usually his partner. When he feels weak and unlovable, he may accuse his partner of being stupid or incapable of doing anything right. If he is having an extramarital affair—or contemplating one—he may become obsessively jealous or accuse his partner of cheating on him. When he feels insecure, he may undercut his partner's strengths or talents;

- *has insatiable needs.* These needs can take the form of sex, encouragement, praise, physical company, or any number of other gratifications. His needs seem overwhelming, and his partner feels that she can never do enough to placate him. He is a bottomless well of need that cannot be filled;

- *exhibits little personal awareness of his own behavior.* He is very keyed into his partner's behavior or children's actions but fails to see how his own behavior impacts those around him. If you point out his poor behavior, he usually blames it on his partner or any number of others;

- *feels strongly that he is acting in his partner's best interests.* If the partner of an abusive man asks him why he calls her sixty times a day, he will say that he wants to make sure she is all right (because he knows how frightened she can get of little things …). When she asks why he needs to know where she is, whom she's with, and when she'll return, he'll tell her that he's only asking on behalf of the kids. If she asks him why he doles out small amounts of money to her as if she were a child, he will whisper in a very confidential tone that she doesn't have any sense about money, and he doesn't want her to be embarrassed by running up the charge cards or having a credit card rejected in a department store. When she wants to know why he stalks her, he'll tell her some guys can go crazy when they see a pretty woman, so he wants to make sure she's safe. He's just being a loving, caring mate and can't believe that she is so ungrateful. He reminds her some women would *kill* to have a guy who cares so much …;

- *experiences no guilt*. Well, if he's not doing anything wrong, and everything is his partner's fault, why would he feel guilty?

- *can have a dual (or triple) personality*. No one believes that this man is abusive. They think his partner is crazy. Why? Because he looks like such a prince when others are around. He may be overly solicitous, helping with the dinner dishes (which is something he does only when company is over) or giving all the kids piggyback rides (ditto). When his partner really thinks about it, many—if not most—times he can be nice and considerate to her. True, there are other times when his cruel and demeaning comments make her feel lower than a slug. True, sometimes he becomes enraged when she doesn't listen to his advice, but then he may express remorse or beg for her forgiveness, and he looks like such a sad puppy dog. She may think, *He's not mean all of the time. He can really be so sweet.* Maddening isn't it?

- *has rigid gender-role stereotypes*. A man acts like and does this, a woman acts like and does that. Man is king of the castle, and woman serves the king. It may not seem that obvious, but when you look behind some of the behavior, you may see that this man has very rigid male/female expectations. For instance, he thinks a man has the right to ask his woman for sex whenever he wants (even if she is sick, or eight and a half months pregnant, or nursing a colicky baby and has had only an hour of sleep in three days). He expects dinner on the table when he gets home (and not the frozen or take-out kind), even if his partner is taking care of three children or works outside the home herself;

- *has a sense of entitlement*. An abusive man feels he has a right to ask for whatever he wants, and he feels entitled to get it from his partner or anyone else. Why? Because he's him, that's why. He has rights others don't have. He has the right to make the rules (and break them, but everyone else had better follow them to the letter), he has the right to expect others to do what he says, he has the right to get what he wants, he has the right to yell at his partner if he feels like it. This may be a personality disorder. However, I've found that many men have been raised like little princes. His mother adored him beyond the point of reason. He never had to answer to anyone, and everything he did was considered absolutely precious. Even if he stole baseball cards from a store, his parent defended him. I mean, if you don't want kids to steal baseball cards, lock them up behind a glass case, why doncha? What do you mean he's not batting first in a baseball game? He's the best player on the team (despite the fact that he struck out the last seven games, but that wasn't his fault). He's getting an F in science class or his teacher sent him to the principal for the fourth time this semester? Then the teacher's an idiot and should be fired. She just doesn't understand how special this little boy is. As a matter of fact, she's probably jealous of him! He doesn't have to empty the trash or make his bed; that's what parents—or older siblings—are for. I can't tell you how many young men I counsel who are abusers in the making primarily because they have such a feeling of entitlement. No one's going to stop them from doing or having what they want, especially not a woman!

- *makes frequent promises to change.* This behavior can be very confusing and upsetting to his partner, because those promises and her hope that he will change may be the driving force keeping her in the relationship. And the truth is, once he makes the promise to change, he may change … for a couple of days. But those couple of days are so terrific, and the memory of how sweet their lives were in those couple of days is so powerful, she keeps hanging on just to get back to those couple of days again.

I cannot emphasize enough the role that alcohol and drugs play in an abusive relationship. The correlation between substance use and partner abuse is staggering. Your man doesn't need to be an alcoholic or chronic drug user for this to be true of your relationship. Think about this concept for a moment: why does your partner drink or use drugs? To forget all that is going badly in his life. Does he have a couple of beers when he gets home? Does he smoke a little—or a lot—of weed on Sunday nights? Does he take a little something before his parents come for a visit or he goes on a fishing trip with his dad? Start being mindful of the times your husband or boyfriend uses drugs or alcohol. You will definitely see a pattern.

Let me make the next point clear, however. Drugs and alcohol do not cause abuse. They do, however, increase the likelihood and severity of abuse. When he is drinking or using, he gives up responsibility for his life for that time. He is not responsible for the way in which he treats you. Don't get me wrong. I'm not at all saying that he has the right to abuse you when he's drunk or high. I'm saying that his substance use is a choice, especially if he knows that he is cruel to you when he's using. If he subsequently chooses to use again, then he knows exactly what he's doing. Of course, he will use the excuse "But I couldn't help it. I was drunk. You can't blame me." Of course you can—and you should.

You've told him—or others have—that he's a creep when he drinks or uses drugs. He continues to do drink or use drugs. Would you call that loving behavior?

Carey smokes pot. I don't see that as a problem, because he just becomes happier when he does it. My parents think it's a huge problem and don't understand that almost everyone in high school has tried pot at least once, and the majority of kids use it regularly. I don't like the fact that he deals it, though. His cell phone is always ringing when we are out; it's crazy. He's got to run over to someone's house or work and deliver it, which takes time away from me. He makes a lot of money doing it, which is nice because he takes me to good places and buys me great gifts. His parents are such idiots; they don't ever ask why he has so much money.

I guess one of the things I really don't like is that he's smoking more and more. Sometimes he's pretty jealous, and sometimes he calls me names when he smokes. He also wants sex all the time when he's high, and sometimes I don't want to, but I do it anyway. He cheated on me a couple of times when he was wasted, but I think it was because I didn't want to have sex, so now I just do it even when I don't feel like it, because I don't want him to go somewhere else.

—Tobie, age fifteen

Don is usually a really nice guy. Well, let me correct that. He's a nice guy a lot of the time. We have a neighborhood poker group, and twice a month, he plays cards with some of the other men on the street. He comes home stinking drunk, and then he's like another person. He finds fault with everything I do, throws things around the house saying it's a pigsty, wants to have sex with me in raunchy ways, calls me names, and all kinds of other stuff. I can't stand to be around him. Even if I try to pretend that I'm asleep when he gets home, that doesn't work. I've told him the next day what he was like, and he apologizes and says it won't happen again, but then two weeks later, here we go again. I hate those poker nights.

—Christina, age forty-one

To sum up who your man is, let me make a few of these points again or in a different way (paraphrased from my book *But I Love Him*):

• Abuse is a learned behavior. It is learned from seeing it used as an effective tool of control—usually in the home in which he grew up.

• Abuse is not a natural reaction to an outside event.

• It is not normal to behave in a violent (not necessarily meaning physically violent) manner within a personal relationship.

• Abusers deny that they have been abusive, or they make light of the abusive episode.

- Abusers blame their partner, other people, or outside events for the abusive incident.

- Abusers don't act because they are out of control. They choose to respond to a situation abusively. They are making a conscious decision to behave in an abusive manner.

- Abusers know what they are doing and what they want from their female partner.

- Abusers are not acting out of anger but out of their need for control and domination.

- Abusive men are not reacting to stress.

- Abusers are not helplessly under the control of drugs or alcohol. They make a decision to drink or use drugs.

- Abusive men may be hard workers, excellent students, or good sons.

- Abusers may be so charming and engaging that others would never suspect they are abusive.

- Abusive men may at times be loving and gentle.

The last three points may indeed be some of the qualities that attracted you to your husband or boyfriend; therefore, you may find it difficult to grasp the concept that he is acting abusively now. He may have once been exactly the type of man your parents said they wanted for you, or your girlfriends may have described him as a "great catch." Add onto that idea that he can be very sweet and charming at times, and it's enough to drive you crazy. Exactly his point, my dear!

Your abusive man understands exactly what he is doing to you, what he wants to get from you, and where he wants the relationship to lead. As long as you allow the abuse, it will *always* escalate. It will never decrease or die on its own.

WHAT HAS IT COST YOU?
HOW DO YOU THINK AND RELATE TO YOUR ABUSER?

I understand how difficult the concepts in this chapter have been to grasp and make real in your life. Busting through denial and seeing your man for what he really is can be overwhelming. Perhaps, on the other hand, understanding who he is somehow comforts you. You have put a name to his behavior and have seen that the problem is not you ... it's him. It may also be a relief to understand that your man is not the only one treating his woman this way and that there are many commonalties to abusive behavior.

Why don't you get your journal out right now and write about these feelings? First, write down all of the behaviors and characteristics you read about in this chapter that apply to your abuser. The following is an example of what your list might look like:

1.   He was raised in an abusive household.

2.   He blames other people for his mistakes.

3.   He has low self-esteem that he covers with bravado.

4.   He drinks too much and then is mean to me.

5.   He pretends like he's a good father when other people are around.

6.   He tells me I'm stupid, when he really feels that way about himself.

7.   His father covered up a lot of the bad things he did when he was a boy.

8.   Sometimes, he can be so sweet and gentle.

9.   He promises to do better next time.

10.   He works hard for a mean boss and doesn't get the credit he deserves.

11.   He thinks I should have sex whenever he wants it and doesn't consider how I feel.

Now, think about some of those ideas and how they make you feel or how you felt when you read them in this chapter. You may feel

• angry that he treats you this way and knows what he is doing to you;

• resentful that he thinks he can treat you like this;

• stupid because you've let him have his way all the time or thought it was your fault;

• sad because he won't get the help he needs;

- frustrated because you can't do anything about it;

- mad at yourself for putting up with all his idiotic pranks;

- weak for feeling like you can't leave;

- worried that his behavior will shape how your children behave as adults;

- scared that it will only get worse, but you feel stuck and don't know what to do;

- relieved to know that you are not the only one dealing with this type of abuse.

Don't be afraid of these lists and your thoughts. They are taking you somewhere important. As you go further in this book, the final destination and what you want to do with these thoughts and feelings will become clear; your path will become easier than it seems now.

Remember on a daily basis—and especially as you go through this book—that LOVE IS A BEHAVIOR. You have learned in this chapter that the ways your man treats you is not loving. It is not loving for him to treat you in these ways, and it is not loving of yourself to accept this behavior. It is also not loving behavior toward your beautiful children—whom you say that you love—for them to witness this type of behavior in your home. Think of Rick, earlier in this chapter, and the legacy not only his father, but also his mother, left for him by making him grow up in an abusive household ...

4

How This Whole Mess Began: Your Original Abusers and What They Told You

When I was a little girl, I guess you could say that I wasn't a real stunner. My older and younger sisters, now they were really beautiful. They were also very feminine looking and I was sort of stocky and, well, I suppose you'd have to call me a "handsome girl." Not too charming, right? My mother and father both valued femininity and girly-girls. I had my strengths—I was very smart and got good grades—but in my house, that didn't hold a candle to looking good in a tutu. My parents put me in ballet and gymnastics just like my other sisters, but they were great, and I just looked ridiculous.

So I heard my parents whispering in worried voices about what would become of such an unattractive girl, what kind of boy would want homely little me, etc. My mother would try to turn me into more of a "girl," but that was fruitless. Don't get me wrong: I wanted to look more girlish and swish my hips when I walked. From the attention my older sister got, I could really see the value in all that. Both of my sisters had boys calling day and night, they went to dances and on dates, they always seemed to be having their hair and nails done for some occasion or were buying some great new dress. When they went out, my parents just looked at me pathetically and asked if I wanted to go out for ice cream with them. It was really horrible, and I learned that my value was in my looks and not my brains. It was pretty bad, and I felt like a freak.

I did eventually get some attention from boys in high school, but it was unwelcome attention. They figured a homely girl would be grateful for a little action, if you know what I mean. I was actually the object of bets to see if they could get in my pants. I heard a rumor going around school that I was really a boy, and so the guys were out to see if it was true. I can't tell you how bad my childhood was. There were many, many times when I thought suicide was a good option but didn't have the heart to embarrass my parents that way.

My parents asked me several times if I was a lesbian. I couldn't believe it. I had a few friends who were ugly girls, too. We all just sort of hung out together in our miserableness.

My mother was what you'd call a real southern belle and even had her "spells" when she'd "take to her bed" for a week or so. I thought it was frightening and tried to help however I could. My sisters were no good; they were pretty, so they were just trained to marry a rich, handsome man who would take care of their every whim. They couldn't make a bed and had no empathic skills. I, on the other hand, would sit at the foot of my mother's bed and listen to her tell me all about my father's infidelities, how he embarrassed her at parties when he drank too much, how flirtatious he was, etc. It was terrible to listen to, but I felt compelled to listen because I had my mother all to myself during those times, and I could be the special daughter.

I was never told that I would marry someone wonderful. I was told that if a boy paid attention to me I should praise the skies and him! I was essentially told that I should settle for any man who would have me, which is what I did.

I've never married, but I have had four abusive relationships with men, each one worse than the last. Basically, they are unfaithful, an embarrassment to me when they drink, flirtatious, etc. Sound familiar? I know I'm not gay, but also I think that because I guess some people might say I look a little "butch," I take any guy who will have me. Sometimes I think that they are attracted to me because they are hoping that maybe I'm bisexual and I'll introduce them into a three-way affair, which I'm not and won't. My few sexual encounters have all been disappointing, and I keep wondering what the big deal is. My mother had told me that sex was all for the man anyway, and it was just a woman's duty to keep him happy so he wouldn't look elsewhere. Maybe she was right.

—**Cicely, age forty-two**

Cicely's story is certainly sad, but I'm sure you have one that is equally tragic. I don't think I've met too many women in abusive relationships who can honestly tell me that their childhoods were something from a Hallmark card. There is always something there in the past.

When you are a child, your home is the most important place on earth. It is supposed to be a sanctuary of peace and harmony, a place where you learn to value and honor yourself because you are valued and honored by your parents. Your birthright is to grow good self-esteem based on your parents' messages and actions. You learn what a wonderful relationship men and women can have together by observing your parents' relationship. Well, that's the way it's *supposed* to be.

Let's discuss what your past may reveal and what you learned as a girl that led to your current abusive relationship. I think you'll be surprised by what you find out.

In my second book, *Destructive Relationships*, I discussed the experiences of girls who were raised in abusive homes. I found that many of these girls shared the following characteristics:

- Higher rates of depression and emotional injuries, such as low self-esteem

- Increased rate of death by homicide and suicide

- Higher risk for substance use

- Earlier marriages and earlier pregnancies

- Early learning of denial as a coping mechanism

- Inability to have a normal childhood and adolescence

- Taking on roles inappropriate to their age and maturity level

When you were growing up, how many times did you tell yourself that you weren't going to create a home like the one in which you grew up or that you were never going to be like your mother? It's almost shocking how those words come back to haunt us, isn't it? Sometimes, women unconsciously seek out abusive relationships in order to resolve the pain of their childhood. You may not have consciously thought, *I couldn't fix Daddy, but I can fix this guy*, but that may nonetheless be a driving factor in your male relationships.

Many behaviors you may have seen in your childhood home might not seem abusive, but they sure did set you up for a future abusive relationship:

- Men call women names, such as *bitch, whore*, or *stupid.*

- Women are the butt of jokes, such as stupid women" or "dumb blond" jokes.

- Women frequently cry over a difficulty with a man.

- Men are considered superior to women, or you may have observed rigid stereotypes of what is acceptable "man's work" and "woman's work."

- Women's body parts are referred to by vulgar words, such as *tits, booty, ass*, and *cunt.*

- The man of the family explodes in anger, and while he isn't physically abusive and may not even yell or scream, he leaves the house.

- It is a woman's obligation to sexually satisfy her man, laugh at all his jokes, not be too smart, defer to his judgment, treat him like a child, make herself available to his desires, take care of him, not complain, forgive and forget, take what she is given and be grateful for it, suffer through life, be a helpmate, and fix whatever is wrong in the relationship.

- There is something wrong with girls if they don't have a boyfriend.

- Men usually have the last word whenever there is a difference of opinion, or the woman remains passive in a heated discussion.

- A woman is nothing without a man.

Do some of those ideas sound familiar in the family in which you grew up? I know many of those were true in my childhood home. One of the clearest examples of these messages is that my mother sent my three brothers to college but didn't think it was necessary for me to attend. My job was to groom myself to be the wife of a successful man. Now, I have to tell you, this wasn't the 1950s I'm talking about. I graduated from high school in 1973! Women's liberation was already in full force. I'd already burned a bra or two and was singing Helen Reddy's "I Am Woman" and dancing to Donna Summer's "I Will Survive"! The whole notion seemed a little turn-of-the-century to me, especially since my mother was a businesswoman. Seeing the way my mother had already gone through several marriages, I wisely decided that I wasn't going to depend on a man, so I put myself through college—whereupon I then got married and became financially dependent on a man! A lot of good that psychology degree from UCLA did me back then.

There are several scenarios, which you may have experienced in your own childhood home, that leave a lasting legacy on a girl and affect her decisions about her place in future relationships:

- A depressed parent

- A substance-abusing parent

- A neglectful parent

- Critical parents

- Sexual abuse

Let's go through each of these situations so you can assess the damage done to you as a child, damage that continues to affect you today. This is not the "parent-bashing" section of the book. My intention is not to enrage you to the point of hating your parents. Quite the contrary. Oftentimes, I think that as women we are emotionally uncomfortable or angry without a cause we can put our fingers on. Some of the pain you feel may be due to childhood situations that were out of your control. If you understand them, you can not only better understand your own life, but also see your parents more clearly as people.

THE EFFECTS OF DEPRESSED PARENTS

Depressed is different from being sad. Cicely described her mother's depression when she describes "spells" in which her mother had to "take to her bed." Depression is not the ordinary sadness all of us feel from time to time. It occurs for at least two weeks at a time and includes behaviors such as

- change in appetite: eating too much or too little;

- change in sleep patterns: sleeping too much or too little or not being able to stay asleep, such as middle-of-the-night wakefulness;

- loss of energy and fatigue;

- difficulty concentrating, focusing, or remembering;

- restlessness or irritability;

- feelings of worthlessness, helplessness, and hopelessness;

- excessive crying;

- chronic aches and pains without any medical cause;

- thoughts of death or suicide, or suicidal attempts;

- loss of pleasure or interest in activities that used to give you happiness (also known as *anhedonia*);

- inappropriate feelings of guilt and being a "bad" person.

Do you recall these applying to your parents when you were a girl? Do you recognize any of these signs of depression in yourself today? Depression certainly has a genetic predisposition, which means that if either of your parents was depressed, you have a far greater risk of becoming depressed yourself. There are many very good reasons to feel depressed, or at least extremely sad, when you are in an abusive relationship, and depression is nothing to be ashamed of. If you are depressed, there may be a genetic component to your feelings as well as a situational component. Both are very valid, and neither is your fault.

Did you know that it is possible for two-month-old babies to be depressed? It's true. If you grew up in a household in which one or both of your parents were depressed, it is likely that you may have been depressed, as well. Just as abuse is a learned behavior, seeing your parents chronically depressed affects the way you learn to relate to your own world.

Perhaps you had a depressed parent, let's say your mother. If so, she could hardly take care of herself, let alone you. Therefore, you may not have been properly cared for or nurtured as you deserved. She may not have had the energy, concentration, or will to do the job she would have liked were she in a better emotional place.

How might your parent's depression affect you and your choice of partners today? Let me list a few situations for you and see if they match your life:

- A girl learns to keep her worries and fears or unhappiness to herself because she doesn't want to further worry her parents or understands that they can't "take it" or help her anyway.

- She learns to fend for herself and not ask for help.

- She feels guilty about her parent's sadness; she develops a helper/rescuer personality and then becomes further frustrated or anxious herself because she cannot fix her parent. This becomes a lifelong pattern for her.

- She learns to become very attuned to her parents' moods and needs, putting herself and her own needs below those of her parents and others.

- She learns to read others' moods and adjusts accordingly, which is the very definition of *codependence.*

- She may fear abandonment due to her parents' early neglect.

My mother suffered terrible bouts of depression. We lived in a community where any kind of mental disorder made you just the same as a devil worshipper. As a matter of fact, it was a sign that the devil had ahold of your mind. Who was going to admit they were depressed?

I can't even remember all the excuses I made as to why my friends couldn't come to my house to play, or why my mother often didn't show up at school to pick me up, or why she didn't come to school plays or dance recitals. It was humiliating. At times, I hated my mother, and then I hated myself for hating my mother. I just wanted her to be like everyone else's mommy. Sometimes I thought that if I were a better girl, she wouldn't be so sad. I didn't know what I had done that would make her cry so much. My dad tried to tell me it wasn't me, but I didn't believe him.

Sometimes, when she'd look at me, she'd just break into sobs. As an adult and a mother who suffers from depression myself now, I can understand that her crying when she saw me was probably guilt and more anguish that she couldn't take care of me. She probably worried about what her depression was doing to me.

She must have been scared a lot, and I know that at times she thought about suicide. She'd say to me, "You'd be better off if I wasn't here." That was a terrible thing to say to a young child, and it scared me to death. I'd go into her room all the time and make sure she was breathing.

Predictably, I went into a helping profession—I became a nurse. I'm good at nursing, but not so good at choosing men. I've been through a handful of bad relationships with men, and my children have different fathers, one of whom I married. The other one didn't want to marry me. I think I find men who have a lot of problems that I think I can fix, which never works out. I try to be the mother I never had, both to the men and to my own children. We'll see how my mothering affects my children when they grow up …

—**Catalina, age thirty**

THE EFFECTS OF SUBSTANCE-ABUSING PARENTS

My dad was a very powerful force in my early life. He was very charismatic and just incredibly handsome. He was my brother's baseball coach and even drove the carpool to school when he had a late start at work. He escorted me to father-daughter dances and made me feel like his little princess. He was successful as a mid-level manager, and everyone was just crazy about him.

What nobody knew about my dad was that when he was home at night, he drank. I don't mean he had a beer watching Monday-night football. I mean he drank and drank until he got so drunk he became someone I didn't know. He wasn't the nice, fun daddy that he was in the morning or afternoon. He wasn't the daddy I loved. He was a monster.

When my dad drank, he yelled at my brother and me and cursed at my mother. He pulled her hair and pushed her into walls or onto the floor. He threw things around and said hateful things about not ever loving us and never wanting to have kids but that my mother tricked him. He said he hated his life and hated his family and wanted to kill all of us.

My dad was a very scary guy when he drank. I didn't know who that man in our house was. He was a stranger wearing my dad's clothes.

Sometimes, I blamed my mother for my dad's drinking, and sometimes I blamed myself. I never blamed him. He worked so hard. He was supporting four people. He was coaching teams and driving us around and buying us gifts. There couldn't be anything wrong with a man like that. It must be the rest of us, who were torturing him so much he had to drink. Well, that's what I thought.

When my dad drank, we tried to stay out of his way, but he'd come looking for us. My mom would do whatever he wanted just to try and calm him down. I hated the way she'd lie though. If he had a horrible hangover the next day, I'd hear her call his boss and tell him that dad would be in a little late because he had another one of his migraines, or she'd tell my brother and me to be very quiet because daddy had a headache.

I couldn't have slumber parties at my house or have friends over for dinner, because he might start drinking. Eventually, he began drinking earlier and earlier, stopping at a bar on his way home. Or if it was the weekend, he'd have a couple of beers in the afternoon. My brother didn't want him to come to any of his sports games, because he was afraid my dad would be drunk and disgusting in the bleachers, which happened a few times.

We all lived day to day, not knowing if, when, where, and how much my dad was going to drink. We were nervous all the time. My brother and I hid bottles and threw beer away when he was at work. That really made him mad. It was very difficult to put our lives together in some logical kind of order with the nice dad/drunk dad.

When I was in high school, my mother began drinking with my dad to keep him company. She never drank as much as he did, but she was a little woman and couldn't drink too much before she was sloshed. I think I hated her drunk more than my dad when he was drunk, because I really saw her as weak.

When my brother was seventeen, he was arrested for a DUI and also, of course, underage drinking. My parents were furious, especially my dad. He hit the roof. That was a big turning point for me in how I looked at my parents. My dad wasn't special; he was just a hypocritical, lying drunk. My mom wasn't the sweet protector; she never protected us from the pain and humiliation of our family life, and I thought she chose my father's alcoholism over the safety of us kids.

I was sixteen, and then began several years when my life went to pot. I became very rebellious and went out with "bad boys." I lost my virginity during that time when I was high, which I was a lot. I never drank, but I did use all kinds of drugs—pretty much whatever I was given. I was a slut and didn't care about school, my life, or anyone else. I tried to stay high as much as possible and avoid my house. My parents were always mad at me, but I didn't care. Who were they to tell me what to do?

When I was nineteen, I had a baby. I was pregnant when I was seventeen, but had an abortion. I honestly can't tell you who was the father of that first baby. I gave my other baby up for adoption and didn't look back until about five years ago when I started turning my life around. I've wondered what happened to that child but won't make an effort to contact him, because he has a life now and doesn't need it complicated by me. I'm probably someone who would just embarrass him anyway. Hopefully he's fine.

My brother has been in and out of jail on petty crimes and is a drunk. I don't know what's happened to my parents. I stopped having a relationship with them many years ago. They sort of disowned me because I was such an embarrassment to them. I'm working through all these issues now and know that I will have to deal with them in the near future. Right now, I'm just trying to get through the day, not make too many mistakes—especially with men—and make a new life for myself. I don't have any idea yet what that life is supposed to look like.

—Emily, age thirty-six

I've met many women in abusive relationships who swear to me that they had the perfect childhood. No, they never saw or heard their parents fighting, dad was always very nice, they went to church together, and on and on. But, when I ask about drinking or drug use in their home, the woman may admit that dad drank a little or that mom had pills for her nervous condition, but it wasn't a big deal. When we dig a little deeper, we find that dad drank a lot several times a week or that mom's pills may have been Valium, which kept her in a stupor most of the time. It still amazes me that women don't consider this type of substance abuse anything that would affect them as girls. After all, they weren't living on skid row or pushing their belongings around in a shopping cart. Dad wasn't drinking cheap booze out of a paper bag under a bridge, and mom still volunteered at school. There wasn't a problem.

In my opinion, parental alcohol or drug use exactly mimics an abusive relationship and is a clear setup for an abusive partner later in a girl's life. Here are the ways in which these two ideas mesh:

1. A substance-using home is a roller-coaster life. There are great ups and downs. When the parent isn't using, the family is up; when he's using, they are down. The family's mood depends on the substance use. In an abusive relationship, a woman frames her moods around the moods of her abuser. He usually has wide and unpredictable mood swings, which keep her on a roller coaster of emotions.

2. There is a lot of secret-keeping in a substance-using household. No one tells the outside world what is going on behind locked doors. Life is a fake, and it's hard for a girl to decipher what is real and what is not. Later in life, she learns to keep the secret of her abusive relationship and not tell anyone what is going on behind her own locked doors.

3. A great deal of lying goes on in a substance-abusing home. The parent who is using lies about how much he's using. His partner lies to others about his use. She also lies to the kids about the substance use or makes excuses for his behavior when he does use, which is a form of lying. Later in life, a girl raised in this kind of household will learn to lie about her abuser's actions and make excuses for his abusive behavior.

4. Denial is a key element of a substance-abusing household. In an effort to quell the anxiety and frustration of being unable to control the partner's substance use, the nonusing partner goes into denial mode: denial that he's using as much as he is, denial that it's hurting her or the family, etc. A girl who grows up in this home may begin using the same denial technique as a coping mechanism to stay in an abusive relationship she feels she has no control over. She denies that he is abusive ("BUT, HE NEVER HIT MEBUT HE NEVER HIT ME!"), denies her unhappiness, and denies the effect the relationship is having on her health, her happiness, and her children.

5. In a substance-abusing household, family members learn to placate the user's irrational wants and desires. They also learn to read his moods at a thousand paces and alter themselves and their wants and desires accordingly. Growing up in this household, a girl then learns to put her own needs below that of her abuser, not ask for what she wants, accommodate ridiculous requests, and read his mood very effectively, which lets her know how she should behave in reaction to him.

6. When a girl grows up in a substance-using home, an upside-down world looks normal, which is what she learns to accept later in a relationally abusive home.

7. The possibility of this girl becoming involved with a substance-using abuser is exponentially higher than for a girl who grows up in a sober household or one in which the parents drink responsibly. As we've already discussed, the correlation between substance use and relationship abuse is staggeringly

high. The chances of the girl becoming a substance user herself also increase greatly.

Do any of these scenarios seem familiar to you? If so, please take a moment and reflect on how your substance-using home may have affected your choices in men. Also examine how those choices are affecting your own children or will affect the children you may later have with your abusive man. How many men have you had relationships with who drank too much or used drugs? When you begin looking at this destructive pattern in your life, I hope you will become alarmed enough to change it.

THE EFFECTS OF A NEGLECTFUL FATHER

> I try to talk to my dad so many times, and he either ignores me or tells me to talk to him later. Now I'm dating a guy I really love. He's good to me and everything. Well, most of the time. Sometimes he can be really hurtful. Anyway, my parents don't like him. The other night they took me out to dinner and were wondering how I could hook up with a guy who treats me the way they think he treats me. My dad actually said, "Chloe, I've always been there for you, haven't I?" I just flat-out told him that he'd never been there for me, and I didn't know what he was smoking if he thought he was. He said, "You're just being deliberately hurtful and lying to yourself. You're trying to make me the bad guy when it's your choice to date someone who's so bad for you." I yelled out in front of the whole restaurant, "Well, at least he pays attention to me even when he's being mean, which is more than you do." I didn't mean to say it that way, but I guess it's true.
> —Chloe, age fourteen

The power of neglect in influencing a girl's feelings about herself and the choices she makes in men later in life: this is an underexplored area of relationships. The title of my doctoral dissertation was "The Effect of Father Neglect on Female Self-Esteem," and the research I found on this subject was so compelling, I'd like to share it with you.

I found that the devastation caused by a father who lives in the home but disregards his daughter or is emotionally unavailable to her is all-consuming. It affects her not only while she is living at home, but certainly when she makes choices in men as she matures. The result is as—if not more—tragic than when a girl loses her father through death. This is because when a girl's father dies, she has lost him forever, and he will never return to her. She can then deify him and make him larger than life in her mind and dreams. Her family, and indeed the community at large, may support these romanticized feelings she has for her dad. Conversely, a girl who has lost her father through neglect cannot confront the finality of true loss. Because he is alive and may even be living in her home, she sees him in front of her and feels that perhaps—if she is very good and tries very hard—he will "come back" to her. She blames herself for his distance.

The loss of a father to neglect or inattention is destructive for many other reasons. Since daddy is the first man a girl loves, he is able to help create good and positive feelings about herself as a young woman. Because he loves her, she feels that she is capable of being loved by another man later in life. It is also Daddy who teaches her about the value of becoming a separate person. Moms and daughters have a very profound and intimate bond, both as woman to woman and mother to child. A Daddy-daughter connection is essentially voluntary. Dads teach daughters self-confidence, security within themselves, and how to succeed out in the larger world. Fathers serve their daughters most critically as role models for achievement, self-esteem, and assertiveness.

Complicate all these feelings with a mother who, in seeing her daughter's disappointment (which may mirror her own), tells the little girl, "Oh honey, don't worry; your daddy loves you very much." Ah, so this is what love looks and feels like!

What becomes of a daughter whose father is there but occupied with things he deems more important than his daughter? He's home but behind a newspaper, TV remote control, or bottle of beer. He appreciates the boys in the family more than the girls. Here are some predictable patterns I have found:

- The daughter may develop a pattern of frustrated relationships with men, both romantically and professionally. She may be unconsciously looking for the approval she didn't receive from her dad and develop a Prince Charming complex, hoping that if she tries hard enough, a man will love her enough not only to notice her but to stay with her forever.

- She may use such words to describe herself as *cautious, serious, guarded, sad, unlovable, not good enough,* and *unattractive.*

- She is insecure about her body image and sees herself as less attractive and less feminine than women with attentive fathers. She is less demanding of others and enjoys sex less than she would like.

- She has a pattern of difficult relationships that include themes of abandonment and infidelity.

- She seems to seek out rejecting types of men who bring out her feelings of self-doubt by seducing and then disappointing her. She then becomes more anxious and insecure about the relationship and blames her partner's unhappiness or the relationship's failure on herself.

- When a woman with this history dates a "nice guy," she may become bored quickly or create chaos. She also both clings to and then pushes away intimacy and kindness.

- She gives up her power to men, becomes emotionally dependent on them for her feeling about herself, and allows them to make most decisions, with which she then complies.

- She may have a fear of her own rage, which plays into her submissive behavior. But this unspoken rage—unconsciously directed at her father—turns inward and becomes depression, anxiety, and/or physical illness, such as headaches, backaches, ulcers, and colitis or other stomach ailments.

If you have recognized yourself and your relationship with your father in the descriptions above, how do you think your experience has affected you in the various stages of your life? What decisions have you made because of your relationship with your father? Are you still looking for your dad's approval (which he doesn't give you) when you get a promotion at work? Do you continue to make excuses for your dad's behavior or blame yourself? What feelings did you experience when you read this section of this chapter? Anger? Sadness? Resentment? Helplessness?

It is helpful if you, as an adult woman, can see your father as another adult rather than a godlike figure. He has frailties and faults, just as you do. He cannot correct the damage he did earlier in your life; however, you can make a decision to change the way you relate to him now.

> My dad cheated on my mother viciously. He was your typical charmer who really couldn't be tied down to one woman. He wasn't even discreet about it, and everyone in town seemed to know what kind of man he was. But they liked him nonetheless, because there was just something so mesmerizing about him. When he gave you his attention, you felt so special; you felt that you were being given a gift.
>
> My two sisters, my mother, and I were all in competition for his time and attention. We were insanely jealous of each other and tried ridiculous ways to win his favor. I remember a time when one of my sisters and my mother were trying to sit on his lap at the same time. Looking back on it now, I can see what an amazing narcissist he was and how much he loved the competition.

We never knew when or if Daddy would come home, and the four of us women spent more than an hour each night preening and primping for his anticipated arrival. It was sick, now that I look at it.

Sometimes, we would see other women in town who'd give my mother a sly little look of satisfaction. We knew later that the woman was someone he was having a fling with, but it hurt us girls as much as our mother, because she was someone who was taking "our man" away from us, also.

I still look to my father for approval and to tell me who I am and make me feel worthy. I don't think I'll ever find my "true love" who will make me feel good enough about myself.
—**Kim, age thirty-seven**

THE EFFECTS OF CRITICAL PARENTS

When I was a girl, my posture was never good enough, my knees were too knobby, my report card wasn't good enough if I got one B, and on and on. Now, my house isn't clean enough, my children's clothes aren't dried the right way, and I don't have my dinner dishes in the right cabinets or spices in the right drawers. When my mother's around, I'm always afraid I'm going to do something wrong, even if I don't do anything at all.
—**Jamie, age twenty-six**

In my professional career, I see so many women who grew up with critical parents who now have with problems in their partner relationships. In their attempt to cover for their mom or dad or make light of the criticism, they may laugh about what their parents continue to say to them or excuse their behavior by telling me that their parents had high expectations or just wanted the best for them. In presenting their parents in this light, they are still trying to minimize the damage they did and win their parent's approval by being a good girl.

In dealing with adult women who are the products of critical parents, the problems I most often see are these:

• They suffer from depression, anxiety, and physical problems whose cause cannot be found.

• They don't trust their own judgment and have an extreme fear of making mistakes, so the action they take is inaction.

• They have an insatiable need to please others and be approved of and accepted.

- They are foolishly loyal to those who do not deserve it and create attachments to anyone who shows them any sort of temporary kindness.

- They don't allow themselves to feel happy at their own successes because they "know" it will be taken away from them at any moment.

- They tend to work for overly demanding bosses without complaint, hoping for a crumb of approval, which doesn't come.

- They are "doormats" to their children, spouse, friends, and anyone else who wants something from them.

- They are the "dumping ground" for anyone's anger and frustration, because they will take it without complaint.

Think for a moment about the criticisms you received as a child and continue to receive today. Looking at the list above, can you recognize some of those behaviors and feelings within yourself? How much of what your parents told you about yourself was actually true? Sit with that for a moment. If you weren't you, but were an outside person looking at you, how much of those criticisms are actually real, and how much might be a projection of your parents' feelings about themselves? Hmmm ...

THE EFFECTS OF SEXUAL ABUSE

According to many reliable national studies, approximately one in three girls will be sexually abused by the time she turns eighteen. Isn't that frightening? The truth is that sexual abuse—like adult nonphysical relationship abuse—happens to girls of every religion, race, economic class, and geographical region. Usually, the abuser is not a stranger, but a father, mother, uncle, aunt, sibling, teacher, caregiver, clergy person, or family friend.

Do not narrowly define sexual abuse as coerced intercourse. In their book *The Courage to Heal*, authors Laura Davis and Ellen Bass define sexual abuse more broadly. You were sexually abused if you were

- touched in sexual areas;

- shown sexual movies or forced to listen to sexual talk;

- made to pose for seductive or sexual photographs;

- forced to perform oral sex on a sibling or adult;

- raped or otherwise penetrated (Dr. Murray's note: penetration may include fingers or an object);

- fondled, kissed, or held in a way that made you feel uncomfortable;

- forced to take part in ritualized abuse in which you were physically or sexually tortured;

- bathed in a way that felt intrusive to you;

- objectified and ridiculed about your body;

- encouraged or goaded into sex you didn't really want;

- told all you were good for was sex;

- involved in child pornography or child prostitution.

The main commonality between childhood sexual abuse and adult relationship abuse is that both are all about power and control. Children who have been sexually violated are truly victims; they didn't have the power to object, and they were not in control of either the relationship or the consequences of nonparticipation. They did not deserve this type of horrible violence, but they carry the shame and guilt as adult women.

The Courage to Heal is a tremendous, groundbreaking book written for women who have experienced childhood sexual abuse. This book helped me in my quest for answers and healing from my own sexual abuse, and I highly recommend it to you, if you were sexually abused. Bass and Davis delineate some of the ways that childhood sexual abuse can affect your relationships later in life. How many of the issues below (taken in part from my book *Destructive Relationships*) apply to you?

- *Difficulty with feelings:* You may have difficulty recognizing your feelings or expressing them. Perhaps you are uncomfortable with negative feelings, such as anger or sadness, or cannot experience a wide range of emotions. You may be prone to depression, anxiety, or panic attacks. Maybe your feelings appear to be out of your control, and you cry "for no good reason" or become irrationally angry or violent.

- *Low self-esteem and lack of personal worth:* You may feel that you are an inherently bad person who doesn't deserve happiness. You may feel powerless, as though you are still a victim. Perhaps if people close to you knew who you really were, they'd leave. You may have a lack of motivation, a failure to succeed, or a need to be perfect at everything you do. Perhaps you exhibit self-destructive behaviors or hate yourself. You may have trouble trusting your intuition or feel unable to protect yourself in dangerous situations.

- *Uncomfortable feelings about your body:* You may not feel present in your own body some of the time; at times you may feel that you've left your body. Perhaps you are frequently unaware of the messages your body sends you, such as hunger, pain, thirst, fatigue, or fear. You may have a difficult time loving and accepting your body, or you may overeat or suffer from an eating disorder, such as anorexia or bulimia.

- *Intimacy issues:* Perhaps you have difficulty trusting anyone and have few, if any, close friends, a fact that leaves you feeling isolated and lonely. It may be difficult for you to give and receive affection and nurturing. You may become romantically interested in men who are unavailable to you either in an emotional sense or because they are married. You may panic when people get too close, either emotionally or physically, and feel claustrophobic at times. Maybe you are clingy and dependent, expect those around you to leave you, or repeatedly "test" the loyalty or perseverance of those close to you.

- *Your sexuality:* You may be unable to remain present and focused during lovemaking, or maybe you go through sex numb or in a panic. Perhaps you use sex to meet nonsexual needs or to keep a man tied to you. You may find that you cannot say "no" to a sexual request, so you end up having sex when and in ways you don't want to. You may not experience sexual desire or pleasure and may believe that such feelings are bad. Maybe you feel that your worth is primarily sexual or have used sex to control men.

- *Children and parenting issues:* You may be uncomfortable or frightened around children or fear that you might be abusive to your own children or someone else's. You may have difficulty setting boundaries for your children or balancing their needs with your own. You may be unable to feel as close to your children as you would like or have a hard time expressing affection, especially with a daughter. You may be overprotective of your children and see danger lurking around every corner.

After reviewing the definitions of sexual abuse and its possible aftermath, do you find yourself in any of those categories? You may want to write down your feelings in your journal and contemplate the unexpected ways that the abuse, which may have occurred thirty or more years ago, still attacks you today.

The way you lost your innocence was unfair and criminal. I have come to see my own sexual abuse as a hole in my heart that will never heal. It is not a life-threatening hole, however, but akin to a hole in a street that I must be careful to navigate around on a constant basis so that I don't fall in.

> When I was seven years old, my mother's boyfriend began sexually abusing me. My father had left when I was two or three and was a cheater and drinker. My mother knew about the abuse and never did anything about it. I guess she was confused and desperate and just happy when he was with her. I never thought that she sacrificed me for her own needs until Dr. Jill brought it up. I guess I just saw my mom as pathetic.
>
> For some reason, when I was twelve, she put an end to the abuse and kicked him out. Dr. Jill thinks that it's because I got my period when I was twelve and was now a woman in competition with her and could also become pregnant. Anyway, I was destroyed that he was gone. I liked the attention from him. I would go out looking for him, seeking him out. My mother never called the police. She'd probably have to admit that she'd known about it for five years, and then what would that say about her?
>
> He and I kept up our little affair behind her back, and when I was eighteen, we got married and had two children together. I know it sounds very strange. When I was married to him, he was very, very abusive. HE NEVER HIT ME, but he was abusive in every other way, to the point where I felt suicidal. He constantly threatened to take my children away in order to keep me with him. He was murdered when my kids were in elementary school, and I was finally free of him, but I went on to have two more abusive marriages and have affairs with married men while I was married myself. The affairs were abusive also.
>
> I think of myself as a very strong and independent person, but when you look at the patterns in my life with men, I guess it doesn't really look that way, does it?
> —**Bridget, age forty-nine**

WHAT HAS IT COST YOU?
THE ROLE CHILDHOOD ABUSE HAS PLAYED IN YOUR ADULT LIFE

You have now seen the ways your parents helped shape you into the woman you are today—and unwittingly helped you make unhealthy relationship choices. When you were a child, you may have been treated unfairly and unkindly. You may have been disrespected and dishonored, unappreciated for the beautiful little girl you were.

As you looked through the sections of this chapter, what areas were particularly significant to you? Take out your lovely journal and write a column on the left side that reads *my abusers*, and list the names of every single person who violated you through neglect, sexual abuse, physical abuse, emotional abuse, verbal abuse, or drug or alcohol abuse. Also list those who harmed you by criticizing you or by living in their own world of depression or anxiety. Who told you that you were bad and wrong or that there was something unlovable about that precious child?

On the right side of the paper, next to the abusers' names, list the type of abuse each one perpetrated. Unfortunately, you may find that some of the people on the list abused you in multiple ways. If so, I want you to list the person's name separately for each different type of abuse. For example, you should avoid doing something like this:

Father: sexual, verbal, emotional, neglect, criticism, drinking

That minimizes the devastation he imposed upon you. In the above example, you should list your father several times; each entry should detail the type of sexual abuse he perpetrated, how often, what it felt like, what you did during and after the abuse, how you felt about yourself, etc. Then, list him again and talk about the names he called you and anyone else he verbally assaulted in your presence and how you felt, and so on. Don't let your abusers off the hook too easily.

This will not be an easy activity; in fact, it may be the most difficult one in the book. It will probably take you several days to complete. That's all right; there is no time limit on this activity. You may feel very tired while and after you write. You may not want to talk with anyone, or you may want to discuss the exercise with a supportive, nurturing person. This may be a good time to begin therapy or bring the results of this work to your current therapist.

If the pain of this exercise begins to feel like too much, remember this: these events have already occurred. The acts themselves are history. You have used denial and repression as effective coping devices to help you get through your life. Although the pain may now be in the present tense, the actions are years old. This abuse has kept you stuck and self-destructive. Abuse lives in the dark and is scary to look at, but once you expose it to the light, which you are doing in this activity, it can begin to recede. You can gain control for the first time in your life.

Do not let fear and past abuse rule your life and your decisions. What your parents did was wrong, and what they may have told you about yourself was wrong, as well.

Once you look the abuse squarely in the eyes, you can begin the exciting path of beginning your life in a new and healthier way—the way you want it to look!

PART II

BUT WHAT IF HE'S RIGHT? UNDERSTANDING YOURSELF AND YOUR RELATIONSHIPS

I've been in this relationship for eight months. The first four months were perfect. I couldn't believe how lucky I was to have the perfect boyfriend. Most of my friends were jealous of me. Then, everything started changing. I don't know what I did wrong. Now, whenever we talk—either in person, on the phone, or online—he's always mad at me.

He blames me for the fact that my parents don't like him, and he thinks I don't stand up for myself by telling them to get lost and butt out of my relationship with him. He doesn't see what having him as my boyfriend has done to my relationship with my parents. My home life is hell. My parents keep telling me how bad he is for me, and they have begun restricting me from seeing him or talking to him. I sneak and do it anyway, but they are always on my case about him.

They don't understand him or our relationship. Sometimes, they see me crying when I've hung up with him, or they say that I don't have any friends anymore since I've gotten serious about him. They think everything that goes wrong in my life is because of him. For instance, I'm getting a couple of bad grades, and they think it's because he's a bad influence and because of all the time we spend together. Yeah, it's true that I used to get mostly As, but now I'm in harder classes and just can't seem to keep up. I guess I'll admit that since I've been with him, I spend a little less time studying than I used to, but am I supposed to be a nun, for God's sake? Am I not allowed to have a social life or a boyfriend? I mean, they keep telling me that high school should be the best time of my life and that they want me to have a good high school experience. Well, isn't having a boyfriend one of those things I'm supposed to have to make it good?

They also say that I used to go to church every Sunday with them, and now I don't, so they think it's because he's not a Christian. He's not, but it's been my decision not to go to church with them. I'm not eight years old anymore; I can make my own decisions about religion now, and they don't seem to understand that. He thinks religion is a big crock and a crutch people use in their lives, and I'm starting to feel that way, too. I never looked at it that way before, so I guess you could say that he may have enlightened me, but I've thought it through. It's not like he brainwashed me or anything.

My parents have an idea that I've had sex with him—which I have, but I'm not going to talk to them about that!—and they think he must have forced me, because I used to say that I was going to wait until I got married. OK, I was stupid and naive about that. I really like having sex with him. It makes me feel closer to him and like we are a real couple. He calls me names sometimes, which hurts my feelings, but it's when he's having a bad day or something like that. It's not all the time. I know he doesn't mean it.

At this point, I don't know how I'm supposed to live out the next three years like this. When we both graduate, we're going to move in together, but I'd never tell my parents about that. They'd probably flip out and send me away to a boarding school. They think I'm under a spell or something and he's being abusive to me. That's so weird; it's like they think he hits me, and he's never laid a hand on me like that.

—**Casey, age fifteen**

When you read Casey's story, could you clearly see that she has been in an abusive relationship and is unable to recognize that her boyfriend truly is brainwashing her?

In the first section of this book you learned what nonphysical abuse looks like and the sneaky ways in which the abuse may have begun in your childhood—or, at least, set you up for future abusive relationships. Now let's talk a bit about other crucial ideas that will be significant in helping you understand more about yourself and your relationships.

The goal of my work with you is not only to describe what your life may look like—and may have looked like for a long time—but to help you understand yourself better. I want you to understand the choices you have made and the ways you can change your life and relationship patterns to achieve a more powerful and contented future.

In this section of the book, I'd like you to open your mind and heart to looking deeper into yourself and your motivations. You already know that I don't want you to regard yourself as a victim, because when you understand the hows and whys of your unwitting part in this—and other—unhealthy relationships, you can not only take charge of your relationships with others, you can take charge of yourself in all situations! How amazing would that be?

We will now begin to look at several important concepts that will allow you to do significant work on the thoughts, ideas, and no-win behaviors that have kept you stuck.

First, we will take a closer look at the many faces of nonphysical abuse. Since you now understand the behaviors and mindset of an abuser, you can grasp important concepts about what that abuse has actually done to your mind, heart, health, and spirit. Abusers come in many shapes and forms. Maybe not all of your abusers are your significant other/partner. The abuser may also take the form of parent, sibling, boss, coworker, female friend, or even your own child. These are also some of the most significant relationships in your life, and—as I've discovered—if you are in a destructive relationship with your male partner, you may also be in multiple unhealthy relationships with others close to you.

Next, we will take a brief tour of "Victim City" and the factors that led you to reside there. You will see that many roads lead into that town but very few leave it. I want you to exit that hamlet as soon as possible; it's not a great place to live, and nothing ever changes when you live there!

A very important section follows, in which we will examine how your abusive relationship affects the way you feel, think, act, and react. You recall that you have 100 percent control over all these behaviors, yet you've allowed *him* to take charge of your precious life force. It's time for you to take back your power, my pal, and that's just what we are going to do several pages from now.

A difficult part of this section comes next, in which we will talk about his way of "loving" you. I know that you are practicing the idea that LOVE IS A BEHAVIOR, so you may want to consider whether or not he really does love you *in the way you deserve to be loved.* Now, you know that I respect the work you're doing in this book, so please take no offense when I pose the question: do you really love him? We will need to take a hard look at that important question before we can move on in a healthy manner.

Next, we'll look at your behavioral patterns with others, particularly men. Are you a people-pleaser/martyr/codependent/drama-and-chaos junkie? That's a mouthful, isn't it? Let's really delve into the ways you act and react with others and the reasons behind your behavior, shall we?

Now, here's a tough question: are you attracted to abusers? For that matter, do you actually choose abusers to be a part of your life? Yikes! How could that be possible? Well, I've found that it's not only possible, it's also probable. You didn't *know* you were attracting and choosing abusers, but you may have been, nonetheless. It's time to check on that pattern, doncha think?

Lastly, you know we have to review your self-esteem, as low self-esteem is not only the root cause but also the outcome of an unhealthy relationship. It may work slow and steady, but it is deadly to the spirit. We will give your self-esteem a checkup, and I'll also give you some nifty plans for lifting it to the skies!

OK, this section is not easy, but I know that you are becoming stronger day by day. You can do it. Let's take a deep breath together and dive in!

5

A Slippery Slope: The Many Faces of Nonphysical Abuse

How many abusive relationships have I had? I don't really know. Are we counting friends and family or just romantic relationships, because the number could change by about 150.
—**Alice, age thirty-seven**

Alice makes a good point there. When I ask women how many abusive relationships they've had in their lives, they are usually quite confused. First, they don't truly understand what abuse looks like, so if they've not been in a physically abusive relationship, they list their number as "zero." If they've been involved with one physically violent man (and pushing and hair-pulling don't count to them), their answer is "one."

Most commonly, when I lecture to large groups of women or work individually with one woman, I outline the types of abuse you and I have already been through earlier in this book. A lightbulb comes on over the women's heads, and they then understand that they've experienced several abusive relationships with men. However, they limit their list of unhealthy relationships to just the ones with male romantic partners.

Then I tell them about signs of abuse from parents, siblings, bosses, coworkers, female friends, and even their children. Their faces inevitably drop, they pull Kleenex out of their purses, and they come to understand that abusers have many names. Then they realize that they may have been in several dozen abusive relationships … in the last year! Many times, they begin to understand that almost all—if not all—of their relationships are abusive. I can tell you from personal experience, that is not a happy realization.

So, let's you and I talk for a few moments about many other types of abusers, rather than just your male partner. Your life will become far easier once you

71

understand how many abusers may be inhabiting your life. When you gain this wretched knowledge, we can take steps together to rectify the situation. Then you will be able to live your fullest and most powerful life.

PARENTS AS ABUSERS

You and I have already discussed the ways in which your childhood home may have been abusive or set you up for an unhealthy adult relationship. Is it possible that your parents are still driving you crazy? Wait, how can that be? You are now an adult. You live in a separate home. You don't have to answer to them, and they can't ground you anymore. Or can they?

> I dread knowing that my mother is coming to my house. I stress about it for days. Sometimes, she "spares" me the anticipation and just shows up unannounced.
>
> The first thing she does when she walks in is stand in my foyer, look around in disgust, and sniff the air. Then, she pretends that she's coughing. That's her little hint that the air is putrid, and even from the entrance, the house is disgustingly filthy. She gives me her cheek to kiss and then makes her way to the back of the house, where the kitchen is. All along the way, she's rearranging things and picking up a spare toy or two.
>
> I have three kids under the age of six, but she's not coming over to help me out with them. No, actually she's coming over to tell me what a lousy job I'm doing as a mother, wife, and homemaker.
>
> Here's her usual list of my problems: I feed my kids boxed macaroni and cheese once a week or so (she made it from scratch), I don't wash their hands every time they touch the floor or the cat, I don't brown my chicken for five minutes on medium-high on each side, sometimes I don't get into the shower until late morning, I don't always use concealer on the dark circles under my eyes after a night up with a sick child, my house doesn't look like a model home, the cat is allowed up on the couch, I don't dress like a Victoria's Secret model when my husband comes home, I can go an entire day or two without putting on makeup, I don't call her twice a day like other good daughters do (gee, I wonder why), and I still haven't lost my baby weight even though my youngest is now eight months old.
>
> I've given up trying to argue with her about any of these things or the hundreds of others she can come up with. Basically, I'm just a complete failure. Lately, my oldest has asked me why my mommy doesn't like me or why she's so mad at me. I really don't know what to say. I talk to my husband about it, hoping that he'll help me out with her constant criticism, but to tell you the truth, I think he gets a kind of kick out of it. When I tell him what happens, he just laughs and says, "You know your mother is like that." Or when she says something about my inadequacy as a wife, he'll pinch my belly pouch and

say, "Well, hon, it has been eight months since the baby was born." I not only don't get any support, but I end up feeling worse about myself. I feel stuck.
—Cheryl, age thirty-two

Do you have Cheryl's mother? I did. I thought I was doing pretty well as a new mother of twins. I didn't have any help, and their dad didn't come home until eight o'clock each night. My mother didn't help me at all. I felt very isolated. They were my first and only children, and I was proud of myself that the three of us lived till the next day! On the odd occasion when my mom visited me, she gave me a look of disgust because there were toys on the floor, dishes in the sink, and nursing pads strewn around willy-nilly. The twins were on different schedules; my daughter had colic all day, while her brother had colic all night. To tell you the truth, I don't have a good recollection of their entire first year. My main goal in life was to stay awake.

So you can imagine how I looked forward to my mother's infrequent but bothersome visits. It was just another thing to feel bad about. I did end up changing that mother/daughter pattern, though, and I'll tell you how I did that later in the book. My current relationship with my eighty-two-year-old mother is one of my choosing and is as satisfactory as it can be. But it is a relationship that gives us both something good, which wouldn't have been possible had I not changed the ways in which I *react* to her. After all, that is one of the three things I have 100 percent control over, right?

So, maybe you currently have a very critical mom or dad who thinks you never do anything well enough, who makes you feel guilty for being alive, who is very demanding, or who has impossibly high expectations of you. Maybe your parents constantly compare you to your siblings or make you feel inadequate. Perhaps you didn't achieve what they wanted for you or didn't knuckle under to their demands or wishes. Perhaps they are verbally unkind or can still give you "the look" they gave you when you were a kid. That look conveys total disapproval and disappointment. Maybe you are considered the black sheep of the family because you married out of your race, socioeconomic class, or religion.

Look back at the signs of verbal and emotional abuse and decide whether your parents fit into any of those categories. I know how difficult that can be. Your parents as abusers? That's not a fun idea, but when you are completely honest about who all of the people in your life are, you can begin to make better decisions. I'm not telling you that you cannot love and honor your parents. Not at all. Just be honest about their behaviors and what you do not want to allow in your life.

SIBLINGS AS ABUSERS

When I'm with my sister, I feel like we are back in our teen years, fighting over who has a boyfriend and who doesn't, who's taking too long in the bathroom, who stole whose pink sweater, whose side mom or dad is taking in the fight. She still tries to one-up me or has this subtle way of making me feel like I'm just the stupid little sister.
—**Gloria, age forty-four**

Gloria is forty-four years old and is still competing with her older sister. Believe me, that's not uncommon. But now, instead of the boyfriend, they may be competing over whose husband makes more money. Instead of the pink sweater, it may be who has the best designer clothes or job or neighborhood. Instead of the bathroom, it may be which sister's children are doing better in school or have been accepted into the better college. They may still compete for mom and dad's designation as the supreme daughter.

Sibling rivalry can be as horrendous at forty-four as it was at four. Although the competition looks different now and may be infinitely more subtle, it's just as serious and meaningful as "who got to sit on daddy's lap." Yes, your child learned to read at three ... but your brother's youngest was potty-trained at fifteen months! You just got a promotion, but he is heading up an entire department! Your family is taking a houseboat vacation this summer, but his family is taking a trip to Hawaii for a week—in a luxury condo! Your baby has beautiful blue eyes, but his child has dad's dimple in his chin! Do you see where I'm going with this?

I have three brothers—one younger and two older. Once all of us grew old enough that our ages didn't matter as much, I found that they shared something I could never be a part of: testosterone. They had a boy's club that was so closed, I was always on the outside. They shared a boy-bond through sports, guy talk, attention to women's body parts ... and making fun of me. Nothing made them happier than having fun at my expense or playing a trick on me. The ultimate source of revelry was if I cried, a reward with which I delighted them quite often. Now, I'm not only talking about when I was eight or ten, but also when I was thirty. I was always a "victim" to these nasty boys and couldn't figure out why. Can you? Gosh, because I let them, and because I gave them such a stunning pay-off for their bad behavior. I eventually cut that off at the pass, but not until I was well into my thirties. Now, our relationship is one of respect and good-natured joking, in which I am not the object of their verbal smacking. Did they mature or become instantly emotionally knowledgeable? I really doubt it; once again, I changed my *reaction* to them.

ABUSIVE BOSSES AND COWORKERS

I worked for a company that gave me a migraine every single day. I couldn't stand it but felt I didn't have any choice but to continue to work there. I was a single mom with two kids, and my child-support checks were erratic. I couldn't just up and leave, even though my boss was Jekyll and Hyde and my coworkers were nasty, backstabbing people who would lie to make themselves look better. My boss wanted me to work two, three, four hours late sometimes without telling me in advance, and then I had to scramble to make childcare arrangements. She'd tell me her personal problems and give me the impression that we were friends, but then she would pull rank on me when it suited her. My coworkers made mistakes and placed the blame on me, sometimes when I wasn't even there, and then they'd act all buddy-buddy with me.

I felt as though I was living in a psychiatric ward! I started taking the problems out on my kids and friends. They were all sick of hearing me complain about work and told me to just quit, which I didn't think I could do. We'd been living in a bad economy, and even though I didn't make a ton of money, I made enough to support my kids if we didn't do anything extra. So, who knows when I'd get another job, especially if I didn't get a good recommendation? I felt that I didn't have any choices, and that was really frightening.

I was sick all weekend, knowing I'd have to go back to work on Monday, so I couldn't even enjoy my kids on the weekends. It was a miserable life.
—**Suzie, age thirty-nine**

I work at a men's clothing store, and it's gotten to be really creepy. I admit that I'm pretty cute, which I'm now understanding is probably the entire reason why my boss hired me. He asks me to wear tight clothes or short skirts that show off my figure. He actually likes it when the men ogle me! He encourages it. Sometimes, when I'm bloated or just not feeling good, I don't want to wear anything too tight. He really yells at me and tells me that I'm ruining his business. I don't know if I should involve my dad in this. I'm trying to handle it on my own, but I'm not doing too well.
—**Callie, age sixteen**

You may be working under similar circumstances as Callie or Suzie's. You've worked in an abusive work environment if you've experienced any of the following:

• An emotionally unstable boss

• A work-at-all-hours boss

- Coworkers who steal your ideas, lie about you, won't leave you alone as you try to work, stab you in the back professionally

- Sexual discrimination or harassment

- Maternity discrimination

As we will discuss in upcoming chapters, once you take your power back, deal with your emotional fears, decide what you deserve in life instead of letting others decide for you, and learn to stand up for yourself, you will very clearly see the myriad choices available to you in your workplace. Your boss may be your *boss*, but as you've undoubtedly heard your kids tell you, s/he's not the "boss of you!"

ABUSIVE FRIENDS

My friend Laura was my confidant and best pal for nine years. We did everything together. We raised our kids together, went to Gymboree together, suffered through potty training together, had parties together, and even got our husbands to like each other so that we could all spend time together as couples. She was the sister I never had. She had a boy, and I had a girl; we imagined them getting married someday and being in-laws and grandparents together! It was the perfect friendship, except sometimes I felt as though I was a little lower than she was. She'd gone to college, and I hadn't. Her husband made a little more than mine did. She had had a career before she had her son, and I had just worked part time at the cosmetics counter of a department store. It wasn't really a career, just some money to keep us afloat while my husband got his career going.

Things between Laura and myself started changing when my husband and I were having marital problems. I had always been able to tell her everything, so I told her about my problems with him. She seemed sympathetic, but as the problems became more serious and ongoing and I became sadder and sadder, she became less and less available.

I might have been using most of our time together in complaining, I don't know. All she had to say was, "Barb, I'm sorry you and Dave are having such a bad time. I've tried to give you all the advice I can, but now you'll really have to make a decision about it. It's hard for me to listen to this all the time." My feelings probably would have been hurt, but I'd have dealt with it. Instead, she just started going further and further from me. Dave and I were seeing a marital therapist and trying to get ourselves back together in a good way. I'd tell her that, and it didn't seem to matter to her. She became closer to other friends that we shared and stopped returning my calls. I felt really alone.

When she and her husband would have fights, she'd confide in me. There were several times when they'd be going at it for days or weeks at a time, and I didn't complain. That's what friends are for: to be there when one is having a bad time. But after a month of Dave and my not getting along, she disappeared off the face of the earth. I heard stories from other people about gossip she was spreading about me and my marriage, some of which was true, and some of which was blown out of proportion. I can't tell you how much that hurt.

The kids would see each other at school but didn't play together outside of that anymore. My daughter really missed Laura's son and didn't understand why they couldn't play together anymore. That wasn't my decision, but Laura just wouldn't answer her phone when I asked about play dates.

I began to wrack my brain and thought about all the times I'd made excuses for her being unkind to me or gossiping about another woman, or the way she was judgmental or the victim in any situation. I started seeing who Laura really was, and it just about crushed me.

—Cyndie, age thirty-six

I can't believe how much my friends gossip about me. It's like the girls are your friends one minute and not the next. I never know who I can trust or believe.

—Lindsay, age fourteen

The phrase *abusive friend* is an oxymoron, isn't it? How could you have abusive friends? I've found that most women have at least a couple of gal pals who are really good for their self-esteem or health. How many times have you given the following excuses for your girlfriends:

- She probably has PMS.

- She was tired.

- The kids—or her husband—must have been driving her crazy.

- I'm sure I heard her incorrectly.

- She had a bad day at work.

- I'm sure I could have been more understanding.

- If I hadn't done_____, she wouldn't have had to _____.

- I'm probably being too sensitive.

- She might have had too much to drink.

- She's my best friend, so I forgive her again.

- She's a little flaky, but that's part of her charm.

- It really doesn't matter to me that much.

- I'm probably making too big a deal of it.

- That's just the way she is.

- She keeps me waiting, but she keeps everyone waiting.

- It's so great to be around her when she's having a good day.

- She had a bad childhood.

I could really go on and on, but I'm sure I hit a few of the excuses you've made for a friend or three … or twelve.

Most of us have had friends we thought we could rely upon—and then, in a pinch, they weren't anywhere to be found. Or what about the pal who drops off her little angels at your house while she runs a few errands and shows up six hours later—after you've fed them lunch and dinner and broken up three crying jags, two tantrums, and four fights with your kids? Have you ever tried to ask them to reciprocate when you needed a hand with your kids for an hour or two so you didn't have to be terrorized by a three-year-old in the market? Maybe you have a friend who dumps all her problems on your slim shoulders, but when you need to talk, she doesn't have the time or interest. What about the "pal" who just can't keep the secret you told her to herself? It's not so much fun when you find out that she told four other women … but only out of concern for you, of course. We've all had girlfriends who are just a tad too honest, haven't we? They will give their opinion on our clothes, furniture, children, figure, and anything else without being asked … but only because they think we need to know, and who else would tell us if not our best friend?

My personal favorite is the friend to whom you tell a big and embarrassing or very personal secret, and you ask her to promise not to tell anyone. She agrees in a very conspiratorial whisper, and then her husband asks you later how that "thing" is going? If you have the nerve to confront her on her broken promise, she'll bat her eyes innocently and turn things back onto you, saying, "You know Steve and I don't have any secrets. He's not going to tell anyone. You know guys don't talk." Wrong! Guys love gossip as much as anyone.

So, what's been your payoff for remaining in these friendships? I find that most of us would rather maintain the illusion of friendships—even if we are being treated like slime—than get out of them and be friendless for a couple of days while we get our own acts together and align ourselves with new, healthier women.

Women are all about relationships. Our lives revolve around relationships. Get a couple or more women together and what do they talk about? Relationships. Work relationships, romantic relationships, parent or sibling relationships, relationships with their kids, heck—even their relationships with their pets.

Men are single-focused and competitive minded. I am always stunned when I ask my husband what he and his friends talk about for five hours on a golf course, and he says, "Nothing." I ask him how that can possibly be. Four men, five hours, and no talking? He swears mostly what they say is, "Good shot," "Too bad," "Oh, you just missed it," "Nasty swing," "You were robbed," and the ever-personal comment, "Nice putter; where'd you get it?"

A woman puts a tremendous amount of stock in her girlfriend relationships. There's something very primal about sharing with a "sister," someone who really understands your experience, merely by virtue of estrogen. So when a woman's girlfriend relationships start heading south, it is very depressing and confusing. If you ever have a few minutes, go to your local middle school, and you'll see girl relationships in their full, abusive prime. Girls gossiping, backstabbing, rumor-mongering, being best friends one day and worst enemies the next—it's a girl soap opera every day, and it just keeps escalating from there.

I think that we have irrationally high expectations for ourselves in the girl-friend department. We have this feeling that everyone who has the same genitalia should think and behave as we would in every situation. We think we should be able to trust them. It makes perfect sense, but I believe that if you have three girl-friends you can really count on, you are a gal-pal millionaire. You are living in girlfriend luxury. Feel lucky if you have these three; enjoy your wealth. The rest are acquaintances at best and should be treated cautiously. We will talk about what you can do to rid yourself of abusive friends later in this book.

ABUSIVE CHILDREN

My son just turned fourteen, and he is a complete nightmare. He had always had sort of a bratty streak when he was younger. He wanted what he wanted and would have tantrums when he didn't get it. I thought he was just being a normal kid. Trust me, most of the time he was really wonderful. He had a huge heart, was very kind to his friends, had a lot of friends, and their parents couldn't stop praising him. He excelled in school and in sports and partici-pated in a lot of volunteer activities. He was a true leader.

When he was thirteen, he started to change. I still can't figure out what that change was, but he started becoming a monster. He's very defiant and refuses to do anything his father or I ask. He's a big kid and can be very intimidating. He's pushed my husband around and terrorizes his younger brother and sister, who just want him to have anything he wants so there won't be fighting. He steals from them and blames them for things he does. They don't even stick up for themselves anymore, because they don't want the consequences.

He calls me vile names constantly. Every word out of his mouth is a cuss word. He doesn't think he should have any rules or restrictions or that we should tell him what to do. He hangs around with a whole new crowd of friends, and I know he's already having sex. He runs away when he doesn't get what he wants and then comes back sweet as pie when he's getting goodies. We impose grounding or other restrictions, but he doesn't follow them.

Ask his friends' parents, his coaches, or the adults at school, and he's a perfect gentleman. It makes us crazy, mostly because we know he can be this way: a good kid, I mean. He can be polite and obey rules with other people, just not at home. He insists he's not taking drugs, and we can't force him to take a drug test. He won't comply.

I'm at my wit's end. When Dr. Jill told him he was an abuser, that seemed to make him think, and he was good for almost a week. We were actually thinking about giving him his computer or phone back, but then he started the abusive stuff all over again. Until she said the word "abuser," it hadn't clicked with me that that's who he is. It made perfect sense and also frightened me.

What did we do wrong, and how do we help him change?

—Kim, age forty-five

Children can be massively abusive to their parents. I counsel a lot of kids and lecture around the country in middle and high schools to about one hundred thousand students each year. I see a horrible pattern of disrespect for people, self, and property in every town I visit. I see huge problems with sex, drugs, and alcohol everywhere I go. Sleazy behavior on the parts of both girls and boys is the norm, rather than the aberration.

What would have happened if you had said to your parents, "I don't have to clear the dinner table. Why should I take everyone else's plates off the table? Why can't they take their own damn plates off the table? I'm tired of being your slave." Well, OK, there are laws in place that don't allow you to hit your kids with a belt anymore, but would you have ever dreamed of speaking that way to your parents? Let me tell you, I hear examples like the one above all the time from other parents.

I blame a few factors for this horrid behavior. Number one, parents don't want to be parents anymore; they want to be their kid's pal. Trust me, your kids have enough pals; they only have you as their parent. A lot of parents want their children to "like" them, or they want to be the cool, hip parent. Nuts to that plan. Your kids won't respect you anymore; they will just see you as the desperate adult you are. Kids need structure, guidance, and adult logic.

Another destructive force I'm seeing is the culture children are being raised in now. Take a look at MTV for a few minutes (take a Maalox first), and tell me what you see and hear. Much of the music your children are being exposed to is incredibly violent, racist, homophobic, *very* disrespectful to women, and so on. The way children dress and who they choose as idols all combines to create an atmosphere of disgusting and disrespectful behaviors. I truly believe that the current entertainment culture is actually hostile to everything we are trying to teach our kids in terms of respect, honesty, and decent behavior.

What can you do? The first thing is to respect yourself. Why should your children respect you if they see you allowing others to treat you disrespectfully? You cannot expect or demand their respect when you don't respect yourself. That would be pointless. Next, have the guts to be a parent. That means walking the walk, teaching consequences and following through on them, imposing rules and restrictions, and being tough when need be and then feeling proud of yourself rather than guilty. That means, if you have a rule that homework has to be done before your kids can play with their friends, that's the rule.

And stop doing your kids' homework or projects for them. Let them fail and make mistakes once in a while. It's not the end of their world; it's called a learning lesson. It's OK for them to be disappointed or not get their way or feel hurt. That's real life. How else are they going to learn? It won't crush them; it will build their self-esteem and character. Your children don't *need* everything they want.

As far as the nasty music and messages, I consider all of that an excellent opportunity to talk with your child about what they are seeing and hearing. Such conversations are a terrific way to reinforce your family's values and expectations. Are you going to take all of that music and disgusting reality TV away? No, but you do have the chance to use it to your advantage.

You can help your children understand the concept of trust and what they have to do to gain and keep yours. You can help them understand the difference between a *right* and a *privilege*. Hint: food for dinner is a right, computer and TV use is a privilege.

You can monitor your children's Internet/instant messaging use. You can introduce yourself to their friends' parents and make sure that when your children visit their house, they always have adult supervision and your basic family rules are being upheld. For example, if you don't allow your child to watch PG-13-or R-rated videos, you should make the child's parents aware of that. So what if they think you're weird or they don't like it! It's your child, and you are his parent. If they don't like it, their child can play at your house instead, right?

What I'm trying to say here is that children like Kim's don't just become "monsters" overnight. At the age of thirteen, her son didn't just wake up and begin the grand change to the young, unruly, disrespectful, abusive child he is today.

If you have abusive children, be sure to read the rest of this book carefully. You don't want them to follow in your footsteps, nor do you want them to become adult abusers.

WHAT HAS IT COST YOU?

Well, this chapter was an eye opener, wasn't it? I'll be you didn't know you had so many abusers in your life. You bought this book to help you understand your male partner and what you can do to change him, I'll bet. Now, you have this whole mess of other people to contend with!

Think about this chapter for a few moments, and get out your journal. Divide the paper into columns: *mom, dad* (*stepmom* or *stepdad*, if applicable), *brother(s), sister(s), boss(es), coworker(s), friend(s), child(ren)*. Under each one, make a check mark if you now consider them to exhibit abusive behavior to you. It could have been past abusive behavior. Now comes the difficult part. Think of every unkind behavior they've displayed that has hurt you. There may be quite a list. If you like, go back only a few years or just to the start of adulthood. Now, state how the abuse made you feel about yourself. Finally, look at every abusive behavior, and make a list of how you dealt with it. Did you make an excuse, and, if so, what was the excuse? Did you let it go? If you confronted the abuser, what was the outcome? Has that affront been resolved, and, if so, have other abuses occurred since? The same type or different abuses?

Do you see a pattern there? This is all very powerful information. Now you can see the ways you've allowed abuse in your life and what your possible payoffs have been. Keep this list nearby and refer to it often in the chapters to come.

In the next chapter, we will take a closer look at the ways you've decided to become a "victim" and how that identity may have served you ... or kept you from looking at reality.

6

Victims?

I don't know what's wrong with me. There must be a black cloud over my life, because I don't know anyone else who has the kind of luck that I do.

My husband is a great guy; don't get me wrong. I'm really grateful for him. Who else would have a mess like me living with them? But he's gone a lot on business, and I feel lonely sometimes.

I used to have a good job, but for some reason I still don't understand, I was laid off. I think it was because I was taking too much time off for my migraines, but what am I supposed to do? Sit in the bright lights of the office all day with a scorcher of a headache? Migraines are a real medical condition; I'm not making them up. If I had a broken arm, would they fire me because I couldn't type for a while? I don't really know if it was that or something else. The management was always so mean to me. I couldn't do anything right. I'll start looking for another job pretty soon.

My son and his wife are expecting their first baby, which is wonderful. I just hope that I'll get to see it. My son hasn't spoken to me in more than a year. I don't have any idea why. He won't tell me. I really think it's his wife. She's very prissy. I've tried to be a good mother-in-law, but everything I did seemed to rub her the wrong way. I can't think of anything I did or said that would have upset her; I think she's so sensitive. Of course, he's siding with her without even hearing my end of the story.

I have some friends. I guess you would call them friends. They are more like fair-weather friends, if you ask me. We used to get together and play cards or go to the movies sometimes or have a cup of coffee. It was nice. One of the girls got a divorce after twenty-three years of marriage. In my opinion, that wasn't a good idea. Men cheat sometimes; you have to forgive them, but she did not. Now, she had to sell their house and get a job. She still sees some of the girls, but I don't see her except sometimes at the market or something like that. I don't know what I did to make her so uncordial. She's having a difficult life, I'm sure of that, but I didn't do anything to cause it.

Anyway, I think I was born under a black cloud. Nothing is going my way, and it makes me very depressed. Some days, I don't even want to get out of bed. What's the use?
—**Nancy, age fifty-two**

Nancy certainly plays the role of victim, doesn't she? Her husband's not around, she lost her job, her son won't talk to her, and neither will her friends.

Do you sometimes feel like your life can't get any worse ... and then it does? I hate to sound so dismissive about all of this, but I don't think there are a whole lot of accidents in life. I also think that you create the life you have. Let me repeat that last part: *You create the life you have.*

You already understand my feeling about victims from chapter one. I believe there are some certifiable victims, but they are not you. The longer or more often you think of yourself as a victim, the longer you will stay a victim, and that is a complete waste of your time and energy.

Let's think again about who victims are: they are folks who are completely hopeless, helpless, and powerless. A sexually abused child fits that criteria. An adult woman in an unhealthy relationship does not.

Please don't think that I have absolutely zero sympathy for your situation. Your situation used to be my situation. I understand the victim idea. I could have won an Academy Award for "Best Victim in a Starring Role." I completely understand your thoughts and feelings that you *can't* leave your abusive relationship. You have been demoralized and demeaned, and your spirit has been crushed into the ground. You have been told things about yourself that are not true (which you will come to understand as you get through this book), you may have been threatened or intimidated, and you don't even know who you are anymore. You may be worried about finances, or your or your children's physical safety. There are 101 good reasons why you are still in your destructive relationship. I understand that.

But ... you still have the ability to get out if you need to. By that, I mean: you are not so mentally impaired that you do not know what day of the week it is, you can still physically get out your front door, you can still use a telephone. While I understand your fear, apprehension, and misgivings, at the very core of the matter, you do have free will and choice. Your will and choice of the moment is to be where you are, and probably for some very valid reasons.

However, you are not in the same situation as a three-year-old who is being sexually assaulted by an adult. Can we agree to that so far?

I have several patients whose identity is that of a victim. They can sit across from me for an hour at a time and tell me why they should get an award for Victim of the Year (or Lifetime). They had horrible childhoods, they seem to work for crummy bosses at every job they have, their children are mouthy and disrespectful, they have physical ailments and their doctors just don't take them seriously enough, they don't have any friends, they got a parking ticket yesterday, and the new shoes they bought at full price last week just went on sale.

It would be enough for anyone to think they should just crawl into a hole and not come out until life magically gets better. The problem is that their lives never do get better. They only get worse. How is that possible? Because *you create the life you have.*

It is not an accident of the universe that most everything in your life is bad. All your friends dropped you, all your bosses have been bad, you've been in one abusive relationship after another, your health is poor, your kids act like little creeps, and you are seventy pounds overweight—but all this didn't just occur out of the blue one day. These actions are all results of choices you have made. How can you be a victim when you've made choices?

Any moment now, you are going to blurt out—to no one in particular—"Dr. Jill, you are really a hypocrite. In chapter 4, you went on and on about the ways our childhood experiences affect the women we become and the choices we make." Shucks, you caught me! This is all true. However, let me ask you an important question. Let's say you never learned about hot and cold or the damage from putting your hand on a hot stove. After you had burned yourself once or twice, how many times would you continue to put your hand there? Let's say you had really weird parents who told you when you were a child, "Darling, burning yourself is fun and something we enjoy doing as a family, much as other families enjoy playing Yahtzee." You might burn yourself beyond recognition as a little girl—if you could tolerate the pain—but when you moved out of your parents' home and lived on your own, you might see that other folks didn't burn themselves on a slow Thursday night. You might get other messages that burning yourself is bad and painful. This information would cause you to look at the whole burning phase of your life and go, "Wow, that was strange. I know my parents told me that burning was a fun family activity, but now that I can make my own decisions, I don't think I want to do that anymore." You'd stay away from fires, right?

When you were a child, you didn't have any outside information that burning yourself was bad. You were a victim. But when you got older and could evaluate your parents' messages, you saw that the whole burning program was not going to work well in your adult life. Who would be attracted to someone who burned herself, aside from a pyromaniac or masochist?

Which turns this story around to you again. You may have gotten rotten information from your parents about who you were and what you want, but when you are an adult and your life is not working, you have the opportunity to make new and better decisions. Because you have that opportunity, you are not a victim.

Let me ask you a very pointed question: let's say a man is in jail for committing multiple rapes and murders. He's a bad, bad dude. Now, during his trial, his lawyer brings up the information that his mother was a prostitute, he never knew who his father was, he was raised in a gang-infested neighborhood, he was beaten up by several of his mother's customers, and he dropped out of school. Oh, and by the way, he started using drugs at the age of ten, but you can understand why: with that kind of life, wouldn't you? Do you give him a pass on the jail time? Do you think, *well he had it really bad when he was a kid and a young man. No wonder he committed all those heinous acts. And anyway, he was probably on drugs when he committed the crimes, so he didn't know what he was doing. Gosh, if I were him, I might make the same decisions. Those people probably deserved to be raped and killed!*

No, you wouldn't think that, and neither would I. Both of us would undoubtedly feel horribly for the child that he was and the kind of life that he had. We might even go so far as to understand how a child with that kind of beginnings could end up thinking that he didn't have a promising future. But we wouldn't excuse the rapes and murders, would we? We'd think, even with that kind of childhood, he still had a choice. His childhood didn't force him to commit crimes. Gosh, I've heard lots of stories in which kids from the streets grow up to be doctors and police officers and have good lives and do good works.

This young man was definitely a victim when he was a child. It wasn't his fault his mom was a prostitute and didn't care for him properly. He was brought into the world in that situation. It's too bad he wasn't given a good home with a nice dad to teach him how to become a responsible man. He shouldn't have had strange men beat him up. Yes indeed, he used to be a victim. Now he's a punk who's made terrible choices, and while he should receive counseling while he's in jail, I don't want him out and living next door to me and my family, do you?

There you go ... no victims.

Let's think for a moment about your heroes or sheros. Who are they, and why are they your s/heroes? Because they've overcome obstacles and done something noble? Because they've been unselfish and done things that have benefited others? Because they've had to work hard to get to where they are now?

One of my sheros is Rosa Parks. You remember her story from school and the civil rights movement. Here was this little African-American (although she certainly wasn't called African-American in those days, but a very vile name) seamstress who refused to give up her seat in the middle of a bus in Montgomery, Alabama in 1955. That was a very bold statement, since in those days, blacks and whites were segregated, and blacks had to sit in the back of the bus. Ms. Parks' action exposed her safety to risk; you know what was going on in the south to African Americans who didn't tow the segregation line at the time. But she had convictions, and she had pride. She saw what was going on around her, and she decided that on that particular day, she was just about fed up, and it was time for someone to take a stand and that it might as well be her. Wow!

She is known as the Mother of the Civil Rights Movement for taking her stand on the bus that day. She lost her job as a seamstress but decided that wasn't going to stop her, either. Remember, she was not a victim. In 1957, with no money in her pocket and no one supporting her, she upped and moved to Detroit and landed herself a job on Representative John Conyers's staff.

Rosa Parks could have seen herself as a victim. She was certainly a victim of intolerance and ignorance. It didn't look like she had a lot of choices. She was raised to be a quiet girl and not make any fuss and go along with what the white man told her to do.

What makes Rosa Parks my shero is that she didn't see herself as a victim. She overcame her fears and the myriad of obstacles in place to keep her down, and she became victorious.

It is impossible for you to be a victim and also be successful and powerful at the same time. It looks like you may need to make a choice. You can remain a victim and go about the rest of your life thinking you have no voice and no choice. You can teach that philosophy to your children and make sure that they are victims, as well. You can stay stuck and powerless, a little woman who has to be pitied and taken care of. Where has that gotten you so far? What kind of relationships have you created and attracted with this mindset? If you were truly happy, you wouldn't be reading this book. It's fair to say that being a victim hasn't worked for you so far.

Here is my simple philosophy of life: If something's working, do more of it. If it's not working, do something else. Sounds easy, doesn't it? Except that most of us do the same thing over and over and expect a different result, which is commonly known as insanity. Simply stated, being a victim and giving up control of your life hasn't worked for you. How would it feel for you to become a more powerful, in-charge woman? To be someone who decides what she wants and how she wants to create her life? To make good decisions and have good friends, a good job, and good relationships? To demand respect—in a nice way—and actually get it? To work toward goals and achieve them? Doesn't that sound wonderful? It's not pie-in-the-sky thinking; it's real. People do those things every day.

Intention is powerful. If it is your intention to create the kind of life you want, you will need to stop being a victim and claim your seat at the table of life. Are you ready? OK then, I'm right alongside you!

WHAT HAS IT COST YOU?
HAVE YOU SEEN YOURSELF AS A VICTIM?

In this chapter, you learned about victims and the ways you may have unwittingly kept yourself down by identifying yourself as a victim. Take a moment and get your journal.

It will be helpful for you to fully understand the ways in which you actually kept yourself a victim and why you chose to do that. Think about all the times in your life when you felt victimized, when you felt you were being treated unfairly, when you were overlooked, or when you felt you couldn't get what you wanted. Write all of those instances down in your journal.

Now comes the hard part: you know my idea that we do everything for a payoff. You will need to look at every one of those journal entries—every time you felt like a victim or that you had no choice—and figure out what your payoff was at the time. That's not going to be easy. You will think, *I didn't have any payoff. That Dr. Jill is just crazy herself. Why would anyone want to feel like a victim?*

Let me give you some hints:

- You get attention.

- You don't have to work hard.

- No one has any expectations of you.

- People feel sorry for you.

- You don't have to make any choices that can come back to haunt you.

- Others "do" for you.

Getting the idea? As difficult as it may be to look at your part in these situations, there must have been a reason why the whole world decided to collide at your stilettos instead of someone else's. When you take a hard look at your part and responsibility in all this bad karma—and what you may have derived from it—then you will be more powerful. You will become very cognizant of making sure it doesn't happen in the next go-round.

When you have completed this activity, make yourself a nice cup of herbal tea, and then we'll talk about the ways that your abusive relationships affect the way you feel, think, act, and react.

7

How Your Abusive Relationship Affects the Way You Feel, Think, Act, and React

I always feel sick. I get headaches a lot, and my stomach seems to be upset most of the time. It's hard for me to keep anything down, and I'm in the bathroom more and more. I don't remember the last time I got a good night's sleep. I have pain in my joints, but it's not arthritis or bursitis. I just feel tired and sick. I feel like I have the flu, but I don't. I've gone to several doctors, and the tests they do all come back fine. A few of them have suggested that I see a therapist, which made me mad, because it sounds like they think I'm a nut job and everything I'm actually feeling is all in my head.

I've been taking antidepressants for almost a year, and that's helped a little bit, but not much. I take a pill for sleep, but I still can't sleep all night. I'm just beginning to feel hopeless. My boyfriend always tells me what a drama queen I am, and maybe he's right.
—**Sarah, age twenty-one**

What Sarah neglected to mention is that her symptoms didn't exist before she met her boyfriend. As a matter of fact, she was the picture of health and had a very active life. Her symptoms began shortly after he began abusing her and intensified as the abuse escalated. Her boyfriend has now—in effect—disabled his young girlfriend, which seemed to be his plan from day one.

There is no doubt in my mind that an abusive relationship affects every part of your life. The way you feel physically, the way you think about yourself and the world, the way you behave, and the way you react to your partner, yourself, and others—all these things are largely related to your abusive relationship. Let's take a look at these ideas.

THE WAY YOU FEEL

You have already read Sarah's health experience. I am completely convinced that there is a powerful mind-body connection. You don't have to believe in Eastern philosophies to understand the impact your feelings have on your health. Have you ever had a tension or stress headache? Have you ever experienced a queasy, fluttering stomach when you were nervous or anxious? How about a racing heart when you were frightened? Then you can easily see that the way you feel physically is deeply affected by the way you feel emotionally. It is difficult to separate the two.

When I was married to my children's father, I was beset with a number of heart problems. I could feel my heart slow down to what felt like a crawl at times, which made me very tired and lethargic. At other times, it seemed as though a hummingbird had taken control of my aorta. I not only felt tired, but sick. I had frequent bouts with colds and the flu and constantly felt I was on the verge of "getting something." I was taking antibiotics at least ten days of every month and then suffering from yeast infections as a result. It was a never-ending cycle in which I felt more and more hopeless and helpless, unable to take control of my health.

I went to a cardiologist, who ran some tests, had me wear a heart monitor, and then told me that, while I had real symptoms she could see, she felt that they were not "organically motivated." That's doctor-speak for "there's nothing wrong with your heart that can't be fixed by fixing your life."

I was hopeless and sick. What was I supposed to do? I felt victimized by the medical system! Hey, I was sick; they told me I was sick. Why weren't they doing anything about it? I can see now that it would have been pretty foolish to do heart surgery on a woman who could fix her heart by getting out of her relationship. Hmmm …

I can't tell you exactly how this thought came to me in the middle of the night, but one sleepless, heart-pounding two o'clock in the morning, I woke up my then husband and said, "You're breaking my heart." He gave me his usual confused look—which I suspect nearly anyone would give upon being awakened in the middle of the night with such news—and said, "What are you talking about? Your heart is *your* problem." I said, softly and sadly, "I know; I haven't taken good care of my heart. I trusted my heart to you, and I've allowed you to literally break it. I can't let you take my heart from me. This marriage is making me ill. It's not fair. It's time for us to end."

Needless to say, a lot happened after that, and our marriage did end. Although there was tremendous stress and horrifying sadness still to come, my heart did mend—and very quickly. My heart, and the rest of my body, continues to be fine to this day.

Here are some of the messages your body may be trying desperately to send you:

- *Stomachaches or stomach distress:* This may be your body's way of telling you that it can't stomach your situation anymore.

- *Headaches:* Could your body be trying to tell you that it doesn't want to think about the bad relationship?

- *Sore throats:* You may have words caught in your throat. I don't mean this literally, of course, but oftentimes in abusive relationships, a woman is not permitted to speak her mind or express an opinion different from her partner's opinion. You still have the thoughts; they just haven't left your throat.

- *Back problems:* Your body may be telling you to get a spine or stand up for yourself!

- *Blurred vision:* Maybe you don't want to see what is going on around you.

As you can see, the problems you are having in your relationships can and usually do have a powerful effect on your health. Often, physicians contact me when they have patients with multiple or chronic physical ailments for which the doctor cannot find a medical cause. After the patient and I talk for a while, we almost always find that a relationship is causing strife and pain, literally. It continues to amaze me that as soon as the relationship issues are solved, so are the physical problems.

This doesn't mean you're crazy or that you're a drama queen. Your symptoms are very real and painful. They are merely a reflection of the real and painful problems you are dealing with in your relationship. When you decide to solve those problems, you will feel better both physically and emotionally.

THE WAY YOU THINK

I was sure I was going crazy. I was having the strangest thoughts. One minute I thought he was having an affair—which ended up not to be so crazy, since I found out he was—and the next minute I was worried that he had been in a car crash—which, unfortunately, was not true. Most of the time, though, I just didn't want to think at all.

My mind was going so fast all the time with so many racing thoughts, I tried my hardest not to think and to switch my mind off. It would race while I was supposed to be working. It would race while I was driving. It would race in the middle of the night. What if, what if, what if … My mind was going all the time. I was worried about everything. Would he leave? Would he stay? Would he be in a good mood when I got home? Would the dinner be good enough, or would it set him off? Would he want to eat anything at all, and if he didn't, what did that mean? Would he want me to talk or be quiet?

I started thinking about getting a breast enlargement. I started thinking about leaving and not coming back. I started thinking about changing my identity so I couldn't be found. Then, I started thinking really hopeless thoughts and began to think that my only way out was suicide, so I started ruminating about that and how and where I would do it. I was truly crazy.

—Desiree, age thirty

Desiree was not all that crazy. Her life and her thoughts were making her seem like she was crazy, though.

When you are in an unhealthy relationship, your mind may seem to have a mind of its own. You worry and ruminate most of the day and night. It doesn't feel like you can control your thoughts.

The way you think about yourself and the way you see the world and your place in it changes. You don't think you have options or choices about your own life. You don't think you can leave your relationship. You have tremendous and irrational fears. You think that if you leave, he'll take your kids. You think that if you leave, he'll kill himself. You think that if you stay, you can help him. You think that you are not worthy of happiness or respect. You think that he is the best—or only—man you can get. You think no one will understand your side if you go. You think you'll be alone the rest of your life.

These thoughts are incorrect but seem perfectly logical to you, because he has worn down your life and self-esteem to the point that they seem reasonable. The fear that you've allowed him to instill in your psyche is so overwhelming that you feel you've lost the ability to think clearly. What may seem even scarier is if those negative thoughts *do* seem clear.

Later, when we investigate the ways emotional fears have kept you stuck, you will learn how to control those fears and illogic. Remember that you have had a cult mentality while in your abusive relationship. You can deprogram your mind from his garbage and have your own realistic thoughts again. It won't be as difficult as you think, and it won't take as long as you might imagine. You can—and will—take charge of your mind and your sanity.

THE WAY YOU ACT AND REACT

A lot of people I know say to me, "Alicia, you just don't act like yourself anymore." I know what that means—I used to be happy and fun. I used to enjoy life and my friends. Since I've been with Alec, I've become more withdrawn and distant. It wasn't always that way. When we were first dating, I went out with my friends, and I was always happy. I was in love, and life was good.

Then, Alec wanted to spend more time together and was suspicious of some of my guy pals when a group of us would get something to eat after work. There was nothing to be suspicious about. They were just friends, and they really respected me. They never tried anything, but that didn't matter to Alec. I couldn't ever talk sense to him. I stopped hanging out with my friends, even the girls.

I don't know. I just started separating myself more and more from everyone. I didn't want to do anything that would upset him. He's very sensitive and protective of me. I guess that's a good thing.

Some days, it's hard for me to get out of bed; I don't know why that is. I don't care if I spend the whole day in my nightgown. I don't answer the phone, because it might be someone I know, and I don't want to have to explain myself to them. Alec calls me on my cell phone, so that's always on. There are so many times when I don't want to answer that either, but I have to or he gets worried or freaks out. It's just easier to talk to him for a few minutes until he calls again.

I keep to myself at work. I try to be friendly and not upset anyone, but they've gotten tired of making an effort with me. I feel bad about that. I miss them, but I don't have any choice. Alec's worry is not worth going out for lunch with a coworker. He's my priority, and they can't seem to understand that. I don't want to try and explain it anymore. I know they all think he's a creep, but they just don't know who he really is. It's nice to have someone who's as concerned about me as he is, someone who wants to make sure I'm all right. Sometimes he carries it a little too far, but he can be so great the rest of the time.

—**Hillary, age eighteen**

The decisions Hillary has made are very common when a woman is in an abusive relationship. They are not the same decisions she made before she met Alec. The way she is choosing to act and react is a direct result of her unhealthy relationship.

Very often, when I am counseling a teenager who is in an abusive dating relationship, her parents will tell me things like, "I don't know what happened to her," "This isn't the child we raised," "She used to be so happy," "She used to have so many friends, and now she has none," "The way she talks to us is not her speaking; it's him," "She's making decisions she never would have made before she met him," "Her morals and values have taken such a dive since she's been with him," "It's like he's taken control of her mind," and more. It's heartbreaking to hear. Basically, the way she is acting and reacting has changed due to the abusive relationship.

Before you were with your current partner, would you have thought of behaving in some of the ways you are now? Had you ever been so depressed, anxious, or fearful? Would you ever have thought that your life would have become what it has?

Your life has changed because you have based your actions and reactions on what he wants, what he expects of you, what you have to do in order to keep him happy—or at least calm—for the moment. The way you "do business" has changed.

Remember as you continue to read this book that you have 100 percent control of the way you choose to X, X, and X (yes, that's right: the way you think, act, and react). He does not have the privilege of choosing those for you. He does not have that power over you—unless you give it to him.

WHAT HAS IT COST YOU?
HOW CAN YOU TAKE CONTROL?

You have just read some interesting, and perhaps troubling, stories of women who allowed their partners to determine the way they feel, think, act, and react. When women are in abusive relationships, self-determination—that is, taking charge of these things themselves—goes out the window.

Of course, control is one of the main focuses of the abuser. Imagine the power you would have over someone if you controlled whether she was sick or how sick she was, if you could control her thoughts and the way she acted and reacted to all of life's situations. At that point, you wouldn't even have to be with her every minute of the day. You would have control of her from afar. You would be a puppet-master pulling her strings whenever and wherever you wished. That's a frightening amount of control! That may sound like far-fetched stuff you see on *The Twilight Zone*. But that may be your life.

Let's take a moment and think about the amount of control your partner really does have over your life.

In your journal write down your answers to the following:

- The last three times you felt sick

- The last five times you had negative or frightening thoughts

- The last two times you acted out of character or out of fear

- The last two times you reacted in a way that you normally wouldn't

Beside each of those answers, think back to what was happening in your relationship at the time. The last time you felt sick, what did that feel like? Did you feel queasy? OK, then let's go back to that feeling. Just before you became nauseated, what had happened? You may think, *well, we went out to eat, and I must have eaten something bad.* That may be true. But what else happened at the dinner table? Did you have a fight? Did he give you a silent look of disgust or disappointment? Did you feel fearful? Did he say something threatening or upsetting? How soon after that conversation did you start to feel sick? You begin to see that it was more likely the partner than the food that made you sick. If you look at the other times you felt sick, you will begin to see a pattern to your illnesses.

Now, let's take the same approach to the way you've been thinking, acting, and reacting. Link each of the ideas you wrote down to your relationship. Do you see any patterns developing? Be honest with yourself. No one is going to see your journal except you. If you have found that your unhealthy relationship is negatively impacting your life, have no fear. Just after we talk about a few more important ideas, we will begin to tackle the problem with full force.

Please don't become impatient and rush ahead. The work you do now and in the next few chapters is the foundation to helping you understand yourself so that you can change. This point of all this is to better your life. Remember that you cannot truly understand him, and you certainly cannot change him. But, thankfully, you can understand and change yourself; that's just what you and I are doing together.

8

Does He Really Love You, and, For That Matter, Do You Really Love Him?

When I started dating Sergio, I thought, this is it; I've found the man of my dreams. He was so attentive and sweet. My family and all my girlfriends really loved him and thought I was so lucky to have him. Strangely enough, most of my male friends felt differently. They thought he was a scammer and a player. They thought he was just working me and everyone else he had charmed. It was strange. I talked to my mother about it, and she said they were probably just jealous because my relationship with them wouldn't be the same since I had a serious boyfriend. That seemed plausible, but it still made me uncomfortable.

Sergio would do little things that annoyed me, but most of the time he was great, so I just ignored those things, or tried to, anyway. He'd look at other girls when I was around, but he told me I couldn't take the Italian out of him. He said it didn't mean anything and that he loved me. I tried to understand that, but he began getting more and more flirtatious with other women. We had been having sex, and most of the time, he was very selfish and not so gentle.

After we'd been dating for a year, I began pushing for marriage. I thought it would solve the roving-eye problem. Also, if I were his wife, he would honor me more in our sexual life, instead of just seeing me as a girlfriend.

He was hesitant about marriage, but then agreed it would be best. He had a bachelor party at which apparently he got really drunk and also a little kinky with the female entertainer. I felt very uncomfortable, but we were getting married in two days, and there was nothing I could do.

After we were married, it seemed like the sweet and charming Sergio left. He was very demanding of me and wanted to know where I was all the time. He cut me off completely from all of my male friends and most of the girls, as well. He gave me an allowance. The sexual part didn't change; it just became worse. He wanted me to get pregnant, which I had been planning and looking forward to most of my life. I really wanted to be a mom, but now I felt panicked about having a child with him.

I started getting sick a lot: headaches and stomach problems, which you'd think would keep him from wanting sex with me, but they didn't. When I'd try to plead with him or push him off, he'd sulk or call me a cold bitch.

A lot of the time, I'd catch him looking at me with the coldest eyes, which sent a chill down my spine. But then, he could also be so nice when he wanted to. Those times became fewer and fewer but were still there every once in a while. They were very powerful connection points and sort of kept me going.

I told him I wanted us to go to counseling, but he just laughed and told me there was nothing wrong with him. I could go to counseling if I wanted, because there was something wrong with me. I did go, and I learned a lot about myself and my marriage. Some of the things made me scared. I started looking at whether or not he really loved me, or if he did, whether he loved me the way I wanted or deserved to be loved. I was also examining whether I loved him anymore. As I said, just thinking about those things was pretty scary.

Three years after I began counseling, I divorced Sergio. It was a long road. Fortunately, I never had children with him. That was probably something in God's plan, because the divorce and the next eighteen years would have been a nightmare. I don't know—I might not have divorced him if we had kids. I might not have been that strong, or I might have felt too guilty.

—Laurel, age thirty-five

Laurel went through a lot of soul searching, defining her ideas of love. When we become deeply involved with a man, we always hope for the best. When we commit to him, we plan on a lifetime of love and friendship.

Our ideas about what love means are formed further back than we can consciously recall and are primarily based on the ways in which we were treated as babies. In the first year of life, all human babies go through a psychological stage known as Trust versus Mistrust. In that time, we learn whether we can trust our caregivers, and, therefore, the outside world. We also learn about love through that trust. For example, when a baby cries, she finds out very quickly whether or not her mommy or daddy—or other caregiver—will come get her. She may need to have her diaper changed or to be fed, held and rocked, talked to, or soothed in another way. She may just want to see a familiar and loving face. If her cries are answered in a timely manner, she learns to trust those people and therefore extends this trust to others. If not, she learns—in a baby sense—that it doesn't matter what she does, she is not important.

We have all seen the horrible photos and videos of babies in foreign orphanages who rock themselves, bang their heads against walls or their cribs, and sit uncomplaining in soiled diapers. They have learned that they are not a priority and that their cries do not matter. Predictably, those children grow up with many emotional problems, attachment disorders primary among them. It is very diffi-cult—if not impossible—for them to trust, give love, or receive love.

As we go on through our childhood years, we continue to learn about love in the ways our parents and other family members treat us and the ways we see them treating each other. If mom and dad disagree and the child then sees them lov-ingly make up, she learns that love is not always cooing and coddling, but that two people who truly love each other don't hurt each other when they argue and can resolve their differences in a loving and healthy way. If mom and dad disagree with nasty words, pushing and shoving, slamming the front door, and the like, but then say, "I love you," that is more confusing to the child. Love involves dra-matic highs and lows, heightened anger, verbal and emotional violence. If these things are also being done to the child, they learn that love sometimes feels good and sometimes feels bad, depending on the way the other person decides to treat her on any given day.

You can see how confusing a setup like this might be for a child. Perhaps this is what you experienced yourself. When you grow up in this environment, you probably bring these ideas about love into your teen and then adult romantic relationships. Feelings of trust, worthiness, fear, and self-respect all play parts in this puzzle.

Love may feel chaotic. Love may feel disappointing. Love may feel confusing or frightening. Love may feel like all of those things—as well as warm and nur-turing on any given day. How in the world could anyone possibly describe love?

Are you just in love with love?

We were all raised on fairy tales of love at first sight, love as sacrifice, love despite incredible odds, love in the face of family disapproval, love being a kiss that wakes us up from a long, stuporous sleep. In our girlhood, we believe that love has a magical way of transporting us from hopelessness and despair to a charmed and exciting life. If we fall in love with a prince, our lives will be com-plete; we'll live happily ever after. A decade ago, we could have asked Princess Diana how marrying the prince worked out for her, but we know how that tragic story ended.

Sometimes, a man who appears to be a prince is actually a frog, and, happily, the reverse is very often true when we give a truly nice guy a chance.

We are also bombarded by articles in women's magazines that tell us how to snare a man and keep a man. These articles tell us that if our relationship isn't going well, it's our fault. "Take our quiz and find out how you can fix your relationship so your man will never leave." *How to kiss him like he's never been kissed before! The ten love moves that will rock his world! Quick dinners he'll adore! Lose those last ten pounds, and make him drool again!*

Teenage girls are welcomed into this club early on with their own magazines, which have junior versions of the same articles. *Lock lips so he'll never look at another girl! Prom dresses he'll love! Ditch that zit and find your man! Sneaky ways to pull him closer!*

We hardly stand a chance when it comes to deciding what love should look like! When you've met your man and settled into what you hope will be a happily-ever-after life that turns out to have an unhappy ending, you may feel emotionally tossed around.

Does he really love you? He's told you that he loves you in the past. Not so much anymore, but he used to tell you, right? You might assume that he still does love you out of default, because he hasn't told you that he doesn't. Why aren't you happy about his love anymore? Why doesn't it feel good?

Because LOVE IS A BEHAVIOR (can you see how I will repeat this line over and over for the rest of this book?). He may tell you that he loves you, or you may *feel* that he must love you, but take a look at his behavior. What are his actions telling you? The reason his "love" doesn't feel satisfying to you anymore is because you're smart. His behavior doesn't match his words, or what you imagine his words would be if you had the courage to ask him if he loved you. That icky feeling in your stomach doesn't feel like love. It's hard for you to believe that he loves you—and you are correct.

I often tell women that he may say that he loves you, and maybe he even means it. Maybe his idea of love is not good enough for you anymore. Perhaps his way of loving you is not healthy and doesn't nurture you. It could be that at the beginning of your relationship, his jealousy and possessiveness felt like love to you, but now they feel suffocating and stifling. Even though he still tells you that he loves you, his *behavior* doesn't feel loving. In fact, you are entirely correct; it's not loving behavior.

If you felt loved by him four months ago, or eight or eighteen years ago, but you don't now, that doesn't mean you are a bad person or crazy. If he is not showing you consistently loving behavior, then he doesn't love you. At least, not in the way you deserve and should expect to be loved.

Now, let me ask you another question: do you really love him? That is the harder question. Maybe you love the idea of loving him. Or maybe you love the idea of being in love. Or maybe you love the man he used to be but is no longer and hasn't been in a long while. That can make you feel confused or frightened.

Are you holding onto a relationship that never really was or that hasn't existed for many years? Would it scare you to imagine that the loving relationship you thought you had was all in your head? That you dreamed it into existence, but it wasn't real? Maybe you wanted it to be real so much that you fantasized it into being. Because it was love as a fantasy instead of love as a reality, it couldn't survive the pressures of the real world. That's a bitter pill to swallow.

Maybe you thought that if you loved him enough, he'd change. He'd see the wonderful woman you really are, feel grateful and delighted, and love you in the way you always knew he could. Or, maybe not … You may have thought that if he made the changes you wanted, you'd fall back in love with him, but he just made minor changes that proved to be temporary, and anyway, it's simply too late.

Now you are stuck in an empty relationship with only the promise or idea of love keeping it limping along, and you wonder why you don't feel happy and fulfilled.

It's all right to know that you are not feeling loved or do not feel love for your partner. It's painful as heck to say out loud "He doesn't really love me, and I don't think I love him, either." That doesn't mean that you are unlovable and incapable of love. It means that, at this moment, he doesn't love you in a satisfactory way and that you deserve to be loved better. Maybe it can be by him and maybe not. Perhaps you can fall back in love with him—if you ever did truly love him—and maybe you can't.

Love as we experience it is a fragile concept. Each of us may define it differently. Maybe love is excitement or contentment or any number of other feelings. But one thing love is for certain is a *behavior*. If neither of you is behaving lovingly, it is time to reexamine the relationship and whether it works for you anymore.

WHAT HAS IT COST YOU?
LOVING AND NONLOVING BEHAVIORS

Artists have written countless songs and sonnets about love. We often look to them to gauge whether we are in love or whether our love is good enough. Good enough for what? Good enough for you.

Did this chapter strike a chord with you? Have you wondered whether your partner is still in love with you and if you are in love with him anymore? How do those thoughts make you feel right now? Frightened? Ashamed? Guilty? Angry? Like you wasted a lot of good years on him? Let's put those feelings down on paper.

Get out your journal and write down all of your partner's behaviors in the last several months that have felt unloving or made you feel you don't love him. As a reality check, write down next to each either L, for loving, or NL, for nonloving. Initially, this may seem like a waste of time, but perhaps you will find that you are still upset by former nonloving behaviors—that even when he is nice to you, you still regard him hostilely. That's OK, because your answers may show you that you are so angry and "done" with the abusive behavior that it doesn't matter what he does; you no longer accept him.

Do you love him? Write down another list of behaviors you've shown him and write L or NL next to them. Write down your feelings about any behaviors that qualify as NL. Why did you behave that way? Because you felt angry, sad, vindictive, hateful? These are all legitimate feelings, and performing this exercise may show you a pattern of push/pull, love/nonlove, anger/sadness that you feel in your relationship. This can help you clarify how you have felt and how long you've felt this way, which will be of great use later in this book when you begin examining decisions you'd like to make about your life.

9

Are You a People-Pleaser, Martyr, Codependent, Drama-and-Chaos Junkie?

Have you ever wondered why your abusive partner chose you? Or why more than one abuser has chosen you? Could there be neon sign over your head that screams "Abuse me! Abuse me!"?

The simple answer is yes. I have found that there are predictable patterns in women who are abused, just as there are predictable patterns in the men who choose to abuse them. It is difficult to know whether women come ready-equipped with these emotional and behavioral patterns or if they develop them the longer and the more frequently they are in abusive relationships. It's a version of the old "nature vs. nurture" question. One thing is for certain: abusers are attracted to these particular women. Likewise, women who behave in certain ways are attracted to abusers.

Let's take a look at four different but similar types of personalities so you can see which category you fit into and why. When you can clearly understand your emotional needs and the unhealthy ways you attempt to get them met, you can then begin finding healthier alternatives.

THE PEOPLE-PLEASER

I enjoy being a wife and mother and living a traditional life. I stay home and take care of the kids and house while my husband works. Maybe it sounds a little *Father Knows Best* to some people, but I find a lot of happiness and satisfaction in it. I worked until James and I had our first child, and then I stopped. It was by mutual agreement, but mostly at my suggestion.

I was raised by a single, working mom, and more than anything else, when I grew up I wanted to be a mommy who was at home with her kids. I'm grateful to James that he works like he does so that I can do this for our children, who are seven, five, three, and nine months old. It's a busy life, that's for sure.

I can't remember the last time I took a shower without a group of kids watching me. I feel like an exhibitionist, but it's the only way I can get a shower and make sure everyone's safe and in one place. I would like to shower before James leaves in the morning, so that he could watch them, but he's too busy getting ready himself.

He likes a cooked breakfast, so I get up at five and get that started. I feel that it's the least I can do for him, since he works all day for us. When he sits down, I wake the kids up and get them going. Shea needs to be at school at seven thirty and Lilly at kindergarten at eight thirty, and then Maddie goes to Gymboree at nine twice a week while the baby takes his morning nap. James leaves the house at seven, and I guess he could take Shea, but he's usually running out the door, so I don't ask. He's so stressed, and I want his day to go well without any additional responsibilities. And, after all, it's part of my job to get the kids where they need to be.

I have a hard time saying no to all of them. I guess I have a hard time saying no to most anyone. I try to work in the older kids' classrooms one or two days each week, but it's hard with the younger ones, so I just try my best. It's difficult to be there for all of them at once. Their teachers will ask me to make cookies or cupcakes for a party, and I do. Teachers have it so hard nowadays, not like when I went to elementary school, so I try to do what I can to support them.

I feel guilty a lot. I know it's hard for James to support five other people all by himself, and sometimes I think about starting some sort of home business, but can't see how I'd fit it into my day with someone wanting me all the time.

Sometimes, my mom just sort of shows up at the front door and wants to come in to chat or something. I don't think she's really grasped that I have four active, young children to watch. She wants me to pay total attention to her, and I'd have to say that she doesn't pitch in to help me while she's visiting. Sometimes, she'll be so frustrated that we can't sit down and have a conversation that she'll leave an hour after she gets there. I guess that's to be expected. I'm not exactly the best hostess.

I try to do fun things with the kids every day, like go to the park or for a bike ride, or to get ice cream. I really want them to remember having a happy childhood. It's important to me that they are happy.

James gets home around seven and expects the kids to be bathed and in their pajamas, so we start that process at five. I think it's a little early for Shea, who still wants to be playing with his friends. I can't blame him, so I get him in the bath last. Then, we begin dinner so that everything's done at seven when James comes in.

There have been a few times when I haven't been able to get everything done in time, and James is not happy. He tells me that he works all day so that I can stay home, and he should be able to expect dinner on the table and the kids ready for bed when he gets home. That's my job. He's right, of course.

This is what I asked for, so I should be able to do it without complaining. Sometimes I don't think he understands what's involved with keeping the house and the kids all going so everyone's happy and everything gets done, but then I don't understand what it takes to get his job done well either, I guess.

After dinner, the kids want to play games and read, so that's what we do. Everyone's in bed—more or less—at eight or eight thirty, so I can get the dinner dishes done and try to have an hour with my husband before I fall asleep.

He'd like sex more often than we have it, but I'm just too tired. I try to give him what he wants, though. He works hard, and I want him to be happy.

—Delia, age thirty-eight

Delia is certainly a people-pleaser deluxe edition, isn't she? Her primary concern is that everyone be happy all the time, which is quite unrealistic. She not only wants her children and husband to be happy, but also her mother, her children's teachers, and who knows who else! The grocery clerk? The Gymboree instructor? The mailman?

It's easy to see where her need to please may have come from: her narcissistic mother, who needs Delia's total attention even though her four young children are underfoot. When that doesn't happen, she pouts and flounces out of the house, leaving Delia feeling like a bad daughter. Delia's mother may have taught her that pleasing mommy is important. James is another demanding narcissist who makes the rules that Delia follows to a T so that he'll be happy. He expects breakfast early in the morning, won't take one of the children to school to help her out, has expectations about the children's being ready for bed and Dhelia having dinner on the table when he gets home. Then, after all that, he still decides to make Delia feel guilty if she's not in the mood for sex!

It's nice to care whether others are happy, but that is not one of the three things you have control over, is it? Spend a moment taking this little quiz to gauge whether or not you are a people-pleaser. Do you

- tend to blame yourself when things go wrong;

- see yourself as a bad person if you make a mistake;

- try to anticipate what others want or how they want you to act;

- placate others, or try to "buy" them, in an attempt to keep harm at bay;

- feel that you've "failed" as a person unless everyone in your life is happy;

- have more concern for others' happiness than for your own;

- only feel happy when others are happy with you;

- have a difficult time with change;

- feel frightened or apprehensive when taking a risk;

- have a history of alcohol or drug abuse, eating disorders, sexual promiscuity, compulsive gambling or shopping, shoplifting, self-mutilation, or suicide attempts;

- often have violent outburst of rage?

(Some questions in this chapter are taken from *The Emotionally Abused Woman* by Beverly Engel.)

At some point—and hopefully this is that point—you will need to look at whether your people-pleasing personality is accomplishing the goal you had originally intended. Is everyone in your life happy all of the time? Is everyone in your life happy with you? Do you find that others become more and more abusive toward you as you attempt to please them more? If so, then your plan is not working as you had intended. The answer is not to attempt to please everyone even more, but to take a look at your need to please and what your payoff for that may be.

THE MARTYR

I don't know why my life has to be so difficult. Don't get me wrong; I love my life. It's just that I don't know anyone else who has to work as hard at their life as I do.

I try to be a good person and make everyone happy and make their lives easier. I help my kids with their homework every night, I make all the meals, I do all the housework, I work twenty-five hours a week so that we can afford extras that my husband would say are extravagant, I drop off and pick up the dry cleaning, I take the kids to soccer and gymnastic practices, I make all the social arrangements, and I do anything else you can think of.

I shouldn't complain, and I hardly ever do. I have a good husband and a good life. I really don't have any right to complain. Sometimes, though, I don't feel like I'm living my own life; I'm living everyone else's. No one says thank you; they just expect me to do everything for them.

Even when I do something nice for my parents, they still have something negative to say about it. Then I end up apologizing for trying to help. I say I'm sorry a lot, not just to my parents but to everyone. I don't know how many times a day I apologize.

I know that my husband and parents can be overbearing and demanding, I just don't want to deal with standing up to them. It's not worth it. I don't know what I'd do if they started getting really nasty. I think I'd just be paralyzed with fear. I know it's not right to be afraid of the people you love. I shouldn't even be talking about this like I am. I'm sorry.

—Barbara, age thirty-one

Women who, like Barbara, see themselves as martyrs may have learned this behavior in childhood when their helplessness and passivity were rewarded in some way. They may have learned that when you put others first, you are viewed as a good daughter and later, a good woman. They may have also been taught that life is hard, and a woman's life is harder; however, it is her duty as a man's helpmate not to complain or ask for what she wants. To sacrifice her own needs, health, or happiness for others is almost noble.

Look at this list of questions and decide whether you have been living your life as a martyr. Do you

- apologize frequently and for almost any reason at all;

- feel that you have to be very careful so that others don't become angry;

- fear confrontation;

- feel that you can't do anything right;

- feel that you can't—or don't have a right to—say no;

- feel as though you're not running your own life;

- feel like running away;

- live day to day without any true happiness;

- constantly put everyone else's needs or desires before your own;

- feel that others don't appreciate you;

- feel frightened when you consider standing up for yourself;

- feel overpowered by significant people in your life;

- always assume the worst;

- become overwhelmed with fear and doubt when you are presented with a problem, or feel helpless when you are in crisis?

Ask yourself what your payoff is for being a martyr. Does anyone admire you, or do they just take advantage of you? Do women pretend to be your friend long enough to ask a favor? Do you ever feel like saying no but are fearful to do so? Why?

When we talk about your emotional fears later in this book, the reasons for this behavior will become clearer, and you can take steps to rid yourself of the fears and stand up for yourself. For now, sit with the idea that you have received certain "goodies" for remaining a martyr.

THE CODEPENDENT

When I met Sam, he was a social drinker. Well, I thought he was, but it turns out that he was drinking socially with me and then more than socially with his friends when I wasn't around. When I got wind of that, I told him that I loved him and wanted to help him stop. He got pretty mad about that and told me he didn't have a problem, that I had a problem, and he'd drink what he wanted when he wanted. He accused me of overreacting because my father was an alcoholic. He might have been right about that, so I tried to keep my worries to myself and just go with the flow.

We got married a couple of years later, and he was a drunken mess at our wedding reception. I was so embarrassed but didn't say anything because—other than that—it was the happiest day of my life, and I didn't want to ruin anything for everyone else.

As Sam began to drink more and more, I tried everything I could to get him to stop. I begged and pleaded, I cried, I hid his bottles. For a time, I even drank with him. I know this sounds crazy, but I really thought that if he saw me passed out in a stupor or throwing up, it would make him feel guilty, and then he'd stop. But that didn't work either.

We got in more and more fights over his drinking. Well, he'd yell, and I'd keep quiet. I tried to keep everything at home together. We had a little boy, and he'd cry when daddy picked him up and was rough with him when he drank. That made Sam mad, and he accused me of brainwashing the baby or turning him into a little mama's boy. I'd have to try and keep the baby quiet when Sam had a hangover. I was the one to call his boss when he was too sick to work. I'd tell some lie about Sam having the twenty-four-hour flu or a migraine. It felt horrible to do that, especially since his boss and his wife had been so good to us and to me in particular.

Sam got into a drunk-driving incident in which the woman driving the other car was severely injured. It was his third DUI, and this time, he went to jail. It was horrible. He was there for a long time, and I didn't know what to do. I was angry with him and scared and sad. I didn't know what to tell people.

I went to see the woman in the hospital and didn't tell Sam. I apologized to her for what my husband did. She was bruised and had broken bones. She looked terrible, and I couldn't help but cry. She told me that her ex-husband was an alcoholic and that, by our brief conversation, she figured mine was too. She said she used to be just like me and that I was in a more permanent prison than he was. She said he'd be out soon and would begin drinking again, but her bones would never be the same, and I would go back to my prison. I didn't know what to say. How could she see right through me?

Sam got out of jail and had to go to an alcohol-abuse program three nights a week, which he complained about. When he came home from the program, he drank and swore and treated the baby and me badly. He called me names and told me it was my fault that he drank and that he had never wanted a kid. He'd tell the baby to shut up when he cried, and one day, he pushed him over.

I don't know what happened to me, but I told him to leave. He just laughed and told me I couldn't take a step without him and that no one else would ever want me because I was homely and scared and bad in bed. He was horrible. I picked up the baby, packed a few things for him, and left the house. My husband was laughing and yelling after me, "You'll be back, bitch. Where do you think you're going?" I called his parole officer and told him that Sam was consistently violating his probation by drinking several times a week and that, if he went to the house now, he could test him, because he was drunk.

A year later, I'm still scared and shaky. He's out again and bothering me. I try not to make him mad and let him see the baby as long as I'm there, too. He resents my supervision and calls me names. I want him to be happy. I don't want him to drink. When I see him, I try to remind him of what his choice of drinking has cost him, but he still won't listen. I know I still love him in spite of everything and wish he'd change. My dad has never stopped drinking, and neither has Sam. What do they have in common? Me.

—Nadia, age twenty-three

You have probably heard the word *codependent* bandied about but may not really know what it means. Does it mean that someone is weak and pathetic, doesn't have a mind of her own, lives to please someone else, and doesn't really know how she feels without another person's guidance? According to Melody Beattie, author of the groundbreaking books *Codependent No More* and *Beyond Codependency*, a codependent woman is "one who has let another person's behavior affect him or her, and who is obsessed with controlling that person's behavior." My own definition of a codependent is "I'm OK if you're OK."

Think of young Nadia for a moment. She let Sam's behavior control her and spent inordinate amounts of time trying to keep him from drinking. When that didn't work, she either drank with him or lied for him. Her moods were fused with his, his needs with hers. She ceased to exist except to please Sam and her son.

Often, codependents were raised in an alcohol-or drug-addicted home; where there were other compulsions, such as food or gambling addictions; or where the parents were severely depressed. Because these girls are often so neglected and their homes are so out of control, they attempt to gain control over their own behavior. They also try in vain to control their parents' behaviors. They become little adults and try to rescue their own parents.

As we talked about in a previous chapter, when you grow up trading places with the adult and caregiver in the family, or have multiple and constant worry yourself, you learn to anticipate the needs of others and attempt to save and help those around you. As a matter of fact, you are not only attracted to people who need your help, you only feel good when you are being of help. The drawback is that you may also at times feel used and resentful because you do more than your fair share with very little in return.

Take this short quiz to find out if you may be codependent. Do you

- ignore problems or pretend they aren't happening;

- pretend circumstances aren't as bad as they are;

- tell yourself things will be better tomorrow;

- stay busy so you don't have to think about things;

- get depressed or sick;

- become a workaholic (at home or work);

- spend money compulsively;

- overeat;

- watch problems get worse and feel helpless to fix them;

- believe lies;

- lie to yourself;

- wonder why you feel like you're going crazy;

- feel responsible for other people's feelings, actions, choices, well-being;

- feel compelled to help others solve their problems;

- find it easier to express anger about injustices done to others than about injustices done to you;

- feel safest or happiest when you are giving to others;

- lose interest in your own life and goals when you are in love;

- worry that significant people in your life will leave you;

- leave bad relationships only to form new ones that don't work either?

Answering yes to just a few of those questions could indicate that you are codependent. Understand that codependent women have very low self-esteem and only feel truly worthwhile when they are giving and doing for others. They have seemingly sweet personalities that mask savior/rescuer complexes. This makes them perfect targets for abusers.

The reason I said they are seemingly sweet is because underneath the sweet persona is a very controlling and angry woman. Since she doesn't express her feelings directly, she silently feels used and resentful. It's not that she doesn't have needs and feelings; she just doesn't feel worthy of making demands. In fact, she really isn't honest with herself or others, so rather than feeling constant hurt and rejection, the codependent woman represses her own anger, fails to complain, pushes her own thoughts and feelings aside, and doesn't allow reality to interfere with her own little world.

Hopefully, you can now see that an abuser seeks someone with the combination of a sweet personality and rescuer complex, someone who puts her own needs aside and never complains directly or asks for what she wants.

THE DRAMA-AND-CHAOS JUNKIE

> I've never had a boyfriend with a normal life. One was a drug addict, one kept losing jobs, one had a criminal record and kept doing stupid stuff that could have gotten him in trouble, another one was a recovering alcoholic, one had a very turbulent childhood, another one was deciding if he should join a motorcycle gang. It's been crazy.

Now, understand that I didn't know any of this when I met them; it just happened. It makes my life hell. I'm always worrying about these guys and trying to help them. I've spent the college savings that my grandparents set up for me springing guys from jail, keeping them from drinking or using, listening to their tales of woe, and just generally keeping them from doing stupid stuff.

I don't know how I find these guys or how they find me.

—Gwen, age eighteen

Listening to Gwen's relationship life is enough to give you a headache. How is it possible that every single significant relationship has been filled with drama and trauma? She's still a teenager. What will her life be like later?

I've met many women who are attracted to "bad boys." Bad boys are exciting and dramatic. Something wild and crazy always seems to be happening in their lives. They need fixing, they have big-time problems, and their lives are bigger than life. Being with them is like being on a roller coaster—you're a little queasy most of the time and don't know when you're going to get whiplash, but boy do you feel alive on this relationship ride! Most of the women I know who think they are sick of the ride go on to date "nice" guys, whom they inevitably find very boring and drop after one or two dates. Then they go on to find another manic fixer-upper and complain about the chaos in their lives.

Chaos and drama can be addictive ... literally. Your body is in a constant state of heightened alert, and your adrenaline pumps. When your body becomes accustomed to this high response state, it's akin to being addicted to a drug that is difficult to quit.

Many women create chaos where there is none. My mother is the queen of that dynamic. She has been involved with a number of men who need her "help," and she also finds female friends who seem to have some sort of problem that requires her attention. Now that my mom is eighty-three years old, it's pretty difficult for her to troll for chaos, so she has found imaginary problems within her own home and with herself. Once a drama queen, always a drama queen? It makes me very sad that my mother is that old and still has nothing in her life except imaginary slights and unhappiness. It would be nice if she could live out her final years in some sort of contentment.

So that you don't end up like my mom, take this little quiz and gauge the level of drama you use in your life. Do you

• almost always find some sort of crisis occurring in your life;

• find that you are almost always angry with at least one person in your life;

- find that you frequently get into heated arguments with friends, coworkers, family members, or male partners;

- see that your reunions after fights or separations from your man are intensely erotic;

- find yourself needing to "stir things up" when things get too calm;

- get bored easily;

- tend to be unhappy with routine and instead prefer a lifestyle that involves continual change;

- ever wonder whether anyone or anything will ever really make you happy;

- ever have fantasies that are filled with violence or illicit sex;

- tend to become attracted to and get involved with men who are unavailable, who aren't interested in you, who are abusive, or who have problems?

Many drama-and-chaos junkies were raised in a chaotic, dysfunctional home with a high level of negative energy. Perhaps there was alcohol or drug use in the home, and perhaps mom was a drama queen. To women raised like this, a high level of drama seems normal.

For many women in this situation, the more unavailable a man is, the greater the challenge to her. The more disinterested he is in her, the more interested she is in him. If he has a highly problematic life, then she knows she can be truly helpful for a good, long time. He will need her, so maybe he won't dump her. It's sort of like job security!

Of course, one of the downfalls is the underlying problem that drives her. Have you ever noticed that, when you're feeling pretty crummy about your life, watching a soap opera makes you feel better? Now, those characters really have it bad. You've distracted yourself for an hour, you haven't had to focus on your problems, and comparatively speaking, your life looks OK. It's the same reason a woman seeks out men with multiple problems or creates drama in her life: as long as she's focusing on the man or the chaos in general, she doesn't have to examine herself and her own inner chaos.

You will need to decide for yourself whether going from one drama to another, feeling irritable and distracted, and never finding contentment is less of an effort than taking the time to look at your life and what drives you. Once you do that, resolution of your problems really doesn't take that long.

My mother is not a happy person. She apparently wasn't a happy young woman, she hasn't been happy for the forty-nine years I've known her, she hasn't had happy relationships with men or women, and she will undoubtedly live out her remaining years as an unhappy, old woman. I hate that this has happened to my mom, and I'd hate to see that happen to you. Why don't you commit to putting yourself first for a few weeks, really working on yourself through this book, and seeing where it leads?

WHAT HAS IT COST YOU?
DO YOU RELATE TO THESE SCENARIOS?

You've taken a good look at four different dynamics of personality and behavior: the people-pleaser, the martyr, the codependent, and the drama-and-chaos junkie. Did you identify with any of the stories you read or the descriptions of these types of women? Could you see yourself in any of these situations? How did you score on the four quizzes?

You may have qualities of each of those personalities. Let's do some work on that.

- In your journal write down each of the four personalities on the left side of your paper.

- Put a check mark next to each of the personalities in which you scored two or more on the quiz.

- Now, write down the items on the quiz that apply to you.

- Under each of the statements that fit you, write down an incident or two that clearly demonstrate why the statement fits.

- How did you feel when each incident happened?

- What did it accomplish for you?

- Did you feel better or worse?

- Has it improved your life?

- What payoff did you receive or do you continue to receive for behaving in this way?

- What would happen if you changed your way of "doing business"?

- On a scale of one to ten, how motivated are you to make that change?

Now that you've examined the personality traits that allow you to easily become involved with an abusive man, let's take a good look at something very crucial to your personality and the changes you can make: your self-esteem.

10

Could Low Self-Esteem Have Anything to Do with This Mess?

When I was a little girl, everything I did was wrong, according to my mom. I didn't look good in pink, which was important to her, because she had three boys before me and had been hoping for a girl each time. I looked good in blue, which wasn't allowed. I had really kinky hair—just like her—but of course she had hoped for the smooth hair my father and two of my brothers had. She couldn't do anything sweet and girly with my hair.

As much as she wanted me to turn into a little ballerina, I was better at sports like soccer and baseball. I could also throw a football very well and soon became the quarterback when my brothers and I played ball. What did she expect? I had three older brothers as my influence. I didn't want to be a girly girl. I wanted to fit in and play with them. We were all two years apart, so I had built-in playmates. I didn't like going on shopping excursions and going for tea. I wanted to get dirty outside with my brothers and their friends.

Needless to say, I was a wash-up as the daughter she'd always dreamed of. Now, I can understand her disappointment and feel sorry for her, but then I just felt wrong as a person.

She started being sort of hostile toward me, and I couldn't even go to my dad about all of this because he came home late and preferred the boys. That was my catch-22: I could play with the boys—which infuriated my mother—but I wasn't a boy, so I wasn't recognized by my father. I was very alone in a lot of ways in my household, as far as my parent's love and approval went. I know it did a big number on me.

I know that today I don't have any self-esteem. I always feel that I have to prove myself to everyone, and I don't feel that I ever do that well enough. My relationships haven't worked out, and I feel I'm at the losing end of most things. I doubt myself and any abilities I have and don't feel like I measure up or am worthy of much. I take a backseat to my friends and am sort of intimidated by strong men and women. I'd like to be happier, and know it's tied to the self-esteem that I never had.
—**Marcy, age thirty-seven**

Self-esteem: how many times have you heard that word tossed around in the last week? What does it mean, anyway? Is it just one of those psychobabble terms that shrinks invented? What bearing does it have on your life?

Like the word *love*, self-esteem can mean many different things. We use the word interchangeably with the ideas of self-worth, self-concept, and the way we feel about ourselves. Sometimes, others may use it as a weapon to make you feel bad about yourself, as in, "If you had any self-esteem, you'd be out of this lousy relationship." Or they may use it to make you feel like a victim, as in, "You can't help being with this creep. It's no wonder; you have such low self-esteem." It can also seem as though it's a magic wand that can cure everything horrible in your life: "If I had better self-esteem, I'd make good choices in men, and I'd be happy."

I suppose the definition of self-esteem can be found in all of those examples to a limited extent, but the way I like to think about it is this: self-esteem is a kind of math problem—self-confidence plus self-respect equals self-esteem. Self-esteem has two separate parts: a feeling of personal competence and a feeling of personal worth. If you are lacking in one or both of these components, you cannot have positive self-esteem.

Let me put it another way: self-esteem reflects in all that you do and in your judgment about your right to be happy. When you have low or negative self-esteem, you not only feel wrong about certain issues in your life, you also feel wrong as a person. You may feel that you are somehow defective, and you could be plagued by feelings of inadequacy, insecurity, self-doubt, and guilt. Does this sound like you so far?

Take a peek at the following forty-nine statements. This list displays feelings and behaviors that are common to women with low self-esteem. Can you see yourself in any of these?

1. I anticipate other people's needs.

2. I try to please others instead of myself.

3. I overcommit myself.

4. I don't really know what I need, or if I do, I tell myself that it is not important.

5. I find it easier to feel and express anger about injustices done to others than about those done to myself.

6. I find myself attracted to needy people.

7. I feel best when I'm giving to others and uncomfortable or guilty when others give to me.

8. I blame myself for everything.

9. I pick on myself for the way I think, feel, look, and behave.

10. I feel different from most other people.

11. I fear rejection.

12. I reject compliments or praise.

13. I think I'm not good enough.

14. I take things personally.

15. I tell myself I can't do anything right.

16. I feel like a victim.

17. I feel a lot of guilt.

18. I tell myself I can't do anything right.

19. I lose sleep over petty problems or other people's behavior.

20. I have a lot of *shoulds* in my life.

21. I believe other people can't possibly like or love me.

22. I'm afraid to let other people see who I am.

23. I don't have the word *no* in my vocabulary.

24. I feel controlled by people or events.

25. I avoid talking about myself.

26. I try to say what I think will please other people.

27. I think that most of what I say is unimportant or uninteresting.

28. I don't trust myself, my feelings, my decisions, or other people.

29. I let other people hurt me.

30. I make a lot of apologies.

31. I am overly trusting of others before I actually get to know them.

32. I lie to myself.

33. I am afraid to make others angry.

34. I am afraid of my own anger.

35. I desperately seek love and approval.

36. I don't remember the last time I felt happy, content, or peaceful with myself.

37. I look for happiness outside myself.

38. I stay in relationships that don't work.

39. I find myself seeking love from people who are incapable of loving.

40. I am afraid or uncomfortable being alone.

41. I try to prove that I'm good enough to be loved.

42. I fall into serious relationships quickly.

43. I don't say what I mean.

44. I have sex when I don't want to.

45. I feel safer feeling hurt than angry.

46. I often feel hopeless about the future.

47. I find it difficult to have fun and be spontaneous.

48. I make lots of excuses for other people's behavior.

49. I remain loyal to people who have hurt me.

How many of these questions apply to you and your life? All of the statements above are indicative of low self-esteem, so if you identified with more than one or two of them, it may be painful for you to see how low your self-esteem has become. Until you read this list, you may not have seen these thoughts and behaviors as abnormal. You may not have recognized those behaviors that prevent you from being as happy as you'd like to be.

You may be wondering how your slide to low self-esteem began. Did you begin with a negative self-concept and thus attracted abusers, or did the messages your abuser gave you kill your positive identity?

The answer is that both happened. It's virtually impossible for a woman with a good feeling about herself to accept degrading treatment from a man, so it follows easily that only women with low self-esteem become involved with abusers to begin with. However, since abusers are very clever, they don't show their target who they are immediately. An abuser takes slow, almost imperceptible steps to lower your self-concept and self-respect. By the time he's "had his way" with you, your feeling about yourself and what you deserve for your life may be 180 degrees different from where you started. You may now stare at your image in a mirror wondering where you went.

Like Marcy, you may have had a childhood in which you were not honored for the person you were. If that is your story, I'm sorry. Planting the seeds of positive self-esteem is the greatest gift parents can give a young child. I believe that it is the parents' obligation to help their child believe that she is the most wonderful and perfect creature on earth and that she is loved and accepted just as she is. They can do this while also setting limits and boundaries and letting her know that while her behavior is not always wonderful, she is a wonderful person, and they feel grateful that she was given to their family. If you are a parent, I hope that even if this gift was not given to you, you are somehow able to give this to your children.

When a child—especially a girl child—doesn't receive these messages early in life, every part of her life can be negatively affected:

- her relationships

- the way she functions in school and then later in her jobs

- her relationships with her peers

- the way she feels she belongs—or doesn't—in her family and in society

- how high in life she is likely to rise

- the types of men she chooses as partners

- the length of time she remains with an unkind partner.

Dr. Nathaniel Branden, known as the "Grandfather of Self-Esteem," holds that apart from biological difficulties, every psychological problem is directly attributable to low self-esteem: depression, anxiety, fear of intimacy or success, alcohol or drug use, underachievement at school or work, spousal abuse, emotional immaturity, suicide, and crimes of violence. Isn't that remarkable?

Let's take another look at your level of self-esteem and the chicken-and-egg theory: whether it was low to begin with and so you chose an unkind partner, or if your partner lowered your self-esteem with his unkindness. Let's also factor into that the previous romantic relationships you've had, as well as relationships with friends, family, and coworkers. Is there a pattern? The vast majority of women in abusive relationships find that they had fairly low self-esteem to begin with, and that the relationships themselves further ground them into the dirt.

The first reason for this is that an abuser knows who he can abuse: a person who doesn't think very much of herself and will comply with his wishes. He will not choose a woman who has true self-confidence and self-respect, because he doesn't want to work that hard. Secondly, the first time a woman with high self-esteem hears an abuser tell her that she's fat, ugly, lazy, and stupid, or that she won't amount to anything or that no one else would want her, her reply is, "And so why are you with me?" Not only doesn't she believe him, she doesn't try to understand, fix, commiserate, or help his troubled little soul in any way. She kicks him to the curb! She doesn't make an excuse for him, allow him to explain, or give him a second chance to make a first impression.

Most commonly, we base our self-esteem on several characteristics:

- *Attractiveness:* People who are very beautiful are often considered to have more positive feelings about themselves and, therefore, happier lives. Compare how you've felt when you've had a good hair day versus a bad hair day.

- *Success:* Our culture emphasizes the importance of productivity and accomplishments.

- *Money:* The acquisition of money and wealth makes many of us feel better about ourselves.

- *Intelligence:* We often think that very brilliant or talented individuals are more worthwhile.

- *Fame and power:* Some people think that the famous, charismatic, and powerful have more fulfilling lives.

- *Love:* We often feel worthwhile if we are loved and cared about.

- *Happiness:* When I ask my patients what they would like to achieve in therapy—what their goal is—the most common answer by far is "I just want to be happy." However, they are not sure what happiness is.

- *Altruism:* We may think that we are worthwhile if we are generous and loving … no matter on whom we are focusing that kindness and generosity.

Let's think about these ideas for a moment. Do you recall that one of the universal truths of life is that each of us has control over only three things: our own thoughts, our own behaviors, and our own reactions? Keeping that in mind, let's take another look at the proposed self-esteem list above. Over which of those items do you have 100 percent control? External things like appearance, money, success, and the love of another person can come and go. You do not pull the only strings on them. You cannot perfectly estimate if your company will downsize, eliminating your job, or when the stock market may go up or down, pulling your savings along with it. We all witnessed the economic crashes and uncertainties after the September 11 tragedies, which were certainly out of our control. After a certain age, you can do leg lifts, run twelve miles a day, and spend the other half of your day at the Clinique counter to no avail. As you may have discovered, you cannot control the love of another person, either, and trying to change, fix, or make your partner happy is a no-win effort.

Basing your self-esteem on factors over which you do not have control is a losing proposition. When we rely on outside forces to determine our level of self-worth, it is called *other esteem*, which is very fragile and blows in whichever direction the wind is blowing today. It is not an accident that the word *self* in self-esteem requires you to feel good about yourself.

Do any of the statements below apply to you?

- I am a considerate and kind person as often as possible.

- I am a person who tries to do what is right most of the time.

- I am a child of God.

- I am a woman who does her best as often as she can.

- I try to be a good mom.

- I am a woman who wants to gain knowledge about myself in order to move ahead and do better in life.

Can you identify with any of those statements? Of course you can. They all share two important qualities: first, they are intangibles—that is, you cannot directly see or measure them. Also, they are things over which you can have perfect control. Isn't that wonderful news? When you base your self-esteem on intangibles, such as the list above, and other statements over which you can have 100 percent control—and not on "stuff" that can be taken from you—you can begin to feel better about yourself, raise your self-esteem, and start to find true happiness.

Now, let's look at another common misconception about self-esteem. It is widely believed that people with high self-esteem do remarkable things. That is, first you need to have high self-esteem, and then you make brave accomplishments. Not so. Actually, it's the other way around. First, you do something that's a little difficult or uncomfortable to you: something you never thought you could do. In doing this task—whether or not you completely succeed—you begin acquiring more self-esteem. As you have the courage to force yourself to take on another difficult task (such as telling your parents you don't like the way they treat you, asking your boss for a raise, telling a "friend" that you cannot talk on the phone with her today, or letting your kids know that you will not allow them to speak to you disrespectfully anymore), you start thinking of yourself as the awesome woman you are. Bear in mind once again, it really doesn't matter if others comply with your wishes—you do not have control over that; what matters is the fact that you attempted the task. Great, huh?

WHAT HAS IT COST YOU?
HOW HIGH IS YOUR SELF-ESTEEM?

Take out your trusty journal again, and let's think about your self-esteem. Write down these thoughts with lots of space in between questions:

- When I think of my self-esteem, how would I currently rate it on a scale of 1–10, with 1 being the lowest it can possibly be and 10 being where I would like to see it to be?

- What situations make me feel less worthwhile?

- Do certain people in my life consistently make me feel badly about myself or tell me negative things about myself? After spending time with them, how do I usually feel?

- How has low self-esteem sabotaged my happiness, creativity, relationships, and personal success?

- What one thing can I do for myself today that will help me begin to think and feel better about myself? Make a list, and do one thing from the list each day for a week.

What affirmations, such as those on the list mentioned earlier, could I give myself each day to counteract the negative messages I usually give myself?

PART III

WHAT ARE THE COSTS? DO YOU HAVE TO GIVE UP ON YOURSELF IF YOU GIVE UP ON HIM?

I don't want to give up. Why should I have to? It's not fair; he's so great most of the time. My parents tell me I can't see him anymore and that they will do everything in their power to protect me. Protect me from what? They have this crazy idea that he could get violent with me because he smokes pot and because of some of the things they've heard him say to me. Yes, I admit that sometimes he gets a little out of control, but I know how to calm him down. Without me around, he could get himself into trouble. I'm the only one who knows how to help him get control of himself. Sometimes he makes me cry, but that's just because I'm an overly sensitive person. Anyone could tell you that, but if I come home from a date with him or I get off the phone with him and I'm crying, my parents go crazy. They don't understand him or our relationship. He'd never hurt me. He's NEVER HIT ME or anything.
—**Gwen, age fifteen**

Why can't he just change and be the person he was when we started dating? I know I'm not exactly the same, either, but he's just so different now. I know

who he really is and who he can be again. I don't want to give up on that. If I give up that hope, what else do I have?
—**Cassandra, age thirty**

Do you feel satisfied with the knowledge you've gained so far? Can you clearly understand what nonphysical abuse looks like and how you may have unwittingly been sucked into this type of relationship? Hopefully, you also understand—and are beginning to live—many of the crucial universal truths we discussed early on and have seen the ways in which a few tweaks in your thinking process can make a huge difference in how you feel. I hope that you've also seen your part in your relationships so that you will avoid feeling like a victim in the future and know that you are powerful and can make stunning choices today.

Let's put your new and improved self-esteem to the test in the upcoming chapters.

In this section of our book, we are going to do some real work on YOU: the way you feel about your partner, your frustrations with him and the relationship, the thoughts and actions that keep you in this rut, and ways you can resolve some unfinished business so that you can move forward. Wouldn't that be great?

First, we're going to take a look at some emotions you may have that—while perfectly normal—are keeping you stuck. Grief, loss, anger, shame, and fear are the most common emotions I see in women who have been trapped in abusive relationships. They are difficult to get past and can have a tight grip on your life. Once you understand these feelings, I will give you simple tools for eliminating them from your life. Wouldn't it feel wonderful to wake up every day without being plagued by these negative emotions?

Sometimes it feels as if you're all alone in the world. No one could possibly feel as badly or as sad as you do. Maybe, with the rush of emotions you have, you feel like you're a bad person or that you're going crazy. Next stop: insane asylum! Because you may also have an abuser in your life who reconfirms your impression that you are a crazy woman, you begin to believe it may be so. Crazy people don't get out of abusive relationships, and you're not crazy. I'd like to spend a few pages telling you how normal you actually are. Wouldn't that be a relief?

Why can't he just change? How many times have you asked yourself that question? You may have asked your therapist, your friends, and even your higher power. If only he would just change a little—or a lot—everything would be perfect. Because really, he can be such a great guy when he wants to. You've talked to him, you've pleaded, you've done everything short of a lobotomy. You've seen the nicer side of him, although perhaps lately it's been less and less often. You have hope. Why can't he just change?

Lastly, in order to move ahead and make good decisions about your abusive relationship with your partner, you will need to resolve some unfinished business with your family of origin … and with yourself.

Three of the next four chapters actually involve your expectations. You may think that they are primarily about your expectations of others in your life, but they really come down to your expectations of yourself. Why? Because you don't have one ounce of control over other people, do you? You do have 100 percent control of everything about *you*.

Let's use that awesome power you possess and get going!

11

Overwhelming Feelings of Grief, Loss, Anger, Guilt, Shame, and Fear That Keep You Stuck

I'm a mess most of the time. I know that about myself, and everyone else just confirms it.

I spend a lot of my time feeling scared, although I'm not really sure what I'm scared of. Do you ever just get that nervous feeling in your stomach, and you're not sure why? That's how I live my life. I feel sad a lot, but I also feel mad. I don't like feeling mad, because I just stay mad, and no one even cares. A lot of people make me mad, and it never changes. They don't change the way they treat me.

I feel like I've wasted a lot of my life being this way and can't get that time back, but I'm more worried about all the time to come that will be wasted. I feel like I'm going to my own funeral and saying good-bye to my youth and probably my later life, too.

I feel guilty for feeling mad at my parents. They can't help who they are. They're old now, and they're not going to change. It gets me mad that they're not going to change, and then being mad makes me feel guilty and ashamed.

I mean, it's not like they never tried with me. I'm just a basket case. I'm the sick one in the family. Everyone knows it. They look at me with either pity or with that sort of exasperated look that's sort of the "we give up" look. As I said, I'm just a real mess. I wish I could get off this roller coaster, but it's been too long. No one treats me well, so how am I supposed to improve?

—Jodie, age twenty-nine

That's a sad way to live your life. Jodie is expressing several feelings at once that are common to almost all women in abusive relationships: grief, anger, shame, guilt, and fear. Do you ever feel that way? I know I spent many of my "good" years in that emotional spin.

129

Earlier in this book, I spoke a bit about being in a FOG, which stands for fear, obligation, and guilt. These emotional-blackmail devices are tools of the abuser's trade—as Dr. Susan Forward explains—and may be a good deal of what has motivated you to remain in your unhealthy relationship.

Let's spend a bit of time looking at these emotions and the ways they keep you stuck.

GRIEF AND LOSS

Whether we realize it or not, we actually go through several minor griefs and losses each day. We may miss pickup time at our children's school, receive a poor grade on a test we studied so hard for, be unable to make it to a school event because we have to work, be denied an important project or promotion at work, find disappointment in something a friend or family member said, or even lose our keys. Each one of those situations is a tiny—or larger—loss that requires a grieving period. When we've been in an unhealthy partner relationship, we grieve for the relationship on a daily basis.

- I wanted the perfect marriage.

- This relationship is hurting my heart and soul.

- This relationship is hurting my children.

- I always imagined that we'd grow old together.

- I thought we'd go to the prom together.

- I'm a better person than this, aren't I?

- Our relationship would be so great if he could just be nice.

- I've spent so many years with him.

- Would he take care of me if I became ill?

I'm sure you have many other thoughts you could add to this list. These are all losses for which you may grieve every day.

There is a semipredictable cycle of grief and loss, which was developed by a renowned psychiatrist, Dr. Elisabeth Kubler-Ross. She studied dying patients and their families and wrote a groundbreaking book, *On Death and Dying*, in the 1950s, which is still widely read today. Her grief-and-loss cycle is now universally applied to not only death, but everyday losses. It is especially useful when we think about relationship loss.

In looking at the stages of grief and loss, it's important to know that you may not necessarily go through these stages in order, although it is likely that you will or have already done so. What is more important, however, is understanding that you will continue to cycle through this process for quite some time. The repetition of the cycle will not necessarily then proceed back to step one and go in order again, but can go from step one to step three to step five and then back to step two or four and around and around—all in the space of five minutes! This is one of the reasons why you may feel like you are losing your mind!

STAGES OF GRIEF AND LOSS

1. *Denial:* In this stage, you can't believe what is happening. Did you mistake what he said to you? He couldn't have cheated on you; you must be wrong. You are not willing or able to look at the entirety of your situation, so you don't look at it at all, or look at it through blurred lenses. If you saw your relationship truthfully, you'd have to face it squarely and make a decision about it.

2. *Anger:* Now, you're mad! How could he have lied to you? What a creep. He does this to you all the time. He thinks you're going to stand for this type of behavior? He's got another think coming. Or maybe you are angry with yourself for putting up with his unkind behavior for so long.

3. *Bargaining:* If only … If only he doesn't cheat and lie, you'll be a better partner and give him what he wants. If he does this, you'll do that. You begin making bargains with yourself, with God, with anyone who will listen.

4. *Depression:* You're sad, devastated, and blue. You can't get out of bed, you don't brush your teeth, you don't have any energy, and you can't eat, sleep, or think straight. You feel hopeless and worthless and don't know how you are going to function today. You can't imagine that your life is going to get any better. You've tried to reason with him, you've tried just to love him and do what he says he wants, and nothing changes.

5. *Acceptance:* You accept the relationship, him, and yourself for who and what they are. You may not like things, but you've accepted the reality of them. You may make a decision to leave or stay. But, for today, you are at a state of acceptance, if not necessarily peace.

I generally add the stage of *Hope*. In this stage, you hope that your life will be better and plan that it will. You can see the light at the end of the tunnel, even if it is a very long, dark tunnel. It may mean that you hope you can live your life in peace, or that you trust that your fears will go unfounded, or that your children will not be irrevocably harmed by your relationship. You may hope that you will be able to make ends meet or that you have decided you will find a more fulfilling relationship in the future.

Can you relate to the rollercoaster cycle of grief and loss? How many times today have you gotten on this ride? I understand the confusion of finally climbing your way out of a depressive period and into acceptance and hope, only to ask yourself, "Am I making too big a deal of this? Am I actually right?" (denial phase). Or maybe you've felt horrible for a week, and now you are making deals with yourself or are just angrier than ever. It can happen in the blink of an eye.

How long does this cycle last? As long as it lasts. No one can tell you how long that will be. There are certainly many factors that apply: how long you've been in this relationship, how many previous abusive relationships you've been in, how severe the abuse has been, what kind of support you have, how quickly you've recovered from emotional injury before, and the like.

You may be wondering why you should be grieving for a man who treated you so horribly. Perhaps others in your life are wondering the same thing. They may tell you, "Get out of bed, and stop crying. I can't believe you're crying over a guy who treated you so badly. You must be crazy. You should be celebrating." We will discuss this in greater detail in our next chapter. For now, the important thing is to understand this cycle of grief and loss, something that you are entitled to go through in your own way, and at your own pace.

WHAT HAS IT COST YOU?
DEALING WITH YOUR GRIEF AND LOSS

You are familiar with the cycle of grief and loss, and now you are ready to use that knowledge. In your journal, write down the main item that you are currently grieving most. If you are in too much grief to identify what you may be feeling, refer to the list at the beginning of this section. Perhaps you will find what you are feeling there. Let's say that one of your biggest losses is the fantasy of being married to the same man for the rest of your life, sharing grandchildren together, walking on the beach together as two old people holding hands, and sharing the contentment of a whole life of history together. That's a tough one. I know. Even though I'm happily remarried, I still find myself grieving that loss with my first husband and father of my children.

Put your greatest loss down in your journal. Now, think of the past week and how you've reacted to that loss. Do you remember the cycle of grief and loss: denial, anger, bargaining, depression, and acceptance? If you wish, you can add hope. Write each of these feelings down in separate columns on your page. Put a checkmark next to each one you felt last Sunday, then do the same for Monday, Tuesday, and so on for the entire week.

Are there more checkmarks on a certain part of the cycle than others? Do you find that this loss is causing you to feel more depressed than anything else, or do you go back to denying the problem or feeling angry a good deal of the time? How often have you accepted your situation or felt hopeful about your future?

Remember that going through this cycle is normal and is a necessary part of your recovery. You will get through this process when you are ready. Right now, be patient with yourself and your healing. At present, it is enough that you recognize your process and are aware of it so that you don't feel crazy and out of control.

ANGER

Anger is a tricky little emotion. When I counsel my patients, I talk to them in quite a bit of depth about anger: their own and the anger of those around them.

When you are in an abusive relationship, you see anger quite a bit. Your partner may not act like a pit bull and throw his anger all over the place. He may be passive-aggressive. He is afraid of or uncomfortable with his anger, so he keeps it veiled. He doesn't get mad; he gets even.

Before we discuss what I think anger really is, it's important for you to look at your own anger and decide whom the anger is directed toward. Are you angry with yourself? At him? At the world and all its injustices? Probably all of the above. If you remain only angry at yourself—for "being such a fool," for believing him or letting your guard down when he was nice, for staying with him for so long and "wasting the best years of your life"—you are cutting yourself off from one-half of the truth. If you remain only angry at him—for not seeing who you are, for not changing, for treating you so carelessly, for lying to you, for ruining your and your kids' lives—then that is the other half.

Yes, you can get angry with your parents for raising you to be a compliant daughter who is afraid to say no. Or you can be mad at the friends who introduced you to your partner, thinking they should have known the type of guy he was in the beginning. You can be angry at whomever you want. I'm not going to stop you. Maybe your anger is good and healthy. Or maybe your anger just keeps you from moving forward.

Let me talk to you about my thoughts on anger and see if they make any sense for you. I think anger is really a cover emotion. We all know what anger is and what it looks like. We may or may not know how to "do" anger. We may be afraid of our own anger and thus display our anger in other ways. We may exhibit passive-aggressive behavior by concealing from people the reasons we are angry with them, which prevents them from being able to deal with or resolve the situation. Or we may gossip and spread rumors about someone with whom we are angry. We may act deceptively sweet toward the object of our anger and then stab him in the back or put pins in the voodoo doll we've made of him! Whatever your version of anger looks like, this is what I think anger really is: hurt, fear, and frustration.

Let's look at that idea. Whenever I see an angry person, I'm *always* looking at someone who is actually very wounded: someone who is in a lot of emotional pain. When we don't want to look at that pain, it is easier to get mad. You've heard many times that juvenile delinquents almost always come from horrible backgrounds. They may have been raised in poverty or had a drug-or alcohol-abusing parent, and they were probably physically or emotionally abused. These are the same characteristics I described to you earlier in this book about your abuser, right? If you talked with this juvenile delinquent and got past his arrogance, bravado, and insistence that he doesn't care, do you think you'd find a child who has been hurt?

When we are angry, we are very often frightened. As we are going to discuss later in this chapter, emotional fear—particularly the fear of being alone—is so powerful and uncomfortable to look at that we very often turn that fear over to anger.

Frustration is another large component of anger. When you think of the reason why you are angry with your partner, what would your answer be? Because he won't change? Because no matter how many times you tell him that he's hurting you or your children, he won't stop? Because you can't get him to see your point of view? Because he acts nice for a short while but doesn't keep it up? Why does he do those things? Because he can … because you allow it. Your anger at him is actually frustration with him … and yourself.

The interesting thing about anger is that the angrier you are, the angrier you get. Have you ever noticed that? It's very difficult to resolve anger. Anger is like wearing a pair of cement shoes. It doesn't allow you to move forward.

However, you can resolve your true anger by looking at your underlying feelings of hurt, fear, and frustration. Let's try an experiment: try to remember the last time you were angry. If you look honestly at it, what were you really hurt about? What were you actually scared of and frustrated about, and with whom? When you've identified your true emotions, you can take steps to resolve them.

GUILT AND SHAME

In his book, *The Feeling Good Handbook*, Dr. David Burns defines guilt and shame in this way: "You believe that you've hurt someone or that you've failed to live up to your own moral standards. Guilt results from self-condemnation, whereas shame involves the fear that you'll lose face when others find out about what you did."

Can you identify with that definition? Guilt and shame are emotional kissing cousins; and while they are related, there are some real differences.

GUILT

As women, we know about guilt, big time. If we work, we feel guilty that we're not home with our kids. If we stay home with our kids, we feel guilty that we're not financially helping to support our family. We feel guilty that we let the kids watch too much television, feed them frozen or fast food. We feel guilty if we miss a school program because we have to work and can't leave the office. All this guilt just with the kids—and there are dozens of other folks in our lives!

We also feel guilty over not buying organic produce, saving the whales, or wearing enough lingerie to make our partners truly happy. We feel guilty because we carry a bit more weight than we'd like, don't wake up with makeup on like the women on TV, don't call our parents often enough, still don't know how to cook a Thanksgiving turkey to look like the ones in *Bon Appetit*, and on and on.

Do you think men feel this much guilt? Well, that seems to be our lot in life, doesn't it?

Guilt isn't always a bad thing, however. Sometimes it motivates us to do the right thing, accomplish goals, or make correct decisions in our lives.

Guilt isn't guilt across the board; that is, not all guilt is created equal. There's good guilt and bad guilt. When you feel good guilt, you feel badly about your actions. When you feel bad guilt, you feel badly about yourself as a person; you feel that you are defective or not good enough. When a woman is in abusive relationships, she is made to feel badly about herself for just being. Nothing she does is good enough, fast enough, smart enough. She is wrong as a person. This may feel comfortable to her because she had critical, neglectful, or otherwise abusive parents.

Did you know that psychologists have found that people who feel good guilt tend to be very understanding and forgiving in addition to having a keen ability to build strong relationships? That's great! However, consider that it may not always be appropriate to be an understanding partner or friend, and it may not be wise to immediately forgive another person's unkind behavior. It is especially unwise to attempt to build relationships with just any ol' someone, especially when he is unhealthy and abusive. This is what I typically see in abusive situations: a woman who is sweet and nurturing and who feels quite a bit of guilt a good deal of the time. She is the woman who may wind up with an abuser.

Not everyone feels appropriate or good guilt. They think rules don't apply to them, and they feel justified in telling others how they feel, no matter how it will hurt that person. They feel righteously correct in making rules for another person who is not their child, perhaps an adult woman. They feel no remorse for their behavior and don't think they need to change. We call these people sociopaths or psychopaths. We also call them abusers.

Can you change a psychopath? The simple answer is no, you cannot. You don't have control over the person's behavior (which leads to hurt, fear, and frustration, also known as anger, on your end). However, you do have control over your thoughts, actions, and reactions to this knowledge.

SHAME

In his wonderful book *Healing the Shame that Binds You,* John Bradshaw offers a wonderful explanation of shame: "In itself, shame is not bad. Shame is a normal emotion. In fact, it is necessary to have the feeling of shame if one is to be truly human. Shame is the emotion that gives us permission to be human. Shame tells us of our limits. Shame keeps us in our human boundaries, letting us know we can and will make mistakes, and that we need help. Our shame tells us we are not God. Healthy shame is the psychological foundation of humility. It is the source of spirituality."

Further in his book, Bradshaw states that healthy shame can be transformed into something else entirely: toxic shame, which is a sense of being, much like bad guilt. Bradshaw writes, "As a state of being, shame takes over one's whole identity. To have shame as an identity is to believe that one's being is flawed, that one is defective as a human being. Once shame is transformed into an identity, it becomes toxic and dehumanizing."

Let's look at the difference between healthy and toxic shame and the way they may have worked in your life and in your abusive relationship.

Healthy shame is beneficial when it motivates you to examine your life and decisions. It can certainly work in your favor as you read this book and perform the activities at the end of each chapter. Self-examination—with appropriate shame and guilt—can lead to introspection and healthier decision-making.

Toxic shame is at the center of depression, feelings of inadequacy and failure, and a whole host of inwardly and outwardly destructive behaviors and thoughts that you may have experienced while in your abusive relationship. Toxic shame also leads to loneliness and isolation. Because you may feel flawed and defective as a person, you might have felt that you couldn't expose who "you really are" to others, or you might have felt that you were untrustworthy in other relationships. You kept the secret of your abuse to yourself—due to shame—and therefore may have inadvertently isolated yourself from others. This isolation works nicely into the abuser's plan to keep you from your friends, family, and activities you love. So you see, toxic shame and abuse work hand in hand in almost every area.

EMOTIONAL FEAR

Of all the thoughts and behaviors that keep women stuck in abusive relationships, emotional fear ranks at the top of the list. When I talk with such women, I hear a long list of fears that keep them where they are, even if they would like to leave:

- I'm afraid of being alone.

- I don't know how to live on my own anymore.

- Have my kids been damaged by my abusive marriage?

- I think a lot about going back to my abusive partner. Does that mean I'm crazy?

- I'm afraid he'll take the kids—he's threatened to do that.

- I couldn't support myself.

- I'd be homeless if I left.

- I'm afraid that no one else will ever love me.

- It's been so long since I've worked, I don't think I have any job skills anymore.

- I feel like a complete mess.

- Sometimes, I think, "It wasn't that bad. What's wrong with me?"

- I'm afraid of everything.

- I'm so depressed that I don't know how I'd function day to day if he left.

- Most days I think I'm going crazy.

- I'm a total loser.

- I feel defective and useless.

- I don't think I'll ever heal from this relationship.

- I can't imagine being in a good relationship after this, which would mean I'd be alone for the rest of my life.

- I don't think anyone else would ever put up with me.

- I feel like a nervous wreck most of the time.

- I don't trust anyone … including myself.

- How can I teach my kids to be strong and be in a good relationship when I've been such a bad role model?

- I second-guess everything I do.

- I can't imagine ever being happy again.

I remember telling myself those statements most days of the week. I said them over and over until chanting them became a part of my daily routine.

I've found that a single unhealthy relationship robs a woman of her spirit. This may occur in childhood, as it did with me and perhaps with you, as well. When this woman finds herself in multiple abusive relationships over the years—with friends, family members, coworkers, supervisors, and romantic partners—the outcome is usually devastating in terms of her emotional health and well-being. As she sinks deeper and deeper into the abuse pit, she begins feeling wrong as a person. Her already fragile self-esteem takes a dive, guilt and shame set in, denial becomes a part of her daily existence, and she begins a cycle of grief and loss. Fear becomes a way of life.

As children, we learn fear as a way of keeping us safe or obedient. We learn not to talk to strangers, because they may be mean people who could do us harm or take us away from our parents. We learn to fear a hot stove so that we don't get burned. We may learn to fear our fathers by hearing "Just wait until your father gets home" when we are misbehaving. If we had an alcoholic mother who was prone to rages, we learned to stay quiet and "invisible" out of fear of her anger.

As we grow, these fears are reinforced, and new ones are added. We fear being the unpopular girl in school, we fear not being asked to the dance, we fear a group of girls whispering, quite sure that the whispers are about us, we fear upsetting boyfriends lest they dump us. As women, our fears—primarily our fear of being alone—prod us into unhealthy relationships in which we make excuses for poor behaviors because we fear the abuser's responses: verbal or physical violence, emotional withdrawal, or even physically abandonment.

Sometimes, fear is rational. You are correct to fear mountain lions, train tracks, and chain gangs. However, in adult life, most of the time fear is irrational and merely a conditioned response. You are used to feeling afraid in certain situations, and so you expand fear's boundaries to include feeling afraid in many other situations.

This is not to say that your fear of your abuser is misguided. I find that most women are not fearful enough of him as a person. While we have not discussed physical abuse in great detail, please always be aware that a nonphysical abuser has the capability to become physically violent at any time. If he has spent a good deal of time being verbally and emotionally violent to you, it's just a skip and a jump away for him to push, shove, hit, choke, and restrain you. I highly encourage you to keep this very rational fear in the front of your mind.

Your abuser has made you jumpy and fearful through his actions: he may have intimidated you with verbal threats against you, your children, outside family members, or pets. He may have threatened to "expose" you to your community, leave you, take the children away, or take all of the joint monies you share. He may have gotten in your face when he was angry or when he didn't get his way. During this time, he conditioned you to feel fearful all the time, never knowing what his mood would be on any given day, what would set him off, or when he would make good on his threats. His threats may or may not be realized. But he is an unstable person, and a certain amount of caution is necessary.

That said, I find that most women in abusive relationships overestimate their abuser's power. He has made so many threats and has such a narcissistic and sick sense of his own power and abilities that he has convinced her he could kill her from across the country just by thinking about her. He has so systematically debilitated her that she believes in an almost Superman-like power on his part.

When a woman combines her primal fear of being alone with a fear for her or her children's safety, she becomes completely debilitated, which is, of course, the initial design of the abuser.

I can tell you one thing for sure: whenever you make a life decision based on fear, it will always be the wrong decision. Think about that for a moment. If you look at a few of the fears that I mentioned earlier, you'll realize that basing the decision to stay in or leave your abusive relationship on those fears would be a mistake.

For example, staying with your abusive partner because you fear being alone brings up new questions to consider: What is your definition of *alone*? Does not being alone simply mean that another person is physically present in your home? Is that physical presence more important to you than the verbal and emotional battering you endure on a daily basis because of that person? To see someone who has nonloving behaviors sitting in a La-Z Boy with a remote control strapped to his hand is more important than your soul dying? I'm not judging you right now, just asking important questions.

Think about that for a moment. If you are physically alone in your home, what does that mean to you? Where is the fear? Do you have legitimate fear for your physical safety if he is not there? In other words, do you live in such an unsafe neighborhood that you have an excellent reason to believe that a stranger may crawl in your window, kick in your front door, or otherwise gain entry to your home? Or is the fear of being alone related to wanting someone to talk with? How much do you talk with your partner now, and more importantly, how much does he really listen to you and respond in a gratifying way?

What I want you to do here is to really examine your fear of being alone in a real-life, nonemotional manner. I truly believe you will see that the fear of being alone is unfounded in the reality of your situation. Why? Because you are completely, utterly, 100 percent alone right now, and you don't even realize it. You have the illusion of not being alone because there is a body in the house, but in every real sense, you are much more alone than if you were physically alone. If he weren't there, perhaps you'd gain the opportunity of finding yourself, and then you'd never be alone again.

When a woman designs her present life and her future around fear, she is doing several unproductive and self-destructive things at once. The major subheading for all of these ideas is *irrational beliefs*.

IRRATIONAL BELIEFS

As you saw in the previous examples, the thought behind irrational beliefs is that our perceptions create our reality. That is, the way that we view the world and our own situations is the only reality that we accept as correct. The most important idea when we think about that concept is this: believing a thought to be true doesn't necessarily make it true. If I were to show you an animal in the zoo that looked like a horse, except it was white with black stripes, and said to you, "Look at that beautiful pelican," you might think, *That girl is gone! She's crazy if she's looking at a zebra and thinking it's a pelican.* I might insist and insist, but you know that we are both looking at a zebra. I might then give such persuasive and heartfelt arguments about the animal being a pelican that you question your own sanity. My reality is that the animal is a pelican, but that is not *the* reality. Just because I think something doesn't make it so.

When you have emotional fears, you may also be engaging in several irrational beliefs that define your reality. Here are the most common ones. See if you can relate:

- *Generalization:* This type of irrational belief sees you viewing a negative event as a catastrophic pattern of defeat. If you find yourself using the word *always* or *never*, you are most likely generalizing, as in, "I always disappoint my family," or "I never do anything right."

- *All-or-nothing thinking:* This is also known as black-and-white thinking or dichotomous thinking. It means that you look at events or thoughts in absolutes in which someone may be all good or all bad in any and all circumstances. When you are engaged in all-or-nothing thinking, there is no room for shades of gray, which is really where most of reality lies.

- *Jumping to conclusions:* This irrational belief system is composed of two parts: mind-reading and fortune-telling. When you are a mind-reader, you make assumptions about the ways others think about you or assumptions about the ways the world works without any concrete evidence whatsoever. This can lead to some paranoia. For example, you are walking in the mall, feeling badly about yourself and your life, when you see a small group of women whispering among themselves and laughing. You may decide that because you are wearing a ratty blouse, your hair needed to be colored three weeks ago, and you didn't have the energy to put on lipstick, they are laughing at you. Of course, that is probably a projection of the way you feel about yourself, but you've jumped to a conclusion about complete strangers. When you are a fortune-teller, you predict that events will turn out badly without any evidence. Before your parents visit, you've already written the script about the day's performance. You absolutely know that there won't be one minute of happiness in the entire visit, and then guess what? You proceed to ensure that the visit goes exactly that way. I have one small question to ask you: if you are such a great fortune-teller, why haven't you won the lottery yet? And, by the way, will you please e-mail me the winning numbers for the next SuperLotto? Thanks so much.

- *Discounting the positives:* You insist that your positive qualities don't count and that any of your accomplishments are unimportant. When I see a woman with this irrational belief, I can work overtime pointing out everything she's done right, and I get an argument about each one.

Me: Your children are so sweet and polite.

She: Oh, they were just born sweet children.

Me: Congratulations on acing your exam. I hear you got the highest grade in your class!

She: Oh, it wasn't a big deal. A monkey could have taken that exam and done well.

Me: That dress is beautiful. It's a wonderful color on you.

She: Oh, this old thing? I got it at the swap meet.

- *Magnification or minimization:* When you magnify events, you blow them way out of proportion. If one of your coworkers is having a bad day and taking it out on you, then no one at work likes you. When you minimize events, you shrink their importance dramatically. In your abusive relationship, you may use minimization very often in order to avoid looking at the way things really are. "My husband said some unkind things to me, but it's not personal. He's just having a bad time at work." "My boyfriend shoved me, but it's not like he hit me."

- *Labeling:* You give yourself labels such as *loser, idiot, lazy, stupid, jerk,* and the like. Oftentimes, they are the exact labels your abuser gives you or the labels your parents gave you as a child. In other words, you are now verbally abusive to yourself.

- *"Should" statements:* You are your best critic … or perhaps second best. You demean and define yourself with words like *should, shouldn't, ought, must, mustn't,* and so on. You make absolute (all-or-nothing) and highly critical statements about yourself. "I should be a better wife and mother," "I shouldn't feel badly about my parents—they can't help the way they are," "I ought to feel better by now," "I must do a perfect job on this report," and so on. When you criticize yourself in these ways, you don't give yourself any wiggle room for human error, improvement, or salvaging a situation. You don't give yourself the same break you would give others.

- *Emotional reasoning:* You make decisions based on your feelings, without looking at concrete evidence. Feelings dictate your thoughts, and then thoughts dictate your actions, so when you make your decisions based on feelings alone, you are putting yourself in danger. You may have been made to feel like a loser and a bad/wrong person for so long that you think of yourself that way. What, then, is the next step? You *act* like a loser or a bad/wrong person, which becomes a vicious circle of abuse.

WHAT HAS IT COST YOU?
ARE YOU READY TO EXAMINE YOUR FEARS?

As we previously discussed, when fears rule your life and make your decisions for you, you will always make a poor decision. When you begin taking control of your fears, you begin taking control of your life. Take your journal out again, and think and write about the following ideas.

- *Examine the evidence:* Fear by fear, ask yourself, "What is the evidence for this fear?" Remember that just because you feel something or that it is your reality doesn't mean it is *the* reality. Let's pretend for a moment that I'm a judge and you are a trial lawyer defending the case that is your fear. I'm a tough judge, so you'll need to come up with some pretty persuasive evidence that your fear is correct and realistic. Remember, feelings don't count in a court of law. Saying, "I just *feel* as if I'll never be happy" is not enough evidence to convince this cranky judge. Hard, cold evidence is the only standard by which a legal case is decided.

- *Look at your double standards:* Think of another fear on your list—let's say, "I don't think I can do anything right." If you heard your best gal pal say that, what would be your reply? My heavens, you'd be shocked and indignant. "Of course you can do many things right!" you'd tell her. Then, you'd proceed to tell her every single thing she does do right, including being such a good friend to you. Now, if you can say that to someone else, what prevents you from saying it to yourself? If you aren't your own friend, why should anyone else bother? OK, so you have some not-so-great characteristics. Who doesn't, including your friend? How many times have you overlooked minor infractions on her part? Would that qualify her as someone who can't do anything right? No, of course not. Why don't you give yourself the gift of applying the same standards to yourself that you would to her or anyone else you love and care about? When your friend is having a bad day, what do you tell her to encourage her along? Why not give yourself the same messages?

- *Conduct an experiment:* Let's look at another of your fears and irrational beliefs. When women have survived abusive relationships, they are not only fearful while they are in the relationship, but also very fearful in the aftermath. They are accustomed to fear as a daily way of life. Why don't we look at the fear, "I'm afraid of everything"? To test whether your fear is well founded, conduct a little science experiment to test out your theory. Take a seat on your couch. Are you afraid of your couch? Do your kitchen potholders make you feel woozy? Is your refrigerator making you squeamish? OK, so we've concluded that you're not afraid of everything in your home. Why not take your experiment to the mall? Sit on a bench in the quad area and look at the people passing by. Are you afraid of each of them? Are you frightened by the mall directory? Are you afraid that you will have a stroke right then and there? No? Well then, given these two examples, I think it's fair to say that you're not afraid of *everything.* Now, since you're at the mall anyway, go look at some cute shoes …

- *Consider the worst-case scenario:* Let's indulge for a moment in your biggest, darkest, baddest fear. What would that be? What are you most frightened of in the entire world? Probably that you or someone you love the most—let's say your kids—will die. This is your worst-case scenario. You can go there just for a moment; you are in a safe place, and you and your loved ones are safe as well. Now, take a look at your list of fears. If you are alone, are you or your kids going to die? If your children are somewhat temporarily damaged by your abusive relationship, will they die? If you are afraid of everything, will you die? If you think of yourself as a total loser, will you or your kids die from this revelation? No to all questions, right? OK, then your worst-case scenario will not come true as a result of any of your fears and irrational beliefs. That means you are in the plus column! Anything else is just gravy now! You're actually doing much better than you think!

Now that you are feeling much better about yourself, let's continue those gains, and I'll tell you how and why you are completely normal!

12

What You're Feeling Is Normal

I don't really know how I should live my life anymore. Nothing seems real or true. I feel like I'm either crazy or depressed all of the time. Everything I believed in is gone; he's taken that from me. I feel as if I'm living in some weird twilight zone ... like I'm looking down at myself and wondering if this is a bad dream I'll eventually wake up from or if this is actually normal and the way I'm going to spend the rest of my life.

I don't know what to think, what to feel, how to act. Sometimes I feel dead, sometimes I feel angry, sometimes I want to give up; and other times I'm trying so hard to make this work. But, the funny thing is that I'm the only one working at it, and I'm also the only one feeling this way. He doesn't care one way or another, so there are times when I tell myself that I shouldn't care, either. But I do, and that makes me feel worse. Mostly, I just feel alone and scared.

—**Heather, age thirty-three**

Heather is feeling a lot of emotions, isn't she? She's experiencing them all at once, which makes her feel shaky and alone. *Could anyone feel this crazy*, she wonders? *I don't dare tell another soul what I'm thinking; I might be committed to an institution!*

Actually, everything that Heather has expressed is completely normal for a woman in an abusive relationship. Let's think about why that might be.

Do you remember when we discussed the different types of abuse in chapter 2? Many of the emotionally and psychologically abusive tactics that men use are designed to make you feel nuts. Couple that with possible spiritual abuse in which your long-held morals and values have been stripped from your soul—which makes you feel like a bad person—and you may begin to see how both you and Heather feel mentally impaired. Now, add into that verbal abuse (which takes away your self-esteem), financial abuse (which leaves you feeling stuck and without options to leave), and then the negative messages you may have received as a child (which reinforce all of the partner abuse), as well as isolation, shame, and guilt, and you can begin to understand how crazy an abusive relationship can make you feel.

It stands to reason that you feel off-kilter. Let's review some of the abuse you may be experiencing and also some of the emotions you may have.

ABUSE

- Putting you down

- Calling you names

- Playing mind games (making you feel crazy)

- Making you feel guilty

- Making all decisions

- Treating you like a servant or "less than"

- Giving you intimidating looks or gestures

- Making light of the abuse or saying it didn't happen

- Telling you that you're too sensitive (after being abused)

- Blaming you

- Threatening you

- Demanding sex when you don't want it or having sex with you in a demeaning manner

- Exhibiting jealousy

- Checking up on you

- Controlling your time

- Telling you who you can see or talk with

- Isolating you from your friends, family, or outside activities

- Threatening to "expose" you or your secrets/weaknesses

- Lying about you

- Forcing you to go outside your religious beliefs or values

- Preventing you from practicing your religion

- Doling out money

- Keeping car keys, telephone, or finances from you

- Subjecting you to uncontrollable rages

- Withdrawing/refusing to talk to you

- Neglecting you

- Engaging in unpredictable or embarrassing behavior

- Hiding important information/leading a secret life

- Humiliating you

- Making unclear "rules" that keep changing or don't apply to him

- Making you look "crazy" to others

YOUR FEELINGS

- Fear

- Grief

- Shame

- Guilt

- Anger

- Denial

- Depression

- Hopefulness

- Acceptance of the abuse

- Hopelessness

- Worthlessness

- Fatigue

- Physical illness

- Confusion

- Inability to go on

- Second-guessing yourself

- Emotional exhaustion

- Humiliation

- Feelings of being a failure

- Foolishness

- Numbness

- "This isn't my life"

- Anxiety

- Unworthiness

- Spiritual abandonment

Have you suffered any of the abuses I just mentioned? How about those feelings listed above? Yes, I thought so. What I want to impress upon you is that everything on the emotions list is normal. Every abused woman experiences these feelings. There is nothing crazy about you; you are in a crazy-making situation!

But how would you know that? Your partner may tell you that you're crazy all the time. He may do things designed to make you feel crazy. Couple that with the knowledge that—due to guilt, shame, and isolation—you are not comparing your reality to other women in similar situations, and that you may not be getting any or substandard counseling ... and you think he's right.

You may have gone to a therapist or couples counselor with him. You thought, *Here's the chance I've been waiting for. He keeps telling me that I'm the one with the problem and that I need help, but I've finally persuaded him that we need to go to a counselor together. Now we'll really get some help, and our relationship will improve.* However, that may not have worked out. Abusers are very charming and manipulative. They know how to work difficult situations to their advantage. Your partner may not have looked like an abuser in the therapist's office. As a matter of fact, when you left therapy, you may have felt worse and concluded that everything really was your fault. He didn't have any problems; his problem was that you don't understand him and are not communicating effectively, just as he told you.

Or, perhaps you went to therapy by yourself, but because of all the abuse you've experienced, you really didn't understand that you were being abused. You may have minimized his behavior, and even if your therapist stated or implied that you were in an unhealthy relationship, you may have made excuses for him. Maybe you even blamed yourself ... just as he does. Perhaps you quit therapy because you didn't want to look at the truth or because you felt that the counselor was pressuring you to leave your partner. Maybe you were too afraid to tell her the truth because you were ashamed or embarrassed to look foolish or you thought she might report your man to the authorities. Could it be that before you went to therapy each time, he told you what you could and couldn't tell your counselor?

I have found that woefully few therapists truly understand abuse, and so they buy his good-guy image, are manipulated by his behavior in session, or side with him due to fear or inexperience. They don't see through the excuses a woman makes for her guy, or they don't understand her fearfulness. Because of therapist bias, she may force a certain personal viewpoint, or she may tell the woman to leave the relationship without considering her feelings or preparing her with several sessions of options and telling her what may happen if she does leave. She doesn't address her client's fears and anxieties.

Here you are with all these feelings and nowhere to go with them except—you think—an asylum. And since you don't have anyone to bounce your feelings off of, how are you to know that other women feel exactly as you do?

Your feelings are normal, but that doesn't mean they are productive. It is difficult to move forward in a healthy manner when you are stuck in emotions that *keep* you stuck.

WHAT HAS IT COST YOU?
WHAT YOU CAN DO ABOUT YOUR FEELINGS

Let's just check out your emotions to see if they are legitimate and therefore worth keeping.

In your journal, list all the feelings you've had about your abusive relationship. You may find a progression from positive to negative and somewhere in between. Some days, you may feel hopeful and good about yourself in your relationship. On other days, you may feel hopeless and worthless. The key is to understand that your emotions are probably dependent on your abuser's moods or what he wants from you.

Feel free to use the list of emotions earlier in the chapter, if they relate to you. Now, take a good look at each one on your own list, and consider it carefully. If you take into account what is being or has been done to you, the abuses you've suffered, and the childhood messages you heard, are your feelings reasonable? Take your abuser's messages out of the equation. For instance, if your parents used to tell you that you didn't have a right to your feelings, or if your current partner tells you that you're crazy for feeling the way you do, do not allow that to influence your individual judgment right now. Today, you are entitled to think for yourself and make your own decisions.

You are able to make good choices. You are a smart and capable woman able to determine whether her feelings are appropriate and chart her own future. Remember one of the universal truths I stated and restated earlier in this book: you have 100 percent control over three things. The first and most important of these is that you can control your thoughts.

13

Why Can't He Just Change?

I used to tell him, "You're destroying our family. You can't talk to me that way. How do you think the kids feel when they hear you do that? It hurts my feelings and makes me feel like nothing." Depending on his mood, he'd either shrug and mumble "Sorry" or he'd say something like "Oh, stop being so dramatic. I didn't do anything wrong. Everything hurts your feelings." Sometimes, he'd change his ways for a couple of days, and the kids and I would be so happy. The house was so calm. Just when I'd let my guard down, he'd go back to his old behavior.

—Linda, age thirty-eight

Once again, here is my simple philosophy of life in general and relationships in particular: If something's working, do more of it. If it's not working, do something else. Linda—and probably you—has been doing the same thing over and over again (begging, pleading, explaining to her husband) and expecting a different response. That's the not-so-clinical definition of "crazy." At this point in Linda's marriage with her husband, she holds an irrational belief that she can change his behavior by talking to him. She's tried that strategy countless times without the effect she'd like.

Let's break apart Linda's statement and analyze what's going wrong for her:

"You're destroying our family." (He's thinking, *No, your craziness is.*)

"You can't talk to me that way." (He's thinking, *Yes I can, and I do.*)

"How do you think the kids feel when they hear you talk like that?" (He's thinking, *They probably think that you're a screaming meemie who deserves it, just as I do.*)

"It hurts my feelings and makes me feel like nothing." (He's thinking, *Mission accomplished! Now, will you shut up?*)

"Depending on his mood, he'd either shrug his shoulders and mumble "Sorry" or say something like "Oh, stop being so dramatic. I didn't do anything wrong. Everything hurts your feelings." (He's either thinking, *Whatever will stop her talking the fastest and easiest* or blaming her for being what he considers to be inappropriately upset. Now, in his view, his behavior is *her* fault.)

"Sometimes, he'd change his ways for a couple of days, and the kids and I would be so happy. The house was so calm." (Her moods are dependent on his moods—codependent—and she's teaching her kids to behave the same. She also sees hope for change and believes he has the capability to be a nice guy when he wants to, which keeps her hanging in there.)

"Just when I'd let my guard down, he'd go back to his old behavior." (Because he can.)

In looking at this example, can you identify many of the same feelings and behaviors in your life? Perhaps—as I did in my first marriage—you are heavily invested in telling your partner how you feel, how his insensitive behavior affects you, and how you'd like things to be different. You actually expect him to change with this not-so-new knowledge. Why doesn't he do that? To answer that effectively, let me ask you an important question: does your partner speak fluent Japanese (or Greek, Farsi, Portuguese, or any other foreign language)? No? Then, why is it that you continue to speak Japanese to him day after day? You are speaking a language that he not only doesn't understand, but one that he has shown you—through his behavior—he has no desire to learn.

You see, you are speaking to your partner in a language of compassion, logic, and good fellowship. It seems perfectly reasonable that he would speak this language fluently, as you do. That is a false perception on your part. You may even have come to the realization that he doesn't speak this language and have thus decided that you would make the perfect professor. You are patient and kind; you can do a great job teaching this new and mysterious language to him. Wrong once again; he is an unwilling student. He is doing an impression of a little child who doesn't want to hear what his mommy is telling him, so he shuts his eyes very tightly, puts his hands over his ears, and yells, "I can't hear you!"

Do you remember our discussion of the ideas behind abuse? The main goals are power and control. I am certain that abusers fully comprehend—and enjoy—how abuse makes their partners feel. Therefore, when the woman explains it over and over—"You're hurting my feelings," "I feel as if I can't take it anymore," "You're killing me," "You make me so depressed that I can't go on this way anymore"—it just reinforces the sadistic joy in their tiny abuser hearts! They've accomplished their goal and have earned bonus points. You couldn't say words any sweeter to him. So why would he change?

Also, understand that when you tell him "You can't treat me that way," he's thinking *Yes I can*. And the fact is, he's correct. He absolutely can treat you that way, and he does—because you let him. What would happen if he began talking to you in a horrible, disrespectful way or treating you in his usual unkind manner, and instead of standing there taking it, crying, pleading, or explaining, you said, "This conversation is over." What would he do? If you fear that he would physically harm you, himself, or your children, then you are in a dangerous relationship that may require the help of an attorney or the police. If you think your statement would increase his vitriol, or cause him to stomp out of the house or do something rash—like taking the children away or harming himself—then you have other, very serious issues to consider.

Do you remember what your worst-case scenario is? Will that happen if you demand some respect and actually treat yourself in a respectful manner by disallowing the abuse? No, probably not. Once again, you are ahead of the game!

So, can your partner change? The answer is yes. Of course he can change. I am a therapist, and if I didn't believe in the power of change, I couldn't work in this profession. The more important question is *will* he change. The answer—statistically and consistent with any study I've ever read on the subject—is probably not. The chances of his changing are quite low. Why?

Well, he has a long history of abusing and being abused. This is how he does business. But—you may be thinking—if this is what he knows and I, or someone else, teaches him a new and better way, then he'll be happier. That may be very true, but remember you are dealing with a man who has a very rigid thought pattern, who is narcissistic, who wants everything his way, and who gets a huge payoff by abusing you. Why should he change? If you knew that every time you bought a lottery ticket, you were going to win, would you stop buying lottery tickets? Of course not. That's what your abuser is thinking as well: *I get a great jackpot every time I mistreat her. I get a terrific payday. Besides, who is she to tell me what I should do!*

Yes, an abuser can change his behavior if he takes the following six steps in order:

1. He understands that his behavior is abusive and inappropriate.

2. He doesn't cast blame for his behavior onto his girlfriend/wife, parents, boss, etc.

3. He takes full responsibility for his abusive behavior.

4. He has a desire to change. He's not just doing it to stay out of trouble with the law, at work, or because his mate nagged him to do so.

5. He follows up his stated desire to change with concrete actions. Love is a behavior!

6. His new actions are ongoing, not just for the moment. Most abusers apologize for their bad behavior and tell their partners it will never happen again. This gives the woman great hope and optimism. But often, the abuser is contrite for only a few days and reverts back to his previous behavior.

That's a long list, but it can be done if the abuser is self-motivated. It takes tremendous effort because it is not just a matter of changing a bad habit. The abuser must do a great deal of work in order to permanently change the lifestyle that worked so successfully for him for so long. It is important to understand that abusing another person and inflicting intentional emotional cruelty is not just a bad habit. It is far greater than that. As you may imagine, in order for an abuser to truly change himself, he must uncover the root of his need for power and control, where it started and why it began. He must process family dynamics to determine what he gets out of it, and then form an entirely new way of relating to others. Kind of like the work you are doing in this book, isn't it? It also requires an entirely new skill: compassion. He needs to completely understand the devastating effect his abusive behavior has on others—and really care. Changing abusive behavior is a very, very long process and takes tremendous effort, with the emphasis on the word *effort*.

It is always a better bet to do significant work on changing yourself rather than your abuser. All of the activities in this book up to this point have led you to be aware of the changes you can make in yourself:

*   Understanding what abuse is

*   Knowing the place your family had in the process

*   Getting a clear picture of who your abusers are and how they act

*   Raising your self-esteem

*   Getting a grip on your fears

*   Dealing with your feelings of guilt and shame, grief and loss, anger and fear

*   Understanding what you can and cannot control

Let's say your abuser doesn't wish to take the steps necessary for real and lasting change. How does that make you feel? Worthless? Unimportant to him? Unloved? Angry? Frustrated? Afraid? The right answer would be yes to all of them. Remember that love is a behavior, so it is entirely appropriate that you feel unimportant to him and unloved. He is not demonstrating loving behavior to you. That kind of knowledge naturally causes you to feel worthless—because you are used to feeling that way, not because you are actually worthless—angry, frustrated, and frightened of the future.

Before you approach your mate with an ultimatum, you must make a crucial decision: are you prepared for him to exit your life? I cannot tell you how important it is for you to think about this in advance, because inherent in every abusive relationship that involves one person who has self-respect (you, or who you will be shortly) is the possibility that the abuser won't want to change. Then what do you do? Stay in the relationship, with the knowledge that nothing will change, or leave? Only you can decide what you—and your children—deserve and how you will accomplish that. We will talk about your options and what they mean to your life later in this book.

WHAT HAS IT COST YOU?
NEW WAYS TO TALK TO YOUR ABUSER, KNOWING THAT HE MAY NOT LISTEN TO WHAT YOU HAVE TO SAY

Sometimes when we are in a very volatile situation, our emotions take over and our brain turns to mush. When you speak to your abuser, he knows your every weakness and uses it to full advantage. He may be a smooth talker who employs courtroom techniques to put you on the defensive, confusing and blaming you, causing you to feel small and hopeless. You need a new plan. You need to be in charge of the conversation. Impossible, you say? He's too loud, too convincing, too forceful, too smart, too intimidating? No he's not. He's just a guy who has practiced his technique and had a lot of success with it. Here is your chance to develop a style that may work for you.

When you speak with your partner, remember that the goal is not to enlighten him about your inner thoughts, make him understand you better, or change him. Based on your past experience with him, is it likely that any one of those things will happen? No. Your goal is to express yourself succinctly and directly, so you'll realize that you can remain in control of your thoughts, behaviors, and reactions and that you can speak/think/behave/react in a way that feels most productive to you. It doesn't mean that speaking with your partner will have a meaningful effect on his thoughts, behaviors, or reactions, or that anything in him will change.

In your journal, write down this statement:

When (name of abuser) *says/does* (words or actions), *I will* (your words or actions).

Let's look at some examples of answers to this exercise:

- When my boyfriend begins to say unkind words to me, I will say, "Stop it right now. I will not allow you to speak that way to me anymore. Either you change the way you act, or you will have to leave. I will give you (X number) days to make a decision, and then I will have to take action."

- When my husband shuts me out and ignores me, I will not talk to him at that point and will either go for a walk, read a book, or call a friend. When we are both calm, I will explain what the consequences of his continued behavior will mean to our marriage. I am prepared to follow through on whatever I state.

- When my mate humiliates me in front of friends, I will tell him that he has hurt me, and I now understand that I cannot trust him, which severely damages our relationship. I will not allow myself to be vulnerable to him until he changes—if he does—and will not tell him anything that is important.

- When my husband/boyfriend demands sex when I don't want it or a sexual act that I am not comfortable with, I will tell him that I am unwilling to do that. If he sulks, I need to understand that his desire for something I don't want is not more important than my need to feel good about myself and us during sex. If he threatens to find someone who will do it, I will tell him that his threat just further demonstrates how little he respects or loves me.

I could certainly give you more examples, but I know you understand the idea. Do you see the commonality in all of the statements above? They come from a place of self-respect and state assertively what you and he can now expect. Try practicing your statements out loud. Your voice may sound strange and scary to you. Just thinking of the consequences of your statements may put you into an anxiety spin. Go back to your worst-case scenario. Will that happen if you express yourself? No? Then go ahead. Remember, your birthright states that you are entitled to be happy, respected, and treated fairly.

Keep remembering that you cannot change your abuser's behavior; you can only change your reaction to it. This knowledge may now give you a great feeling of calm and composure. Why? Because you have undoubtedly spent a good deal of your life trying to either fix abusers, understand them, or adjust your life to fit their expectations, no matter how cruel or unreasonable. Your life has just gotten 100 percent easier!

14

Resolving Unfinished Business with Your Family of Origin so That You Can Move On

I can't say enough all the ways my childhood—well, my mom, really—has messed up my life. I don't even know where to begin.

My father died when I was a baby, and my mother never remarried. She's always been a controlling tyrant. Appearance is everything to her. I'm her only child, and I guess I've never matched her idea of perfection. She's always been not only highly critical of everything I do, but she's constantly criticized the way I look. I always thought I was the ugliest girl in the world. It wasn't until a few months ago that I looked at some photos she stashed away of me when I was elementary and high-school age. I was really beautiful; stunning, actually. But, in all the pictures, I'm never looking directly at the camera, and I'm wearing baggy clothes, because I can remember that she always told me that I was fat. I wasn't! I had a darling figure. I also remember that she made excuses about why I couldn't date every boy who asked me. She'd tell me, "He just feels sorry for you and wants to use you for sex. He dates the popular, pretty girls. What would he want with you besides sex?" Can you believe that? Now I think she must have been threatened or jealous of me.

She'd berate me and talk about me to other people as if I wasn't even there. Nothing I did was ever good enough. She chose to spend her time with her friends' daughters, as if they were her own.

She also went into horrible rages and would hit me with objects. Until recently I had repressed all those memories, but now I remember all of them. I finally confronted her about them, and she was very shrill and insisted they never happened. But I know they did happen.

She demands that I call her every day and tell her everything that's going on in my life. Then she somehow uses any problems I'm having against me at a later time. I can't trust her in any way. I used to think that she wouldn't want me if I was successful and needed me to be sick and a failure. I'm not sure that's wrong to this day. But she also punishes me emotionally and verbally when I do well, so I can't win with her.

Everyone else thinks she's wonderful and believes what she tells them about me because she's so convincing, and they've heard the stories for so long.

I'm forty-two and have never been married or had children. All of my relationships with men have been abusive, and my jobs don't work out well, either. I feel totally stuck in my life and don't know how to get out of all this. I know it stems from my relationship with my mother, but I don't know how to fix it. I don't have any optimism that I'll ever be happy or free from her, even after she dies.

—Meredith, age forty-two

I hear many stories similar to Meredith's. In fact, a good portion of my book *Destructive Relationships* focused on breaking your abusive tie with parents who continue to dishonor who you are. I've found that when a woman has suffered through an abusive childhood and does not resolve that abuse, she goes on to replicate that relationship with male partners, friends, coworkers, bosses, siblings, and her own children.

She continues to deepen the gaping wounds left by her parents, which she may express in present-day anger, shame, fear, false hope, resentment, depression, joylessness, physical illness, and, of course, abusive relationships.

Therefore, it is crucial to resolve past hurts with your parents in some way. In her book *The Emotionally Abused Woman*, Beverly Engel reminds us of many signs of unresolved business with family-of-origin abusers:

- Involvement with abusive people

- Spending a great deal of time thinking about the childhood abusers, which may include vengeful thoughts or ruminations about what you'd say to them today

- Inappropriate anger outbursts

- Repeating the same relationship patterns today that you had with your childhood abusers

Many women with abusive childhoods maintain the abuse status quo with their parents in some way in the present. Even though they are adults with lives of their own, they become young children again when faced with their abusive parents: cowering, feeling fearful to speak up, not wanting to upset their parents, resenting them and hating themselves. They put their parents' need to continually abuse them ahead of their own right to happiness!

As I was growing up, my mother was not only critical but also very narcissistic. Now that she's in her eighties, sadly, I think it's fair to say that she has not mellowed much with age. I recall so many times when she'd project her own feelings of worthlessness onto me—although I certainly didn't know that was what she was doing at the time—and told me things about myself that simply weren't true. Being young, and only having my mother as my female role model, I believed her abuse wholeheartedly. She'd tell me I was weak, among other observations. I don't recall being a sickly child and was actually quite strong and resilient, considering my life. But even today, she tells me, "I don't think you're getting enough rest. You look terrible. Remember, you're not a strong person." My mother has dementia now, and I think of her as a sad, pathetic character who has wasted her life on drama, chaos, fear, anxiety, and unimportant things. I feel very sorry for her. Up until a dozen years ago, when she'd tell me I was weak or criticize my appearance, I would shrink, not speak up for myself, and resent her. I now see her inaccurate critique as a total projection of the way she feels about herself; I feel pity that in the waning years of her life, she still needs to live in her personal hell. Do I like her comments? No, of course not. Sometimes—for my benefit alone—I thank her for her concern and tell her that I'm actually very strong and that I'm taking good care of myself. Because of her dementia, I know that she will say the same thing several more times in our conversation, but it makes me feel better to address it once.

My mother's behavior doesn't change, even though I now assert myself. Why is that? Because I don't have control over her thoughts, behaviors, and reactions and never have, right?

Beverly Engel has a wonderful exercise in her book that can help you discover where to begin resolving your unfinished business with former abusers. The first step is discovering what the business is.

1.   Answer the following questions: What is your relationship with your original abuser now? Do you ever see him/her? Are you close? Do you still feel abused by him/her?

2.   List all the reasons you are still angry with your *original* abuser. List all the reasons you are still hurt.

3.   Make a list of what you want from your original abuser now.

4. List the reasons you feel angry with and hurt by your *current* abuser.

5. Make a list of what you want from your current abuser.

6. Compare the lists from #2 and #4. Then compare the lists from #3 and #5.

This exercise is very effective; I encourage you to use your journal for this exercise. You will see that one of the fallouts from childhood abuse may be your hesitance to express your feelings in many situations. Part of resolving your unfinished business is learning to express these feelings.

Now, before I lose you on this subject, let me assure you that I am not suggesting you have an angry showdown with your parents. However, it is important for you to acknowledge your feelings, if only to yourself in the privacy of your own home.

I know that when I was a child, I was afraid to express my feelings. Besides, if I did, who cared? I learned to push down unpleasant thoughts due to frustration, hopelessness, and minimization. I went through my childhood in a sort of sleepwalking stage, trying not to feel anything too intensely, including happiness—for that very joy could be pulled out from under me at any moment. It was safer not to experience happiness at all.

This philosophy came back to bite me in the derriere when I met my perfect match: my children's father. He, too, didn't express emotions, which nearly drove me mad! The more I tried to get him to open up, the more he shut down. Go figure. I became angrier and angrier and felt as if I was in the marriage alone. I tried several times to express my feelings to him, thinking that as my husband he must be a safe person, but I found that he continued in shutdown mode. Eventually, I just reverted back to old childhood behavior: concluding that because yet another person did not care about my feelings, my feelings must be bad. Controlling my emotions—and all the havoc that came with them—became a full-time job.

This became a good plan for me at the time, a nifty survival tool. When I expressed my emotions, my former husband had told me that I was too sensitive and dramatic and that I was blowing things out of proportion and generally overreacting. Maybe I was; I still can't say. Next to a person who expressed zero emotion, any emotion may have looked spectacularly threatening.

The longer I spent in that marriage, the more numb I became … or so I thought. All of my feelings were going somewhere—just as yours have—even if I refused to let them out. As I said earlier, my emotions went into heart problems and other chronic physical illness. What began as a great coping mechanism when I was a child was now doing me in.

I would ask you to take a moment right now to think about where your emotions are sitting in your body. Your body remembers every feeling you've had and stores them as what is called body memories. As we talked about earlier in this book, you may get tension headaches, stomachaches, sore throats, stiffness, backaches, fluttering heart, or any number of other body cues telling you that your feelings are attempting to speak up. As you think about your childhood abuses and begin the healing process, your body will make itself known in a strong way. Allow these signals to envelop you, even if they are unpleasant. They will subside as you do the work. You've spent many years denying and pushing down these feelings that were trying desperately to get out and be heard. Working through them will not happen overnight or without some pain.

CRUCIAL STEPS IN RESOLVING YOUR UNFINISHED BUSINESS

You will need to do some difficult things in order to get past the unresolved issues with your family: you must learn to release your anger, hurt, and resentment, and you will need to confront your abuser, although not necessarily in person. I will be with you every step of the way. Here we go.

Were you able to identify the areas of hurt and anger you've held with your parents? Did you see that some of the core issues you've been holding onto arose because your abusers

- emotionally, verbally, sexually, or physically abused you;

- did not listen to you;

- did not allow you to have your own thoughts and feelings;

- punished you with silence and withdrawal;

- were too enmeshed in your life;

- were poor role models;

- were narcissistic;

- were absent emotionally or physically;

- did not make you feel worthwhile to them?

It is important that you sit with these feelings for as long as possible and give yourself permission to be angry—that is, experience feelings of hurt, fear, and frustration—with your abusers. What they did to you was criminal. It was felonious, not merely a misdemeanor. You deserve this time, not only so you can process your hurt and resentment, but also because this is the loving time they should have given you when you were a child. While you cannot change the fact that they didn't give that time to you then, you can give it to yourself now.

When you refuse to express your hurt and anger in the present, you remain negatively emotionally tied to your parents. You invest a tremendous amount of energy in resenting and blaming them for the past when you could be using that store of energy to make your current life better. You continue to allow them to control you every day.

It is natural and normal for you to have deeply negative emotions about them and their actions. You would not be human if you didn't; however, when you persist in blaming them for all your failings—and doing so would certainly be understandable—you remain an emotional child under their thumb. When you were young you didn't have your own power; your abusers took advantage of that fact. Today, however, you are an adult woman who can make her own decisions about the length of time she wants to remain emotionally shut down, bitter, powerless, childlike, and depressed.

Give yourself permission to be angry with your abusers, whether or not they know of your anger. In this instance, your anger—that is, your hurt, fear, and frustration—is completely justified. Once you let it out, you will feel lighter in spirit; perhaps that will encourage lightness of physical being if you have been an emotional eater most of your life in an effort to stuff your feelings down. You will be able to feel a full range of emotions and become a stronger woman. Acknowledging your anger will also give you the courage to make painful decisions about your current abusive relationship.

How can you release your anger most effectively? Here are a number of proven tactics:

- *Have an imaginary conversation with your parents:* Wouldn't it be great to confront your abusers and tell them anything you'd like, however you'd like, while they are unable to respond? Now *you* are in charge, and they are powerless! You might want to set up a chair and put a picture of your parent on that chair. You can either sit across from "her," or you can pace (anger has a lot of energy) while you talk. Let every single thing out: every infraction, every hurt, and every resentment. Your abuser cannot talk back.

- *Write a letter to your abuser:* I have personally found this very effective. You can write this letter by hand or type it on a computer. I recommend hand-writing, which makes the experience very personal; you are able to remain slightly detached when a piece of technology is doing the writing. Handwriting is a physical and sensual (not to be mistaken with sexual) act. You can use plain, white paper or lined, yellow or white paper, or you can buy yourself beautiful and elegant paper. Whatever feels right to you is what is right. You can use a pen, pencil, crayon, or marker (to further express the child's view). Write down the ways your abuser hurt you, what that abuse did to your life and your decisions, and the way you feel about him today. Come from an "I" place; that is, begin your sentences with I. For example, "I'm angry with you for——," "I can hardly believe that you would think it was OK to——," or "I'm sick of you doing——to me."

When you have completed your letter—and you may want to write a letter to several people—you can do any number of things with it: tear it up into little pieces and throw it away, crumble it up and flush it down the toilet (whether you use the toilet before you flush the letter is up to you!), burn it, or mail it. When I wrote my letter to my father, who sexually abused me, I tore the letter into very small pieces, dug a hole in my yard and put the pieces in the hole, and then planted a lemon tree there. It was wonderful to have a living and beautiful thing grow in place of the pain. The tree smelled wonderful, and its fruit nurtured my children and me. Hey, when you've literally got lemons, make lemonade!

- *Get physical:* As I said, anger has a lot of energy. Instead of keeping all that energy inside, release it through healthy physical activity. We now understand that physical exercise is very effective against depression and other emotional difficulties. Use your energy to its greatest advantage. Ask your body what it feels like doing with its anger energy. Would it like to run, walk, swim, bike, kick, throw things, or scream? How about all of the above? Fine, go ahead. By the time you are done with your anger release, you may have a healthier body as a side benefit. You can also cry. Crying is very healing to your body. Your tears have stored toxins that you can now release. While crying will not help you release your anger per se, it would certainly be understandable if you felt like having a good cry, or twelve, when doing this work. You are uncovering and processing very painful areas of your life. Go ahead and cry for the little girl who was treated so unfairly. She deserves it.

• *Direct confrontation:* You can directly confront your abuser in the letter that you mail, through e-mail, over the phone, or in person. If you chose to do so over the telephone or in person, you will need to prepare yourself very well in advance of your meeting.

Before you attempt a direct confrontation, be honest about your current level of emotional strength and stamina. You may decide that you are ready, or you may decide that you would like some additional preparation before making this contact. Either way is fine and is your perfect way.

Write a script of everything you'd like to address with your parent. This is an important step; not only does it put you in charge of the meeting, but you will not be caught off guard and vulnerable should your parent become defensive or act pathetic or confrontational. Your script should include the following areas:

• What he did to you—this may be a very long list, but state each incident that you can recall

• How you felt as the result of each of the abuses

• The effects his behavior had on you as a child, and the ways it continues to impact you today

• The way you feel about him today and why

• What you would like from him now

Practice your script into a tape recorder, in front of a mirror, or with a friend so you can get feedback. Be aware of how you feel, and take a break if you need to. How is your body reacting? Is it tense? Is your stomach doing flip-flops? Do you feel like crying, or are you actually crying? It is not weak to cry in front of your abuser when you are discussing such painful topics; however, if you think that tears would be ineffective or would cause you to appear small and childlike, you will need to practice until you are able to "talk" to your abuser without crying.

Call, e-mail, fax, or write to your abusive parent, and state your desire for a meeting. Understand that he may not want to do this. Just because you request a meeting doesn't mean you can control whether he will feel like attending. If he does not wish to participate, understand that you will need to deal with your grief and sadness in one of the other ways we've already discussed. Then you will have to decide whether you want to keep this person in your life in any way. He still does not wish to hear your voice or acknowledge the abuse. This knowledge reinforces your legitimate hurt. We will discuss that later in this book.

If your parent agrees to the meeting, make sure that you are clear about the reason. Don't be coy and say you'd just like to get together. That's dishonest and abusive in itself. Set whatever ground rules feel comfortable to you, such as looking you in the eyes when you talk, not interrupting you when you are speaking, not defending his position or minimizing your statements. Make sure that your parent agrees to the ground rules, and be clear about the consequences for failing to comply: for example, you will need to leave. Set the time and place for the meeting. It should take place on neutral, public ground so that you feel safe and can leave if you wish.

Despite all of this preparation, expect your parent to rationalize, blame you or someone else for his hurtful behavior, deny that the abuse took place, try to make you feel sorry for him, try to make you responsible for the actions, or make you feel guilty for bringing this up or for being a "bad" child. All of this is untrue. Do not "bite"; that is, don't address his claims. Just quietly interrupt his chatter, remind him of the ground rules, and continue your script until you are finished. I think it is wise to have a supportive friend drive you to and from this meeting and wait in the car for you.

Remember that despite the fact that you will be clear, honest, reasonable, and correct in your statements, you haven't any control over the way your abuser will react. That is not yours to control. It may end with your parent's gratitude that you resolved the cold war between you, surprise that you've felt this way for so many years, or self-blame. On the other hand, his reaction may also be defensiveness and incredulousness that you have the audacity to make up such stories! He may try to make you feel as crazy as he always has; you may actually find it reassuring to see that he is still the same person you've known him to be: an abuser. However, also know that even though the confrontation may end badly, positive changes can take place between you with some time and healing. Do not use your old standby—false hope—to keep this thought alive, however. Put the idea out of your head, and then you can be pleasantly surprised if it eventually takes place.

WHAT HAS IT COST YOU?
RESOLVING UNFINISHED BUSINESS

Since you have already spent so much time making lists, letters, and scripts, you have completed the activities necessary for success in this chapter. Take a few days and then look at your writings again. Is there anything you forgot? Is there anything you'd change or amplify?

How are you feeling at this point in the book? If you've had some new revelations about yourself or your process, write about them now. You are halfway through the book, and we are going to make a sharp turn now; this is your chance to review all that you've written thus far, take a few more days to understand your feelings, and then move forward.

Congratulations on your insights and for sticking with this often difficult work. I honor your commitment and hope that you honor yourself as well.

PART IV

WHAT ARE THE STEPS TO GET OUT? MAKING DECISIONS AND TAKING A STAND

He told me that if I leave, he'll make sure the courts and everyone else knows how crazy I am, and I'll never have custody of our kids. He also said that if he has custody, he'll be able to take them to live anywhere he wants, which would be out of state. I couldn't live with that, and he knows that. I can't live without my kids.
—Theresa, age thirty-six

My boyfriend told me that if I break up with him, he'll tell everyone at school all the things we did sexually. I'm sort of ashamed of some of the things I did with him. I only did them because he really wanted me to, but I didn't like doing them. I wasn't exactly forced, but I was, if you know what I mean. I did them because I love him, and I knew it would really make him happy, but I wouldn't have wanted to otherwise. My parents don't know I've had sex, and that would be hard for them to hear. And then how would I go back to school with everyone knowing what I did? It's just so confusing to me, because I know he's not this person. He's not the type of person who would do something like this to me. I know he loves me. He tells me all the time, and we have so much fun together. He's not like my best friend's boyfriend. My guy doesn't hit me or anything like that; he's just a little moody. I figure if I can just go along with him when he's in a bad mood, none of this sex stuff has to ever come out, and we'll be OK.

—Becca, age sixteen

It's so difficult to know what to do now that you have more information about yourself, your family of origin, your current abuser, your children, and your relationship. Should you stay? Should you leave? If you decide to leave, how should you go about it? And what will happen to you and your children if you do leave? What will happen to him? Oh, the confusion! The guilt! The shame! The fear! The unknowingness of it all!

Here you thought knowledge gave you power, but right now, all you're feeling is a whole bunch of bad, scary feelings that seem out of your control.

Wait! Of course they are in your control. Remember, you have control of what? That's right: your thoughts, behaviors, and reactions. Take a deep breath, and come back to this page when you are ready. I'll wait.

I understand all the feelings you are going through right now. It's one thing to have all the intellectual information, and it's quite another to really think about what you should or need to do. You may be thinking, *OK, I know my relationship is bad. I even know it's abusive. But my children are small/I don't have a way to support myself yet/I'm still nauseated when I think about telling my parents I'm leaving him/my parents told me to leave him so many times, and I didn't, and now I don't want them to be right.* I get that. No one is pushing you. No pressure here.

Every woman needs to decide for herself what her life should look like. No one else lives in your home and in your head. Only you can decide if you should stay or go. Maybe you should go, but not today or next week. Maybe you should wait awhile and get better prepared. That's all right. We are going to talk about whether or not you should leave soon and, if so, what actions you should take to get all your ducks in a row and leave wisely instead of haphazardly and foolishly. We will also discuss the likely steps he will take if you do decide to leave. I have found that an abuser goes through a very predictable pattern when his partner takes back her power and control. Needless to say, he isn't happy and doesn't cheerfully wish you well. It is crucial that you consider the likely aftermath during your decision-making process. I truly want you to have all the information beforehand.

First, we will twirl around the idea of rights—your rights. Yes, you do have them! For the longest time, you may not have believed that you have certain fundamental rights, but you have loads of them. That's another important concept to understand before you make the big decisions you are about to contemplate.

Let's get going on this section. At the end of the next four chapters, you will indeed know what to do next, and you'll feel capable of making a decision and taking a stand.

15

You Have Rights!

I have rights? You must be kidding. If you're correct, this would be the first time in my life that anyone's told me that. I just sort of assumed that everyone else had rights, but I just had to go along with their plans.
—**Jesse, age seventeen**

What Jesse is saying may sound strange or humorous to you, or it may sound like your life. I can certainly relate. I can't tell you how many times in my first marriage, when I attempted to share with my mother some of my grief over my relationship with my husband, she said to me, "Oh, that's just crazy. You have a perfect life. You have no right to feel that way." Yowza! And here I thought I was living in a free country. Who took away my right to feel any which way I wanted? Sounds good and strong now, doesn't it? But back then, I truly did think that I hadn't any rights to my feelings. Long story—it started thirty years before those conversations.

Anyway, I'm wondering if you've had similar thoughts. When you are in an abusive relationship, your abuser decides what your rights are and are not. He makes the rules, and your job is to follow them. He undermines your good thinking processes and makes you feel more than a little crazy—and we all know that "crazy" people have fewer rights. Isn't that what you see on television and movies? Do you remember the movie *One Flew Over the Cuckoo's Nest?* Jack Nicholson's character didn't have as many rights as he thought he should have. And what about *Girl, Interrupted?* Certainly, Winona Ryder's character didn't understand why her rights were taken away. We could go on and on referencing all the "asylum" movies, but let's just agree that the "prisoner" doesn't have as many rights as those in charge.

When you begin an abusive relationship, you may already have very low self-esteem. Your parents or previous abusers may have told you that you don't have rights, so you are malleable as far as thinking you don't deserve as much as your partner. Or maybe you had been pretty strong up until you met him, and you've even fought him on the rights issue, but now here you are wondering what you deserve.

Let's be clear: you do not deserve fewer rights than your partner or any other abuser in your life. You are living in a free country and are guaranteed certain "inalienable rights" via your Constitution. You have free will and have a good mind. No one but you can decide what rights you do and do not have in your personal life and in relationships with others.

Why don't we examine some of these rights? In my opinion, you have tons of rights. Some of them include the right to

- be happy;

- have your own opinion;

- say no;

- choose your friends;

- make your own decisions regarding your life and your future;

- speak your mind without penalty;

- be treated with respect and affection even when your partner is angry or disappointed;

- have an equal relationship in which neither of you is the "boss";

- compromise fairly;

- engage in consensual sex;

- refuse to do anything that makes you feel uncomfortable;

- refuse to do anything that compromises your beliefs/values/morals;

- protect yourself emotionally and physically;

- have different ideas than your partner;

- not become pregnant if you don't want to;

- spend time alone or with your friends/family without him there;

- have your own private thoughts;

- make as many decisions about finances as your partner;

- have male friendships without explaining endlessly to your partner, feeling guilty and afraid, or keeping your friendship a secret;

- experience your feelings;

- reject violence;

- say no to sex when you don't want to engage;

- feel honored and cherished in your relationships;

- educate yourself and hold a job, if you would like to;

- be treated with compassion;

- be loved;

- live without fear;

- be respected at all times.

How many items on your list are currently full-time parts of your romantic relationship? If you didn't check all of them, then you need to ask yourself an important question that only you can answer: why not? That may sound like a simplistic question, but it is actually very profound. You see, at some place in your soul, you decided that you weren't worthy of every single one of those rights. You decided you didn't have the right to them.

However, just by being born, you have most of the rights I've listed above. The United States Bill of Rights states that you have the right to "life, liberty, and the pursuit of happiness." You have freedom of speech, freedom of religion (to believe and practice whatever religion you choose), and the right to assemble—that is, to hang out with whomever you wish. The Fourth Amendment states that you have the right to be secure in your home.

The Canadian Charter of Rights and Freedoms stipulates that everyone has the following fundamental freedoms: freedom of conscience and religion; freedom of thought, belief, opinion, and expression; freedom of peaceful assembly; and freedom of association (you can choose your own friends).

The French Bill of Rights guarantees religious freedom, freedom of speech, and personal security.

You see, no matter where you go, everyone is on the same bandwagon. You have certain rights that are true and clear and cannot be taken away from you.

The right to be happy may sound strange to you. I was miserable in my first marriage for so long that I no longer had any concept of my right to be happy. What was "happy," anyway? Shouldn't I have been happy? It wasn't until a very wise therapist told me, "You know, Jill, you have the right to be happy," that I stopped and thought about that idea. What made me think I didn't have that right? And, more importantly, if I exercised my right, who was going to be unhappy? Did I have the right to be happy at other people's expense? What about my children's right to be happy? They had the same right, and I thought that if I divorced their father, that would make them the opposite of happy. What about my husband? I knew that divorcing him would make him very unhappy. Sure, he wasn't happy in the marriage, either, I'm sure, but divorce would be worse for him. Did I have the right to make him unhappy after I'd promised to stay with him forever and ever? After all he'd done for me and all the time we'd spent together?

I'll bet you've asked yourself some of these very same questions, haven't you? Here is the answer I gave myself after a tremendous amount of thought: I decided that I did deserve to be happy and that I'd spent all my life trying to make others happy, with varying degrees of success. Sometimes, making them happy made me happy, as well, and sometimes their happiness came at my expense. I had tried very hard to be happy at the same time but couldn't understand why that didn't happen. The common denominator I kept coming back to was my marriage. At that point, I'd been married nearly twenty years. I had to decide whether, twenty years from that moment, I would not only be unhappier, but would feel that for another twenty years I had denied myself my right to be happy. Would it be all right with me if I had been unhappily married for a good portion of forty years? Is that what I would want for my children? In another twenty years, I would be sixty-one years old. Would I feel capable of starting over at that point, or would fear hold me back forever?

The right to be happy is basic but very difficult to put into action when you are in an abusive relationship. It doesn't seem possible that you have the right to your own opinion, the right to have private thoughts, the right to respect or affection. It doesn't even seem possible that you have the rights to compromise in your relationship or make your own decisions. Such ideas may seem absurd. They may seem downright nuts. After all, when was the last time you exercised those rights or any of the others on the list?

Because you may not have known you had these rights, or if you did you haven't insisted on them, it may seem difficult for you to begin asking for—no—demanding them. What will happen if you do? I will tell you: you will be thrust into realizing that some of the people in your life do not want you to have certain rights. They will chastise you, demean you, or call you names. Does that make you fearful? Are you willing to risk their reaction? Can you say to those people, "Why do you think I'm not entitled to this? It is a basic right. Why shouldn't I have it?" As for their reaction to your questions, expect more uncomfortable fumbling around than actual answers. But in asserting your right to fair treatment, you will have made a very positive step toward a healthier and happier existence.

WHAT HAS IT COST YOU?
WHAT ARE YOUR RIGHTS?

You've taken a good look at the list of your rights in this chapter, and now it's time for you to do some work. Take out your journal and jot down any other rights you know you have that aren't on the list.

Now, look at the entire list—mine plus yours—and checkmark all that you lack in your life. After the checkmark, write the names of the person or persons who have violated those rights. You may have quite a long list of people.

How does it make you feel to know that so many of your rights have been violated? How do you feel about the people on the list who have not honored your rights?

Here's a name you may have forgotten to put on your list: yours. This is an important step. If you have not honored yourself and treated yourself respectfully or with affection and compromise, then you have violated your own human rights. With that example, why would others treat you differently? If you don't stand up for yourself and your beliefs, should anyone else give them to you as a gift? Remember that you teach people how to treat you.

Now, look at your own long list of neglected rights and pick the one most important to you. What one step can you take today to begin moving closer to making sure that right is honored?

For example, if you've chosen the right to have your own opinion, perhaps one thing you can do today is express a political opinion or an opinion about a movie or television show you saw. That may sound silly to you, but let me assure you that it's not. Starting with very small steps in expressing your opinions—and only to people you consider safe—will allow you to find your own voice without penalty. Telling your abuser that you are not going to tolerate his demeaning comments, that you refuse to have sex with him just because he feels like it, or that you are not going to make dinner or do the laundry anymore may be too large a step right now!

Begin small, and grow from there. Take one right at a time, and work through it in very small ways. That is, take one right today, and begin to assert yourself with a tiny step. Tomorrow, choose another right, and do the same. Figure out for yourself what you can do—without anyone else's permission; remember that these are rights, not favors—to begin demanding the rights you were born to have.

16

Should You Stay or Leave?

I've been married for nine years, one and a half of them good. Good as in his not yelling at me or making me feel wrong about everything. But, not good as in making me feel loved and good about myself, either.

Did I know he was this way: controlling, selfish, wanting everything his way and thinking my opinions are stupid? In the beginning, when I'd ask myself if this was true, I'd answer that when we were dating, he was wonderful and generous and very loving. I'd say that I had never seen the other side of him, and I was shocked to see it. That was a lie, though. I guess I wanted to believe it at the time, because I felt stupid and ashamed.

The truth is that when we were dating, he'd win the arguments, he'd choose the movie or restaurant, he wanted to be with me all the time to the point that I felt guilty if I saw my own friends, so I didn't. I knew that when he was really angry, he'd punch holes in his walls, BUT HE NEVER HIT ME. Once, when I thought we should take a break, he told me that if we weren't together he didn't have any reason to live. Or, sometimes, he'd drink himself almost into a stupor, because he said that I acted like I didn't love him and he was worthless.

This probably sounds ridiculous, but a lot of that junk he did when we were dating made me love him more. I mean, a guy who would kill himself over you is pretty heavy shit. And, who doesn't like a strong, macho man who orders for the lady at a restaurant like in the old movies or wants to spend every moment with her? He told me he loved me all the time. It was really heady.

Sometimes I felt overwhelmed by his neediness, but that was counterbalanced with his being so strong and in control. I thought it was the perfect balance of masculine and feminine, and I considered myself so lucky to have him.

So, yeah, there were signs beforehand, but I didn't know what they meant. I was only nineteen—almost twenty—when we met, and who the hell knew what the perfect relationship was? Not me; my parents were always miserable with each other, and his weren't any better. There were things about his personality that made me uncomfortable, but I discounted my feelings and kept

179

reminding myself of all his good qualities—and there were lots of those. No one's perfect, I'd tell myself, least of all me.

We got married. Slowly but surely his bad behaviors became worse, and he got a bunch of new bad behaviors to keep them company. I tried hard to understand him. I tried to be loving and sweet and just go along. I called my mother for advice, and she told me that she couldn't help me, because she was struggling with my father and didn't have any emotional energy left. My mother-in-law told me to try and love and understand him more and be more supportive. She said he had been high-strung since he was a child, and that's what she did. I didn't understand her advice, because number one, that obviously didn't work for her, and number two, that's what I was doing, and it obviously didn't work for me.

Like a ninny, I thought that if we had a child, he would ease up. He used to tell me that he hated listening to his parents fight, and he wouldn't ever want that for his child. I thought that was a good sign, right? We had Chloe, who is adorable and the apple of her father's eye. He really does love her with all his heart, and she does him, but it sure didn't change the way he treats me. It's only gotten worse, and now he gets Chloe to be his ally. He'll say things like, "Let's try to understand mommy today because she's acting a little crazy." Then, they laugh together, and she's now calling me "Crazy Mommy." Or sometimes she'll ask me if I'm feeling crazy today. I want to shout, "Uh, yeah, because your father makes me crazy!"

We have the house, the beautiful child, the two cars, the weeklong vacation in the summer, and I can't stand my life. I feel wrong and bad. I feel ungrateful. But he's the cruelest person I know. Well, I guess I'd have to say he's the nicest person I know to other people and the cruelest person I know to me. He saves all his venom for me when we are alone. Everyone else thinks he's a prince. For example, on the way to a party, he'll degrade me, call me names, play mind games with me until I'm spinning, and then when we're at the party, I act like either a madwoman or a total recluse, and he's Mr. Life-of-the-Party. Either way, I can't compete with him.

I've talked with my girlfriends about him until they can't stand me anymore. First of all, they don't believe a word of what I'm saying. Let me check that—they would believe me, but they see something completely different, so they have no reference point except what I tell them. I think they think I'm nuts or just very overly dramatic. Second of all, they've told me time and again, "Janie, if you're that miserable, just leave." Sounds easy, and it's very logical, but for some reason, I just can't do it.

I've tried to leave. I've even packed my bags and Chloe's. He's come home and seen them and said, "Just where do you think you're going? If you're stupid enough to leave, go ahead. But, you're not taking my daughter with you. I'll hunt you down and find you and slap handcuffs on you for stealing my child. I'll have you locked up. Everyone knows you're crazy, anyway. It shouldn't be anything difficult to prove." Or sometimes he'll tell me that he'd have to kill himself if Chloe and I left, that he'd have nothing to live for.

Now, almost ten years later, I'm still here deciding what to do. I keep waiting for the guy everyone else knows to come home to me. I take his mother's advice and try to love and understand him more. That helps for a few days, and I see what a nice person he can be.

I don't know what to do. It's not as if he's ever hit me or anything like that. I know that if he ever laid a hand on me or Chloe, I'd be out of here in a flash. Maybe I'm waiting for that to happen so I'd have an excuse to go or to kick him out. Sometimes—if I'm really honest—I think I provoke him to hit me so I can tell him to leave, but he never does. I think he's caught onto that idea because once he told me, "You think I'm going to hit you? You really think I'd go to jail for you or ruin my reputation or give you ammunition to take my daughter? You're not worth it to me."

I sit on this fence all day, and the thoughts of staying or leaving consume me. I look at my daughter and think I can't do this to her. I look at the house she lives in and her relationship with her daddy and think I can wait until she's out of the house. That's in thirteen years. That's not such a long time.
—**Janie, age thirty-four**

You may be exactly where Janie is. You've agonized over your relationship, you've read books, you've talked to friends, and you've gotten counsel from clergy, your family, or perhaps even a therapist. Maybe with the accumulated knowledge you've gained, you've been able to affect some small changes—if only temporarily—in your mate. Still, you're reading another relationship book and trying to figure out what you should do.

You've sat on the same fence as Janie for so long that your glutes are sore. What should you do? Should you continue to stay with him and hope that things will get better if you are more patient, loving, and kind? Or have you given him more chances than he deserves while you get little in return, so it's time to make a graceful exit?

This is a life-changing decision, not just for you, but for many others around you. Because of that, no one else can tell you what the right answer is for you and your life—not your friends, your parents, your clergy, your children, or me. None of us is living inside your head, your heart, or your life.

WHAT IS YOUR ACCEPTABLE BOUNDARY LINE?

Only you can decide where your "line" is. What do I mean by your line? Every woman should really have a line that cannot be crossed. It is the boundary between what is acceptable and what is not. By acceptable, I don't mean perfect or even very good. Acceptable is *acceptable enough*—the bare minimum that will keep you in your abusive relationship. One woman's acceptable may be that she is not physically abused. Another woman may feel that since physical abuse—to her—means a broken arm or black eye, perhaps pushing and shoving is acceptable, but the other more discernable signs of abuse are her line that can't be crossed. His calling you a bitch or insulting your cooking may be acceptable, while infidelity may be your line. Not letting you see your friends or family, checking up on you, and other jealous behaviors may be acceptable, but demeaning your children and seeing them personally suffer may be your line.

Developing your line between what you will "take" and what would cause you to leave without hesitation is crucial to your decision-making process and your life in general. Developing boundaries is perhaps the biggest contributor to emotional health that I can think of. I find that most women don't have healthy boundaries, and they certainly don't have a line. I know that in my first marriage I sure didn't. I just felt bad pretty much all the time, because I never told him or myself, "If I do/he does this … I will tell him he needs to leave." Looking back, I know why I didn't do that. Number one, no one ever told me that I needed to have some boundaries and some pride, and number two, I was too afraid. I couldn't envision my life as a divorced woman of two children. I couldn't even go there in my head; it was too scary. Why draw a line when I was going to allow him to cross it anyway?

SOCIETY'S REASONS WHY YOU'RE STAYING

Why are you staying when the little voice in your head may be telling you that you should be leaving? There are many good reasons why women stay in abusive relationships. You know that, and I know that. Society in general has a difficult time understanding why you would remain with a man who treats you cruelly. They've surmised many reasons, and perhaps at this point, you believe some of them yourself.

She must like the abuse. How many times have you heard this one? This is a popular reason, because it moves the blame from your abuser to you. Women make this cruel comment about other women to make themselves feel safe, and men say this about women because it makes the woman sound crazy and takes a man's aberrant behavior off his shoulders. Another variation of this warped concept is that "no one can abuse you unless you want him to." Huh? I've counseled literally thousands of abused women, and I'd have to say that I haven't met a masochist in the bunch. Not one of them wanted or enjoyed the abuse. They've submitted to it, or allowed it, but not one of them wanted it, liked it, or asked for it. Every single one of them did whatever she felt she could to stop it but was unsuccessful.

She must have done something to deserve the abuse. Abusive men feel completely justified in their abusive behaviors toward their mates. They think it is their job to train and teach their misguided woman, since she is so ill-equipped to get along without his knowledge. It is his job to punish and reward her depending on the behavior he wants. If she does something he decides he doesn't enjoy that day, she has to learn the proper way. If only she'd learn, he wouldn't have to punish her. What you need to understand is that no matter what you've done, you don't deserve to be abused. I repeat: there is nothing you can do that makes you deserving of your man's abuse. You are a human being, and as such, you are entitled to your rights of life, liberty, and the pursuit of happiness.

WHY ARE YOU STAYING?

It was easier to stay than leave. I wasn't happy, that's for sure, but it was still easier. My husband made good money, and we lived in a very nice house in a great, safe neighborhood. I had a lot of security in that way. I had two children, and it had always been my dream and plan to stay home with my kids. His income allowed me to do that. In exchange, I took care of everything else. I didn't mind or resent that. I actually liked being a housewife more than any other job I'd ever had before and maybe since then, as well. It gave me a tremendous feeling of satisfaction.

He'd come home late every night and was exhausted and noncommunicative, not only during the week but on the weekends as well. I felt very lonely and alone almost all of the time. I felt neglected, and he was withdrawn a lot. I'm sure he wasn't happy, either, but when I asked him what was wrong or how I could help, he didn't have an answer. I was helpless. He told me many times that he didn't love me anymore and didn't know why, but he would not work on trying to get our marriage back on track. He disrespected me as a woman in every way that was important to me. I didn't have a life with him.

I traded my self-respect for physical comfort and financial security. I thought to myself, I can leave him and live in a tiny place with my kids, put them in daycare all day while I work, not be able to go to many of their school events or be the type of mother I had planned, or I can stay and live in this home, take care of my kids, and not have financial stress. Either way, I won't have a marriage. What to do? I knew I was selling myself out by staying, but I gave myself all sorts of timelines for my own change to take place.

I began seeing a therapist, reading books, and making plans to go back to school so I'd have a career that could sustain me. Slowly, when I felt capable, I began taking action on my schooling plans and setting into motion a time for leaving. It worked. I began feeling more hopeful about my future and my abilities. I finally did ask him to leave, but it was at my time when I was able.

—**Jill, age forty-nine**

Yes, ladies, that Jill is me. That was my story and my reasons for staying. Trade-offs: they are a big reason to stay. You get this but don't get that. You get money, but you don't get love or respect. You get security, but you don't have self-esteem. Trade-offs are very powerful and can be extremely legitimate for quite a while. As I've said earlier in this book, you can't rely on them forever, because the mind-body connection comes into play at some point and doesn't allow you to deny, minimize, or make excuses. There will be a time when your body says, "That's enough. You've degraded yourself long enough. I've hung around serving you to the best of my ability, but I can no longer do that. You have to make a choice." Mine was when I weighed less than ninety pounds and my heart was about to give out. Then, all trade-offs were over.

WHAT HAS IT COST YOU?
WHAT ARE YOUR TRADE-OFFS?

This is a very important exercise that will help you see what you are trading to remain in your abusive relationship. In your journal, create these columns: *trade-off* and *cost of trade-off*.

In the first column, write down what your trade-off is and in the second column, what you are trading. Let me help you with some examples that may be issues for you:

TRADE-OFF	COST OF TRADE-OFF
Money	He gives me allowance.
	I feel like a prostitute.
	I feel like a child.
	He can give or take at will.
My age	I may not get another man.
	He accepts my age.
	Insecurity—what if no one wants to hire someone my age?
Not being alone	Companionship
	Being yelled at or disrespected
	He treats me like a servant
Intact family	Illusion of a nice family
	Children see me hurt

Children see poor role-modeling

Societal/family acceptance

Do you see the idea? With each trade-off, there are good and not-so-hot reasons to stay. Examine your trade-offs and make some decisions about whether these are still valid reasons for you to remain in your relationship. For example, at this point in your life, keeping your family intact for the sake of what your family or society will think—despite the fact that your children see you hurt and are witnessing poor role-modeling—may or may not be reason enough to sick with it. As I said, you are the lone decision maker, because you are an adult woman who will need to deal with the aftermath in a strong and determined manner.

OTHER IMPORTANT REASONS YOU MAY DECIDE TO STAY

In their informative book *When Love Goes Wrong—What to Do When You Can't Do Anything Right*, authors Ann Jones and Susan Schechter chart out seven common reasons why women remain in abusive relationships. I wholly concur with their assessment and would like to share their wisdom with you:

1. I'm still hopeful that he'll change.

2. I'm afraid of my partner.

3. I'm afraid that I can't make it financially.

4. I'm afraid of being alone.

5. I'm staying here for my children.

6. I'm bound by my sense of responsibility.

7. I'm still in the process of making a choice or plan.

I held many of these beliefs myself. Let me share with you some truths about the reasons for staying that are listed above. My experiences may help you become more clear about what is and is not real, identify what is in your power and control, and determine whether these are reasons or excuses.

• *I love my partner.* Do you remember what love is? A behavior. In chapter 7, we discussed whether what you are feeling for him is love or many other different emotions that have very little to do with love.

- *The good far outweighs the bad.* But what is the bad? If the bad parts include demeaning, disrespectful, soul-destroying behaviors, does it really matter how good the good is? Additionally, he may be "good" 85 percent of the time. Is there some reason you should not expect fair and respectful treatment the other 15 percent of the time?

- *I believe the control is not really my partner's true nature.* It doesn't matter whether it is his nature or not. He makes a decision to act in certain ways, so perhaps his true nature really is cruel ...

- *I have a special bond with my partner that I'll never find with anyone else.* No one is that special—not even you or me. If your special bond also includes his degrading you, then I do hope you'll never find that with anyone else. You deserve a much better bond than that.

- *I believe I can help my partner.* No, you can support his positive growth, but only he can help himself.

- *I refuse to fail.* Which one of you is failing? He has failed to provide an emotionally safe environment for you. Do you consider yourself a failure if you don't take everything he dishes out?

- *I want my relationship the way it used to be.* You don't have control of that, and in any case, if you look at the way it actually was, you may find that for a long time you have internally nurtured a fantasy of how you wished it *could* have been.

- *The abuse is not that bad.* Here's where we go to your line. How bad is bad? How bad does it need to be? Do you deserve any abuse at all?

- *I'm afraid he'll———.* Do you remember the chapter on fear? Fear is extremely powerful, and the threats it creates are overwhelming. Look at your various fears, and decide whether they are irrational beliefs or not. If you find fears such as, "He'll get custody of the kids, or kidnap them," "He'll hurt the kids, other people, himself, me," or, "He'll track me down wherever I am," then you have a legal and mental issue on your hands. You are with a very dangerous and mentally unstable person who is using emotional blackmail to control you. Is that someone worth staying with? You have many legal options, which we will investigate further. Very likely, he has made these threats to control and intimidate you. In any case, you have the full protection of the laws of your state.

- *I have fears about finances.* As I've told you, I had huge money fears and was terrified of becoming a bag lady. I have to be honest: despite the fact that I am doing fine financially, the bag-lady fear is very powerful. Instead of giving in to what could become a paralyzing fear, I use it to my advantage. I look at my financial picture every month and decide in which areas I have control over my finances. I am a psychotherapist in private practice, and when I don't see patients, I don't get paid. I don't have control over patients canceling appointments, if a patient will decide to leave counseling prematurely, or if I will acquire new patients. Since I attribute my success as a therapist primarily to "extinction" of patients—that is, I don't want my patients to see me for long periods of time; I want them to feel and do better quickly and leave counseling—it is inevitable that I will lose patients as part of the program. This unstable financial stream could make me feel very uneasy, so I have spread my income streams in other directions as well: presentations and book publishing. That way, I have three different sources of income, and more importantly, I have three different ways of helping others, which gives me tremendous satisfaction. I never could have imagined this type of satisfaction when I was married the first time and living in financial fear.

- *I'm afraid of being alone—at least I'm used to this life with my partner.* Do you recall the quote I used in the early chapters of this book: "Most people prefer the certainty of misery to the misery of uncertainty"? This applies to most of your fears of being alone. Examine the aloneness you feel. Remember, there is "alone," and there is "lonely." I suspect that even though you are not technically alone, you are more lonely than if you were alone.

- *I don't want to have to raise my kids alone.* If your partner is a decent father to the children, you will not be raising them alone. You can even arrange joint custody. However, if your children are not seeing good role-modeling, please consider the repercussions of him in the house "raising" them with you.

- *I'll never find anyone better out there. He's the best I can do.* That is true only if you decide that you don't deserve any better.

- *He loves the kids so much and is so good to them that I can't take them away from him/I don't want to ruin my kids' future and deprive them of nice things or a good education.* Please understand this clearly: no matter how many baseball games he takes them to, no matter how video games he gives them, no matter how much allowance he is able to provide them, no matter how many ice-cream cones he buys or family vacations he's a part of, no matter how many iPods he gives them, absolutely nothing will make up for your children witnessing his cruelty to you. You may think, *They don't hear us fighting. We do that after they are asleep*, or, *He doesn't hit me. If he did that, I'd leave, because that would be horrible for the kids to see. The way things are now, the kids aren't really being damaged.* I can only tell you that this is one of women's biggest delusions when they are in an abusive relationship.

Study after study has demonstrated the enormous damage that a nonphysically abusive relationship has on children. Most indicate that it is just as harmful to children as witnessing physical violence. Having worked with many of these children, I can tell you that they *always* hear the fighting. They are attuned to it: they stay awake at night—pretending to be asleep when you come in to check on them—waiting for the fights to begin, or they turn their television or radio up loudly to drown out the noise. They hear the fighting and are completely aware of what is being said. It devastates them. Using the children as an excuse for staying is unfair to them.

Will your children be upset if you leave their father/stepfather? Yes, of course they will. They will cry, beg, and plead with you to stay. They are children and don't want their lives to change. I saw this when I worked in a domestic violence shelter. The children there had witnessed terrible abuse; many of them were physically abused themselves. They still considered it their mother's fault for leaving, still cried about missing their father, still worried about his welfare, and still wanted more than anything to see him. You are your children's mother. You make the decisions about what is best for them.

- *A good wife stands by her man/I vowed we would never be a divorce statistic; I refuse to give up/I can't bear the responsibility for the relationship failing.* How about these ideas: a good husband stands by his wife; he vowed he would never do anything that would make you a divorce statistic; you are not giving up—he gave up on the relationship when he refused to stop treating you in a cruel manner; the relationship's failure is not wholly your responsibility—in choosing to engage in bad behavior, he is responsible. How do those ideas sound?

- *I'm not so easy to live with, either. The responsibility for this is mine, too.* That's right; you are not a victim. However, even if you are not easy to live with, there is absolutely nothing you could have done to warrant the type of behavior he's inflicted. Get into individual counseling and understand your not-easy-to-live-with behaviors, but don't use them as an excuse to take abuse.

- *I will never break my marriage vows; they were given to God.* That may be true, but he also promised to love, honor, and respect you. He's broken those vows to God many times over. Some religions have reasons why a woman may divorce her husband: abandonment, addictions he refuses to address, adultery, emotional cruelty, and so on. Certainly, your husband has been emotionally cruel and has abandoned you emotionally and spiritually. He has also broken his own vows. Oftentimes, if you seek pastoral counseling, clergy members have very good intentions but do not understand the dynamics of abuse and so encourage a woman to stick with it and actually put the brunt of the responsibility on the woman. This is misleading. I encourage you to seek secular counseling in addition to any clerical advice you may be receiving.

- *I can't leave him—he's not well/I support him—he needs me.* Often, a man will drag out his illness or physical limitations to keep a woman in the home. He may be capable of some sort of work or government assistance, and if you check your insurance coverage, you may also find that he is eligible for nursing assistance.

- *I'm trying to stop the abuse but keep the relationship.* This may seem reasonable to you, so I encourage you to put a time limit on your watching and waiting. If he is in serious counseling, have stringent methods for evaluating his progress. If he is not in counseling or otherwise consciously addressing the reasons behind the abuse, you will see only small, temporary changes that are ultimately meaningless. You can only stop the abuse in one way: by leaving. There is no incentive for him to discontinue the abuse if you are with him. Why should he? All he has to do is make a few promises of change, not act on them, and you'll still be there, thereby giving him everything he wants.

GOOD REASONS TO STAY

Any or all of the following actions on the part of your partner may be good enough reasons to stay with him for the moment:

1. He has acknowledged he has a problem and that he is 100 percent responsible for his behavior. He doesn't blame you or anyone else—not even his bad childhood—for the abuse.

2. While he doesn't blame his childhood, he recognizes that he is repeating a pattern of abuse. He talks about the ways he felt hurt by this when he was a child and also sees how this same abuse is hurting you and/or your children.

3. He has agreed/proposed that he needs to go into counseling. Since this is a problem of his behavior, he will go to individual counseling and not ask you to go with him until he is well into positive progress and his therapist calls to invite you. He agrees that at that time, the counseling will still be focused on

him and not things you could have done to help him. You will receive your own personal counseling to help you understand your part in putting up with the abuse and your patterns of abuse.

4. He will stick with counseling for at least one year (the usual amount of time a judge would mandate for counseling, if he were to appear in court for abuse) and will go each and every week without excuses.

5. You can see concrete examples of consistent behavioral changes.

6. If he has an addiction problem, he makes inquiries about self-help/twelve-step groups that can help him, and he goes to them several times a week. He gets a sponsor, works with his sponsor, and pursues the program with fervor. If his addiction requires in-patient treatment, he checks himself into a rehab program.

Those six steps are necessary for women to stay with their abuser. In each one of them, the responsibility for change is squarely on your partner's shoulders, not yours.

Remember, however, that many times, a relationship is too emotionally "gone" to be revived, no matter how you would like to change that fact. You may have suffered too much abuse to ever respect or love him again.

I think of relationships as African violet plants. If you've ever had an African violet, you know that while they are beautiful plants, they are also very fragile and require a great deal of extra care. They need special food and must be moved around into different light. They like to be sung to and treated more lovingly and gently than a potted plant. If you don't take these steps, they die. Then it doesn't matter how much food or light you give them or how many songs you sing; they're dead and may never come back. The same is true of relationships. They require extra love and attention. Once they are dead, however, it may be impossible to revive them. Only you can decide if your relationship is or should be over, even if your partner takes the steps above. Only you can decide what you want.

WHAT HAS IT COST YOU?
REASONS YOU HAVE USED FOR STAYING IN YOUR ABUSIVE RELATIONSHIP

In looking at the lists of fears, reasons for staying or leaving, and excuses, which struck you as the closest to how you are currently feeling? Write those in your journal, and then attack your belief system with concrete actions you can take today. For example, if you are afraid to leave because he is not well and not working, you can call his doctor to learn more about the problem and its prognosis. Is there anything that can be done to hasten his recovery? Does he need different medication or physical therapy? In the doctor's opinion, how long does the average patient take to get back up to speed, or why does the doctor think your mate has not reached that place in his recovery? Will he need long-term care, and if so, what kind, and can the doctor connect you with resources for that type of assistance?

Do you see where I'm going with this? Put yourself in charge; not of his recovery, but of the information you will need to make an informed decision.

In the next chapter, we will talk about actions you should take if you decide to leave. This information will help you make a logical, not emotional or fearful, decision for yourself.

17

Actions to Take before You Leave

It took me twelve years. I had been married for sixteen years, and I cried for about twelve of them.

At that four-year mark, we had a one-year-old, and I knew I couldn't leave then. I thought that once we got past the initial first, hard year of the baby's life, things would get better. Bobby was a colicky baby and cried most of the time. It was just really horrible for both of us, but mostly for me because I stayed home with him. I wanted to go back to work when he was four months old; we needed the money, and I was losing my mind. But Steve insisted that his son wasn't going to be raised by other people. Since we made almost the same amount of money, I suggested that he stay home with the baby and I go to work. He just told me I was crazy.

It's not that I didn't love little Bobby; I did very much. But I was raised by a single mother who worked two jobs so that we could get by, and I had worked since I was eleven, so working was what I knew how to do. It felt right to me to be contributing to a household. When I was a kid, I hated that my mom worked all the time and vowed to myself that when I had a baby, I'd stay home and be a "real" mommy. Funny thing was, a couple of months after Bobby was born, I didn't feel comfortable staying home. I realized I was a working person, and that's what I needed to do.

I interviewed all sorts of wonderful women and only planned on working half-time at work and the rest of the time at home. My company was willing to do that for me. I thought I was getting the best of both worlds. This may seem cold to some women, but working and being a mother was what I wanted to do. I knew I'd lose my mind if I stayed home full time. I'm not saying anything bad about women who do; I think that's great for them and their family, but I couldn't do it.

Anyway, as I said, Steve put his foot down about that. Actually, he started putting his foot down to a lot of things, mostly involving the baby and the house, which he hadn't done before. I asked him why he had the final say in what we decided, and he said, "OK, go ahead and leave my son with a stranger, and you'll see what happens to your little job." I didn't know what that meant, but it felt like a threat. He had a look in his eyes that was scary. I stayed home.

I wasn't miserable at home. I just missed being with adults part of the day and using my brain in ways I was used to doing. I joined playgroups and little baby gym classes. I even went to a gym myself that had daycare for the babies while the moms worked out. But I couldn't stand that everywhere I went, everything was about the baby. My female friends couldn't discuss what was happening in the world or our community. I started going batty.

I begged Steve again to reconsider when Bobby was three, and he again refused. As a matter of fact, he wanted another baby. I wanted to give the idea more consideration. After all, it was mostly my life being impacted, not his.

During all this time, he would call home or my cell phone at least eight times a day to see where I was and what I was doing. He gave me money to buy groceries, which was weird since I used to write a check. But now he was giving me cash. I asked him why, and he said that I couldn't manage money well, and we needed to tighten our belts a little more without my income, so this would help with the budget. This way, we'd know exactly how much we were spending. It all sounded very logical. Of course, I once again volunteered to go back to work at least part time to help out our finances, and he said it wasn't necessary. I didn't understand any of it. Here he was, saying we were having a tough time financially because I wasn't working, but he wouldn't let me work, so now he was giving me an allowance. The allowance thing felt very fatherly to me, and I didn't like it.

I didn't say much about any of this because Steve seemed to constantly be on edge in those days. His company was downsizing, and he had a threat of being laid off most of the time. He'd come home very stressed every night, and there was nothing I could say.

He wanted to have sex more often, which was quite rough and had so little connection to me that it felt like rape most of the time. Sometimes I cried in the bathroom afterward, but I figured that this was how he was working out his stress, and in a way I was glad that he looked to me as his support. I know that sounds crazy.

When Bobby was three and a half, I found that I was pregnant again. I became very depressed. I wasn't ready for another baby yet. Steve was acting so weird and treating me badly. He'd started criticizing everything about me, like my appearance—he thought I was getting fat—and the housework—I didn't keep house as well as his mom—and he thought I wasn't paying enough attention to Bobby. I tried telling him that I spent every waking moment with Bobby but thought that he was missing his daddy. That didn't go over well.

Anyway, I was pregnant and not happy. I didn't see how I could raise another child with Steve. Our married life had gone so far downhill so fast that I had been thinking of separating. I had decided that if things didn't get better by the time Bobby was four, I would do that. Now I was stuck again.

I suggested counseling. He told me I was crazy, so if I wanted counseling, I could do it, but he wasn't going. I read books about marriage and tried to do what they suggested. I tried harder, I listened more, I made myself available to him sexually, I praised almost everything the man did, and all the rest. By the time Lizzie was born, I was done. I finally realized that the problem was him—and also me because I continued to put up with his behavior.

I once again wanted to go back to work but decided to just arrange everything myself and call my former boss to see if there was still a place for me in the company. He said he'd find something. I was overjoyed. I found a wonderful, older, grandma type to care for the kids, bought a few new items of working-women clothes, and on the eve of going back to work, I told Steve what I was doing. He hit the roof. I thought he was going to hit me, and I was scared of him. I told him that I didn't consult him because the last time I did, he put a stop to it and that I was an equal partner in the marriage and had as much say as he did. I told him about the woman I'd hired and said that my salary would more than pay for her as well as the food bill and some of the household bills. He wouldn't have to bear the entire financial burden.

He kept on looking at me with venom in his eyes and told me what an uncaring mother I was and what a fool he was for having children with me. He said he felt sorry for our children that they had such a selfish mother. He said he knew they would hate me when they got older because I liked work more than I liked them. He went on and on until I couldn't stand it. I asked him why he was saying such mean and untrue things. He said, "Look at you; you look like a little slut. All tarted up to go off to work. You think I don't know why you want to get out there? How many men work at your company? How many men do you plan on f***ing on the first day back, sweetie?" I couldn't believe him!

Even though it was hard, I went to work the next day. He called fourteen times. My boss told me that I couldn't get personal calls unless they were emergencies, and I told my husband that. The next day, he called seventeen times. The third day, he called twenty times. I kept telling him not to call, and most of the time, I just hung up on him as soon as his call was put through, or I told the switchboard person not to put it through at all. This made him angrier, so he'd call more. I was fired by the end of the week. My boss told me she hated to do it and understood what was going on, but she couldn't be involved in our personal problems. This was Steve's plan all along.

That was really it for me, and I started planning my escape from him. I now saw what he was capable of and that he would go to any lengths necessary to get what he wanted and to destroy me. I became very frightened of him and knew that I had to get away from him.

I had talked to my sister about this a few times. She was sympathetic but said she didn't want to get involved in our personal stuff. My mother said she understood because my father was very similar but didn't think she could go through this again with me. She said she'd support whatever I wanted to do. I didn't have any friends to speak of. I'd pissed all of them off by refusing to just talk baby talk with all of them. I think they thought I thought I was too good for them or that they were simple and stupid. I didn't think that at all. I just thought we didn't have much in common except that we were all mothers.

I was really alone. Since Steve gave me money and he had the checkbook, I didn't have access to money in the bank without him knowing what I was doing. I didn't have money, I didn't have a place to go, I didn't have a job, and I couldn't even go ten feet without his calling and wanting to know where I was. I didn't know how I was going to leave, and that made me very depressed.

Some months, I would think, *It's not so bad ... I can live through it until the kids are out of high school.* I'd actually count the months and days, but that would get me even more depressed because it was so far away. At other times I would get myself together and make plans to leave soon.

I had a lot of fear. If I left with the kids, would he try to take them away from me? What would he say about me to them? Would he leave me penniless and unable to get a job? Would he draw out a divorce proceeding so long that there wouldn't be any money left, and we'd have to sell the house just to pay the lawyers? Where would I go, and how would I live? I couldn't imagine being alone and started questioning myself about a lot of things that he told me. Was I a bad mother? Would the kids be better off with him? Was it really that bad? Did I just expect too much from him? Was I trying hard enough myself? I'm sure I wasn't any picnic either, so maybe if I just tried to accept him as he was, I'd be happier. At least we had a home and food and anything else we needed. How could I take children out of this environment just because I couldn't stand it? Maybe I really was as selfish as he said.

The fear paralyzed me some days. I was torn and stuck. That went on for about eight years. But somehow I knew I'd have to leave him if I were going to survive and be sane. When Bobby was eleven and Lizzie was seven, I made a final decision that I was out of there. Life with Steve just kept getting worse and worse and more and more restrictive. My world was closing in so much that I hardly had room to move around without him knowing every single thing I was doing. Plus, he was more and more verbally and sexually abusive. The kids were going upstairs and closing their doors and turning on music very loudly when they thought he was going to start yelling at me. Lizzie had stomachaches all the time, and Bobby was doing badly in school and making trouble. Their lives were falling apart because of the marriage, and I now saw it as selfish of me to stay instead of the other way around.

I looked in the newspapers and started interviewing for jobs again. My skills were very rusty, and I didn't know computers as well as I should, so I bought a computer program to teach me what I needed to know. I would practice when the kids were at school and then hide the program in my trunk when they got home so Steve wouldn't question me about it. It took almost a year and several programs, but I learned what I needed to know. I called my mother and told her what I was doing and said that the kids and I needed a place to stay. She only lived a half hour away, so I wouldn't be taking them far from Steve; I didn't think he could complain about it. She told me again that she didn't want to get involved, but I reminded her that she told me she would support my decision; this was it and how she could support it. I told her I didn't want to get her involved in the divorce part, but we needed a place to stay, and I had to depend on her. She agreed, and then I had to deal with my sister, who called to tell me the strain it was going to put on our mother. I finally had to tell her to keep out of it; that's what my sister had told me she wanted from me—to stay uninvolved in my marital life.

I told the kids one morning that we were going to stay with grandma for a little while, but they would still be going to their own schools and would be able to play with their friends. They could take whatever they wanted to grandma's. They asked why, and I told them that I hadn't been feeling well and that grandma would help take care of me since daddy was too busy working. They had seen me sick a lot and bought the excuse, but they were not happy about leaving their home and their dad. I told them they could see daddy as much as they wanted, but we were leaving that day. I think they knew more than they told me.

Steve, of course, went crazy when he answered the phone at work, and I told him where we were. He came right over, and I told my mother to leave. He made a huge deal and threatened to take the kids since he told me I had kidnapped them. I was all set with my responses, because I knew in advance what he would say. I had researched every legal angle on the computer while I was learning the programs!

He made the divorce very difficult, as I knew he would. He put the kids right in the middle of it, as I knew he would. He took all the money from the accounts and closed them, just as I knew he would, but I asked my lawyer to hire a forensic accountant, which is a person who uncovers all hidden monies and discovers how much your spouse really makes and how he spends the money, etc. It was very expensive, but my lawyer told me I'd get it back when the case was over, and Steve would have to pay for the service. I gave Steve all this information, letting him know that the longer he dragged out the case, the more expensive it would be for him. We didn't have a lot of money, so this hit home with him. I told him I wouldn't put restrictions on his seeing the kids; I didn't want to do that and punish him or the kids that way. I just wanted him to be respectful in the way he spoke about me, and I promised to do the same. I just wanted to get on with my life.

I can't tell you that it wasn't horrible and painful. It was the worst thing I've ever done, and I can't imagine anything harder. He immediately began dating a lot and would let me know about it. I was very hurt and jealous. Even though I didn't want him, I guess I didn't want anyone else to have him, and I didn't want the kids to be with another woman who might end up replacing me in a way.

I got a job, but it didn't pay nearly the money I used to make. My old boss wouldn't take me back because of what had happened. By that time, she had moved way up the corporate ladder, and I have to admit, I was envious of her and what she had done in her career. She told me that because of Steve's insta-bility, it would be unethical for her to recommend me to other companies. She couldn't put her name on the line like that. I was initially very angry with her, but I came to understand her point of view. I didn't blame her; it wasn't personal. She was just exercising personal boundaries, which I guess I had to respect. We continued to talk sporadically, and she eventually became my mentor.

With the proceeds from the sale of the house, I was able to buy a two-bed-room condo, which was far smaller than what we had lived in, but we were out of my mother's house, and I felt proud that I had my own place. Steve, of course, had the bigger income, and even with child support and the very mod-est alimony he paid me, he still made much more than I did and had a nicer place. The kids had their own rooms over there and were in almost the same neighborhood as our old house, so they sometimes preferred to spend a half week or a whole week over there with their father and his girlfriend. It really hurt me a lot.

It's been two years, and I'm getting through this with some help from a therapist. I've made my own friends, and that feels good. I like going to work and to the kids' sports games on the weekends, when it's my weekend to be with them. I don't have any interest in dating yet. I don't know if I ever will. I'm still young enough that I hope there will be love in my life someday when I'm ready for it. I know I'm not ready yet. I feel I'm at the point where I can look forward to waking up each day, at least, which I couldn't have said a few years ago.

—**Gayle, age forty-three**

WHERE DO YOU GO FROM HERE?

Like Gayle, you may have finally come to the conclusion that it is time to move on from your abusive relationship. Or you may have decided that this is not yet your time, and you still have hope. You may have concluded that your relation-ship still has positive aspects that you and your partner can work on, or perhaps your partner or both of you are in counseling, and you are seeing some forward progress. Maybe you are in school or vocational counseling and are waiting until you have completed that process until you make a final decision. You may still have many personal, emotional issues to work out before you feel ready to make a competent decision.

As I've said many times before: this is your decision alone, and there is not a right or wrong decision. No one else is living in your life; no one else can judge it or tell you what to do.

If you have decided that you will leave at some point, you cannot just up and walk out. Well, let me rephrase that. If you have been with this person a relatively short amount of time, have your own source of income, have your own place to live, and do not have children to consider, then yes, you can probably make a decision today and act upon it immediately. In the next chapter, we will discuss what your mate will do when you leave him—and that is a very important chapter for everyone to read no matter the circumstances—but if you are in the situation described above, you can leave more easily.

However, let's say that you don't have enough income to live independently, you don't have your own home, and/or you have children to think about. If so, your decision will, of course, be more difficult. Finding a way to leave in a *prepared, intelligent* way will take some planning.

Let's take a look at what you may have to consider and what you can do now to be fully prepared.

YOUR LEGAL RIGHTS

It is always a good idea to understand what you can expect from a legal standpoint. You can make more informed decisions when you know what course your life will take in the aftermath of leaving your partner. Abusers very often threaten to take children away, to leave the woman penniless and homeless, and so on. The fear of the unknown frequently paralyzes the woman into staying.

The best way to curb your fears and understand your legal rights is to consult a family law (divorce) attorney. If you are not married to your abuser, but have lived with him for a long period of time, you may be eligible for common-law marriage status in your state. If you have contributed income to a shared household, you may also want to determine your financial rights. Even if you are unmarried and have maintained your own household, you may want to consult an attorney to find out what you can do if your mate refuses to leave you alone after the breakup or spreads untrue rumors about you, which may impact your livelihood.

You don't have to shell out big bucks for a consultation with an attorney. You can ask friends for referrals or look in your telephone book for a legal rights advocacy organization. Then you can request a twenty-minute consultation with a per-hour attorney. Women's rights groups, which you can find on the Internet, may also be able to help you.

Once you schedule your consultation, be prepared in advance with a written list of questions you may want to ask. Don't go in unprepared and come away without addressing your specific concerns. It is your meeting, not the lawyer's, and the attorney is working for you during that time. She needs to adhere to your agenda, not hers, so put yourself in a place of self-assuredness and authority by being prepared with your list. You may have specific questions unique to your situation that an attorney wouldn't think to address. Put those at the top of the list. Here are some other questions you may want to ask:

- How much should I expect in alimony and child support? My monthly/yearly income is (x), his is (x), and we have (x) number of children. We have been married/living together for (x) number of years. How long will I receive this income from him?

- I put him through school/helped him start a business/paid off his debts; will that have any impact on the amount of settlement I can expect?

- Will I need to leave my home? If I want to stay in my home until my children are (x) years of age, how will we go about doing that, and will I have to give up anything to do that?

- If I am going to receive a settlement, about how much can I expect? We have bank accounts totaling (x), investments totaling (x), his retirement account totaling (x), my retirement account totaling (x), and a home valued at (x). We also have furniture and cars (are they leased or owned, is there an outstanding balance on a car loan, and if so, how much?), as well as jewelry. The total amount of debt we have is (x).

- What about health care and insurance?

- What can I expect in terms of the children? They are (x) years old. Will I get full or joint legal and physical custody, and what does that mean?

- What can I expect in terms of visitation? What if I want monitored/supervised visitation? What evidence do I have to submit?

- How long should I expect this process to take? What if he fights me every step of the way?

- What do you estimate my attorney's fees to be, do you require a retainer, and will we be able to ask him to pay all or a portion of my attorney's fees?

These questions seem to be the most important to women, but as I've said, you may have others that fit your situation specifically. As you can see, many of these questions will require you to do some advance preparation.

Another word of advice: you have a set amount of time to spend with the attorney or legal adviser. It will go by very quickly and may cost you money.

While your attorney may be a very pleasant person, she is not your friend, confidante, or therapist. Save your sad stories of the horrible ways he treated you for your friend, confidante, or therapist. Attorneys are businesspeople, and they're there to help you legally, not emotionally. Your job in that meeting is to be quick and prepared and to come away with crucial information that will help you make good decisions. This may sound callous to you, but learning these boundaries is crucial to getting what you want and deserve.

Once you've investigated what your legal rights are and what you can expect in that arena, there are a few other areas to plan out before leaving.

WHERE WILL YOU GO?

You can ask him to leave—and if you have children, the only decent thing would actually be for him to go so that your children don't have to be further upset. However, remember whom you are dealing with. If he were a decent person, you wouldn't be thinking of leaving, right? When you decide to take back your own power and control, this sets off switches in an abuser that put him into full commando motion. How dare you leave him? Who do you think you are, anyway? You are now his enemy, and he will do whatever he can to ruin you and incapacitate you emotionally and financially so that you have to return to him. That's his thinking. Expecting him to leave the home may not be realistic. You can talk to him—you're good at trying to appeal to him emotionally or logically—but it may not have any effect except to anger him further. A smart woman always makes her own plans for shelter.

If you have your own income that can support living in an apartment or other type of home, begin looking around now. Get an idea about rents and space as well as neighborhoods. If you have children, you may want to find a place that allows them to remain in the same school and be near their friends and father. Remember, you don't want to live with him, and perhaps you don't even want to see or talk with him, but don't project those feelings onto your children. In the majority of cases, your children will want to see him and spend time with him. You may even be surprised or hurt if they tell you that they want to live with him instead of you. Remember that they are children and see you as the instigator of their world being turned upside down. They may not like you too well right now.

If you are pinched by finances or you'd prefer not to live alone, I'd like to clue you in to a wonderful organization I've recently found. The name is Co-abode.com, and it's a very successful roommate-matching service designed for single moms. Did you know that there are more than ten million single mothers living with children under the age of eighteen? According to the Department of

Justice, nearly one-third of these women live below the poverty level. Co-abode.com will help match you and your family with another mom and her kids in a shared living situation. Many women who have taken advantage of this approach have found it tremendously helpful and rewarding, not only financially, but also emotionally. They have a "sister" in strength and support, someone to rely upon who really understands their situation. I encourage you to investigate this resource.

If you have an acceptable and respectful relationship with family members, you may want to contact them to see if you can live there for a short while. If you have children and your family is a fair distance away, do not use this avenue. Their father may accuse you of kidnapping them, and he may have legal recourse to prosecute you. Ask you attorney in advance, but in most states, you cannot take the children away from their father without permission. You wouldn't want him to take your children six states away to live with his family, either, so be fair, even if he was never fair to you in your relationship. It's about the kids now.

Friends may be able to help you with a room in their home for a specific amount of time. Before you make this request of a friend or family member, you should set a very specific time limit that you plan to be in the home. That means, before asking this favor, you should have visited your legal adviser and have a good idea of how long the divorce process will take, when you can get a job or settlement that will allow you to support yourself in your own place, and so on. It isn't fair to expect your family or friend to foot the bill for you and/or your kids just because you have a creep of a mate. All of this is ultimately your responsibility, and no one owes you anything. Keep this in mind when you are asking the favor.

You must also reassure the people you stay with—and stick with the promise—that you will not allow them to become involved in the messiness of your separation. You should have your own phone number, so he doesn't call their phone asking for you or the kids, and you should have a plan to contribute to the household, whether that be by providing money, doing chores, or helping out with their children. You are not a guest, and you are not staying at a resort. These people have real lives they need to go on with, and they are graciously offering you a place to stay. You should also let them know that you will not talk to them night after night about your relationship and what happened—in detail—and what is going on with your legal process—in detail. They will begin to feel used and resentful. You do need to talk, but you should be doing that with a therapist who can give you unbiased and knowledgeable advice that can help you move forward.

If you don't have a friend or family member who can help shelter you, you can go to your house of worship and ask for help. Your pastor or spiritual adviser may be able to put you in contact with other resources and may even help you financially.

The last resort—but by no means a bad resort—is a women's shelter. There are domestic violence shelters right where you live that you don't even know about. They are secret, safe houses. Remember, a domestic violence shelter isn't just for people who have been beaten up. Go back and look at chapter 2 of this book to remind yourself that you, too, have endured domestic violence.

Most shelters are very clean and comfortable, and all those that I've had the pleasure of either working in or visiting have been very lovely homes. Most offer not only a place to stay, but also psychological counseling and help finding a job, schooling, and a place to live. It is a very supportive environment with a lot of camaraderie. You can find a domestic violence shelter in your area by calling the National Domestic Violence Hotline, which is 800-799-SAFE. Remember, these are not homeless shelters, and all have specific requirements of the residents. There will be rules and a program to follow. Understand that going in. Do you remember when we talked about trade-offs in the last chapter? There are also trade-offs for living free of charge in a shelter.

MONEY

Let's be realistic: you need money to survive. Just as when you started out with your abuser, you needed more than love to get by, it is also true that when you break up with your abuser, you need more than hope to survive. You need hard, cold cash.

During your time of preparation, you may want to begin putting away a certain amount of grocery or clothing money, if you are able. If you have access to an ATM card, you may want to take out a small amount each week that goes into an envelope to be used for the first month or two of your departure. To be fully prepared, you will want to estimate the total amount you will need for two months—whether living on your own, with a friend or family member, or in a shelter situation—and save for that. It may take a while, depending on your current financial situation and your access to money.

You will need to find work so that you have an income. If you are already working, you may have an easier time leaving from a financial standpoint, while emotionally you can find leaving just as, or more, difficult than the woman who doesn't work outside her home. If you are a middle-aged woman who has never worked outside your home, you may be able to support yourself through your expertise in cooking, cleaning, and caring for children. Do not look down your nose at these prospects; you have highly prized skills that are in great demand in our society of upwardly mobile, two-paycheck families.

The idea of working in a fast-paced, high-technology world may seem daunting and perhaps even impossible. Understanding computers may appear an overwhelming task, and I have to confess to being computer-avoidant myself. When I decided to write books, I had to train myself to use a computer, and let me tell you—it was very difficult! However, I can share with you that mass retail stores such as Best Buy and Comp USA offer many fine computer classes. These stores, and others, also sell programs so that you can teach yourself; they are remarkably simple to understand. Of course, you must already own a computer or have access to one in order to take advantage of the programs, though your public library might very well offer training programs or, at the very least, computer access.

All of this may seem overwhelming to you, but I advise you to be realistic about the world you will enter when you leave your abuser. It is not wise to assume that he will take care of you financially. Perhaps he will be legally ordered to give you assistance, but I've rarely met a woman leaving an abusive situation who wishes to remain fully financially dependant on her former mate. Part of her idea of leaving is to be independent and at least partially self-sufficient. That said, don't go to the other extreme and deny monies to which you are entitled.

Oftentimes, a woman who has been with an abuser is cowed by the man into a "deal." He tells her that the two of them can best make financial decisions, not an attorney, who he claims will take all their money. Then the abuser works out a financial agreement himself, which he pressures the woman to sign. Do not go there. Tell him that you have to show any agreement to your attorney first. He will balk at that—because he's drawn up something that will only benefit himself—saying that you will waste a lot of money if you consult an attorney. Don't give in. It is money well spent and will protect you and your children.

Very often an abuser will draw out the legal process so long that a woman will become exhausted and tell her attorney to settle for whatever she can get. That, too, is a mistake—it is definitely part of his abusive financial strategy. Look to the future and decide that you and your children are worth the extra time and aggravation in the long run. Since your legal adviser will tell you what you can reasonably expect, stick with that plan. Don't rush things; in the process of trying to eliminate a few days, or months, of frustration, you might actually be setting yourself up for years of financial hardship.

WHO WILL TAKE CARE OF THE CHILDREN?

Of course, if you have to work and you have children, one of your main concerns will be their welfare. If you are currently working, you probably have a child care arrangement in place. However, if you have been working part time and have to now work full time, you may need another plan. Or you may have worked at a job you liked that didn't pay as much as you will need once you leave, so you may have to find another job.

Can your current child care provider offer you more time and benefits? Do you want to find in-home child care, after-school child care or full-time child care in a large setting? Can a parent or friend help you at least some of the time in exchange for your helping them on the weekends—or your days off—with something they need? Is there a mothers' co-op for child care in your community?

Finding competent child care is the biggest single worry working mothers have. It doesn't matter if you are making seven dollars per hour or one hundred thousand dollars per year.

If your children's father is going to share custody with you, then make sure that he is responsible for not only getting your children to their child care provider during the time they are staying with him, but that he pays his share, as well. This may be structured into the amount of child care funds you receive, or he may pay the provider directly. If he is going to pay directly, it is important for your provider to understand this monetary situation: you are only responsible for your share, should he not pay. What is their policy when parents share the cost? What will happen to your child if you pay your portion, and he does not take care of his obligation? Child care providers do not want to be involved in parents' legal and financial squabbles. They care for your child, but they are also business-people and require compensation for their services. Frequently, an abuser pushes the "kid button" as a way to continue to exert power and control over the mother. He may know that even if he doesn't pay his portion, you will end up paying it so that you can go to work and know that your child is cared for. You can go to your legal adviser with every complaint like this, but know that you will be paying for your attorney to send a letter to his, to garnish his wages, and so on. This is why it is important to understand your provider's policy in advance.

Once you have found a child care situation you feel comfortable with, make surprise visits. Pay attention to what your children are saying about the environment; notice if they have a change in behavior after the settling-in period.

If you have stayed home with your child until this point, it may be difficult for both of you to separate from the other, and you may go through a period of guilt.

You may doubt yourself and your decision to leave your abuser. These feelings are normal and natural and may persist for some time. You may feel that you've ruined your child's life by making this decision. Your abuser may reinforce this opinion by telling you what a bad mother you are or that you are selfish—that leaving will scar the child for life.

Actually, you should understand that staying in an abusive relationship is what permanently scars a child. I counsel many children, primarily teens, and not one of them has told me that having a working mother has ruined their lives. However, they do tell me about living in a home where their father and mother fight or about seeing their father destroying their mother's self-esteem day after day. That kind of environment damages them.

ASKING FOR HELP

Are you too proud or too frightened to ask for help? If you have been keeping your abusive relationship a secret from your family and friends, you may feel embarrassed or foolish now, because essentially you have been lying to them by omission. That is, you may not have blatantly lied to them—although when you're asked how things are going and you say "fine," that's lying—but by concealing information you have lied by omission, which means you lied because you left out facts and didn't tell the whole truth. You had your reasons. Not everyone is entitled to know every private aspect of your relationship. I understand that, and I'm not judging you. Just know that if this has been your pattern, your friends and family may not only be shocked but might also feel betrayed.

You can still ask them for help. They are the people closest to you in your life. They may challenge you on that point, asking you why, if they were so close, you didn't confide in them. You can see their point. Domestic violence is difficult to explain to others, and secrecy and shame are a common part of the problem. Apologize, and try to explain in very few words. They still are not entitled to all of your private life unless it is your choice to give it to them.

You may need to ask your community or state for financial assistance. Going on welfare short-term is not the very worst thing that you can do, as long as you have a financial plan in place that will get you off assistance. You have your pride, and leaving your abuser and going on an indefinite course of state assistance will not help you feel better about yourself. But you and your children need food and a place to live. If welfare is your only way out for a couple of months, do not be too proud to accept it.

Your religious community may be able to help you in several ways: food, shelter, counseling, child care, and more. Even if you presume that your clergy head will not approve of your decision, give him or her a chance. Once you explain your situation, you may find your clergy member more gracious than you had imagined. I have given lectures and trainings to clergy members who were formerly ill-informed about domestic violence and are very grateful for the information and anxious to help their parishioners in this situation.

Online women's sites such as ivillage.com are tremendously supportive of women and offer great resources.

You may have been in the dark when you were being abused and your abuser told you not to tell others about "family business," but he is no longer your decision maker. You are. You don't have to be ashamed of anything you've done or of the decisions you are making. They are the right ones for you. You have prepared yourself carefully for these decisions and are now ready to fly!

WHAT HAS IT COST YOU?
MINIMIZE THE COSTS BY TAKING STEPS BEFORE YOU LEAVE

As you've seen in earlier chapters, understanding your abusive relationships takes an enormous amount of work. Making a decision to stay or leave depends on many factors and requires tremendous effort. Actually leaving your abusive relationship cannot be an impulsive decision; you must prepare very carefully in order to do so wisely and safely.

In this activity, you are going to do as much advance work as possible to prepare yourself. Get your journal, and write down these ideas, leaving a good amount of space between each one—or better yet, put each concept on a different page: *job, legal, housing,* and *child care.*

Now, under each category, write down a vertical list of what you need to find out. Beside each of those ideas, write down a resource person or agency that can help you. This will prove to be a time-consuming activity, but once you have completed it, you will feel prepared to take positive action.

I have already given you an example of some of the questions you will want to ask your legal adviser. However, before you ask those questions, you need to have information. Let's say you are going to tell him how much money you have in a joint savings and retirement account. How will you get that information? Do you have financial records at home? Have you signed joint income-tax returns? The information will be on that. Where is that kept? If you have a loan or lease on a car, you need to find out what the monthly payment is and the length of the obligation. Where is that information kept? If your partner takes care of the family finances and keeps you in the dark, you may have to play detective and snoop in an area that is usually off-limits to you.

Finding housing or a job may take a while. Finding training so that you can get a job may also take time. Write down the steps you have to take and the resources you need, and begin slowly following through. Allow yourself a reasonable amount of time each day to work on this project. You may become frustrated at how slow this work actually is. Understand that you are preparing yourself for success, so be patient. You are worth the time.

18

What He'll Do If You Leave

Alex had told me on several occasions that he couldn't live without me, that his life would be pointless without me, or that he'd kill himself if I ever left. He'd say it just before I planned to surprise him with the statement that I couldn't handle the relationship anymore and was going to take a break. It's like he had radar. I couldn't stand the guilt if I knew I was the cause of his hurting or killing himself, so I haven't left yet.
—Angela, age seventeen

Angela's story may be your own. It is very typical for abusers to threaten to hurt themselves if you leave. Actually, if you are contemplating leaving your abusive mate, or have already made the decision to do so, it's important for you to understand what his reaction will be. That way you won't be surprised or shocked when some or all of the behaviors I discuss with you in this chapter come to pass.

Abusers have typical patterns, and I don't need to know your abuser in order to tell you how he will behave if you leave him. All abusers are basically the same person: they have controlling behaviors but are actually extremely dependent people. Even though they exhibit great bravado or charisma, they have very low self-esteem and lack self-confidence. Although they appear to have all the answers, they are very frightened most of the time. They project blame on you that they don't want to own in themselves. They seek power and control to bolster their fragile self-confidence, and project onto you the bad feelings they have about themselves.

Put all of this information together, and you can see that your abuser will not take it well if you tell him you've had enough. He will not be gracious and good-natured and work out an amicable settlement with you. You have taken back your own power and control, which leaves him feeling frightened, dependent, and insecure—all emotions that are intolerable to an abuser.

Will he act frightened? Absolutely not. He will be far more abusive than ever. This is crucial for you to know. How dare you take back your own power and control! Who do you think you are?

Many women think that they will be able to part as friends once they break up with their abuser. This is a seriously irrational belief. Let me ask you two questions: If he can be such a terrific friend, why isn't he still your boyfriend or husband? Do you have any other friends who treat you this way?

In my experience, the following are the typical behaviors of an abuser when he is threatened with his partner leaving, or after she has left. Please read them carefully and with an open mind. I can absolutely guarantee you that your partner will do at least one of these and probably several others. Do not continue to live in denial that none of this applies to you or your situation.

1. He will cry, beg, plead, and promise to change. He will tell you that he loves you more than anything and that he will do whatever he has to so you will stay. If you suggest counseling, he will tell you one of two things: (1) He will promise to call a therapist and then will either put it off until you forget—because in the meantime, he will have made changes to his behavior (that are not permanent), so you will not bother him about the appointment—or he will actually go to therapy once or twice. I can guarantee you that he will not stick with it. He will either tell you after the second session that his therapist told him that he's fine now and doesn't need to come back, or you will see such "miraculous" results after one or two sessions that you fall back in love with him and won't insist he go back. (2) He'll tell you that he doesn't need a therapist and can make the changes on his own with your support. Let me ask you, if it was so easy for him to make all these changes by himself, why didn't he do it earlier when you were so miserable? And your support? No, you've supported him year after year; now it's time for him to get the individual help he needs and for you to go on with your life. You should determine, after he's been in counseling for a solid year, whether he's actually made significant enough changes that have stuck. He may also suggest couples counseling. Don't fall for that, either. He is an abuser. He is dependent. He doesn't really want to change all that much. He wants to use you. You undoubtedly suggested couples counseling to him many times, and he balked at it, possibly telling you that you're the one with the problem, right? He needs to get his own, separate help to uncover why he enjoys abusing you. You could probably benefit from your own therapy, as well.

2. He may further separate you from your support network: family, friends, and house of worship. He is beginning to feel desperate and needs to isolate you from outside help that can guide and support you.

3. He may insult and demean you even more, telling you that you're fat, stupid, and lazy, or that you can't survive without him, or that no other man would want you. They are not true statements. After all, if they were, why would he feel so threatened that you are leaving?

4. He will threaten you with cutting you off from money or taking away the children or your home. He'll tell you that you won't get any money and that you'll be living on the street alone because he'll take the children so far away you'll never find them.

5. He'll threaten to expose something about you that would be humiliating for others to know.

6. He'll start spreading rumors and gossip about you. He may tell everyone that you are an abusive mother and beat your kids, that you're a kleptomaniac, that you had an affair, that you like weird sexual practices, and the like. Let's hope that the people in your life couldn't possibly believe any of this. If they would believe his lies, then perhaps they, too, are abusers.

7. He'll begin seeing other women immediately to make you jealous and let you know that not only can he easily replace you, but that you were never that important to him to begin with. What kind of man is that cruel? Yours.

8. He'll call your cell phone or home phone and leave threatening or disgusting messages. I had a female patient whose abuser called her voice mail and let her hear him having sex with another woman. That wasn't pretty.

9. He'll call, telling you that he's sick, he's depressed, he can't go to work. Basically, he'll sound pathetic and needy. Being the sweet rescuer that you are, you may feel very guilty and nurturing and want to run to his aid. Think about it all you want—and then don't do it.

10. He may threaten to hurt you or your children, family members, or pets. This is called a "terrorist threat" and is highly illegal. Report these threats immediately to the police, even if you think he wouldn't do anything harmful. I cannot tell you how many women I've counseled whose mates were non-

physically abusive while they were together, but who became physically violent when the women left. Remember, he is out of control now, needy, and very angry. He may do anything. Please do not be fooled or stay in denial about this important fact.

11. He may threaten to hurt himself. He may tell you "I can't live without you," "I might as well kill myself," "I wish I were dead," and so on. Please listen to me: this is not romantic or flattering—it's sick. As wonderful as you are, no one should be killing himself over you. This is the biggest manipulation an abuser can dish out, especially to a woman who has made it her job to take care of her man's every little boo-boo and bad feeling. If you are actually concerned that he might kill himself, do not engage in conversation with him. Instead, call a member of his family or a friend, or you can call the police. Either way, it will take care of your concern for his safety without your becoming involved. By the way, if you take this approach, expect a phone call from him in which he calls you a selfish, uncaring bitch because you didn't grab the bait and come running back to him.

12. A friend or a member of his family will call you and tell you that he's depressed, that he hasn't eaten, slept, or gone to work. They are so worried about him. They will suggest that you call him. "Just once; I know you don't want to go back to him, but it would make him feel so much better if he heard your voice one time." Nope; once again, a manipulation to woo you back.

13. He may stalk you, break something—like a lock on your house, a window on your car—or otherwise keep you off guard so that you remain nervous and on edge all the time. Now he thinks he's back in control! Once again, call the police and make a report.

Please know that these are typical behaviors for an abuser when his female partner decides she's had enough of his act. However, that doesn't make them pleasant or right. If you know what to expect in advance, you can make advance preparations.

A word about police intervention: as I told you earlier, you may actually be in some real danger. The police are there to help you.

You may want to investigate an order of protection, also known as a restraining order. It is a legal protective order issued by a judge. With it, your mate cannot contact you by phone, letter, or e-mail; he cannot molest, strike, attack, threaten, or sexually assault you, or otherwise disturb your peace. He must stay a specified distance away from you at all times. This, of course, becomes a bit more complicated if you share children with whom he has visitation. If he is harassing you, you may want to exchange your children at a safe location, such as the parking lot of a police or fire department. If he is abusive, however, you must also look at whether he is a healthy presence in your children's lives. We will discuss in the final section of this book. You are eligible for a restraining order (known in some states as an Order of Protection or Protective Order) under the following circumstances:

- He has assaulted or attempted to assault you or another member of your family.

- He caused, threatened, or attempted bodily injury to you or another member of your household.

- He made you or a member of your household afraid that he would commit physical or emotional harm to you or them.

- He sexually assaulted or attempted to sexually assault you or a member of your household.

- He has stalked you.

If you decide that you need a restraining order, do not hesitate to get one. He will receive a copy of it and will be apprised of his rights and the consequences of his violating the order. Many women are afraid of taking this legal step, because they are worried that it will make him even angrier. They are correct. He will be angrier; you've caught him and made it clear that you will not tolerate his behavior. You are letting him know that you are stronger than he thinks and that you will hold him accountable for his actions. Abusers don't like this! He wants you to remain a frightened, cowering, little bug that he can squish at will. The restraining order shows him that you are no longer that person, and he cannot treat you that way.

This next information is very important, so please read it carefully: If you get a restraining order, and he violates it (for example, he continues the abusive behavior), you must contact the police immediately each and every time he violates it. Failing do this lets your mate know that you didn't really mean what you set out to do. It makes him think that he is above the law, no one can stop him, and he hasn't any restrictions. He will become even more dangerous. Also, and this is equally important to you, if you contact the police, and they take him to jail for the night or longer, *you* have not put him in jail. His abusive, illegal behavior has put him in jail. It is not your fault that he may be in trouble with the law. It is 100 percent his responsibility. A judge specifically laid out for him what he could and could not do, and he decided that he would disregard a legal order. This is what abusers do.

Many women tell me, "I don't want him to get in trouble; I just want his behavior to change." That's true, but that is not one of the three things you have control over. He has complete control over his thoughts, behaviors, and reactions in response to the legal order. He can decide that he will comply and act lawfully, or he can decide to break the law. Either way, it is his decision. You cannot influence his thought processes or save him from making a bad decision.

In the next section of this book, we will look at your decision to move forward in a healthy way in your new life. You're doing great work!

WHAT HAS IT COST YOU?
PREPARING FOR A POSSIBLE STORM

How did you feel about the prospect of your mate trying one or more of the predictable behaviors I listed? Did it make you feel anxious, frightened, angry? Did it make you decide to stay, if leaving is going to be that difficult? All of those reactions would be reasonable for you and your situation.

Why don't you take out your journal and do some advance preparation for what you'll do if he takes any of those actions?

Write down each of the behaviors you believe may be possible. Then, write down three that you think he would never do. Beside each of them, write down your plan for dealing with each behavior. For example, let's say he threatens to take away your children and your home and leave you penniless. What are some good actions for you to take? You could call your lawyer—or get a lawyer if you don't have one—and discuss the likelihood of this actually happening. I would suggest that one of your responses to this scenario should be to not engage him in a discussion. This is what he wants. He wants your attention, and he also wants to see how anxious and scared his threat makes you. Why? Because then he has power and control over you again. Don't think he's going to give it up easily, my friend. If he makes that threat, you can calmly (like an actress; of course you're not calm) say, "Oh, that's interesting. Good-bye." With that, you will have frustrated the living heck out of him. After he's gone or you've hung up the phone, you can cry your eyes out, wring your hands, or pace. A better plan would be to immediately call your attorney and get a quick reality check.

Go through each scenario and plan your response, especially to the three you think he'd never try. It doesn't matter if you think they are outrageous. I just want you to be prepared in case of something shocking and unforeseen.

Remember, you are now his mortal enemy. If you tell him that the relationship is over, do not expect him to respond "Oh, all right; I can see your point. I am abusive, and you deserve something better, so let me leave you the house, the cars, the furniture, and all the money." He abused you while you were together—and that's when he liked you and you were compliant. Now, all gloves are off! Just because he's never hit you while you were in the relationship with him, don't think for a nanosecond that he would not physically hurt you now. Don't be naive and allow yourself to become a statistic …

PART V

GETTING BETTER—CHANGING YOUR LIFE! MOVING FORWARD INTO YOUR NONABUSIVE LIFE

I don't think it really matters all that much whether I stay with my boyfriend or leave him. I like having a boyfriend, and all guys are the same, anyway. I've had three boyfriends before Sammy that treated me the same way he does. What would be the point? It's not so bad; HE DOESN'T HIT ME.
—**Vanessa, age seventeen**

This is a very important section of our work together. At this point, you understand your former abusive relationships and what kept you in them. You've had to make horrendously difficult decisions about whether you should stay in your current relationship or leave. The process involved in making that choice can cause more than a few gray hairs and can age you like nothing else … except maybe being in an abusive relationship. It's fair to say—speaking from personal experience, my dear—that you may have already acquainted yourself with semi-permanent hair color and wrinkle-fighting potions!

In the next five chapters, we will talk about the fears every woman has when she is newly on her own and has finally rid herself of a lifelong pattern of unhealthy, destructive relationships.

First, we will investigate who you are. That sounds easy enough, doesn't it? Well, you may be surprised. If you've spent many years allowing others to tell you who you are and what you deserve, you've now acquired a number of new voices in your head. No, that doesn't mean I believe you are mentally deranged ... just that you may have your parents' voice telling you who they believe you are, a former mate's voice telling you something else, and your current mate telling you yet another. That's a lot of opinions, and none of them may be true. In the first chapter, we will talk about getting to know the real you again—the one you were before so many other folks rendered an unwelcome opinion. You will also begin discovering what you want in your life. Wouldn't it be sweet if you made all your own decisions? Well, guess what? You can!

Secondly, you are going to want to change your relationship patterns and the cycle of abuse that you've lived with for so many years. That may be tough and uncomfortable. Remember, most people prefer the certainty of misery to the misery of uncertainty. However, it's not enough for you to ditch your current abuser if you just go on to yet another abusive relationship. What's the good of that? You have so much knowledge and an amazing amount of power now. Learning to identify the types of people who can support, nurture, respect, and honor you is crucial; the work necessary to achieve it is very worthwhile. Imagine not feeling nervous and depressed in a new relationship, whether it's with a mate or a friend, in a working situation, or in a new type of relationship with your family members. Wouldn't that feel great?

Thirdly, we will talk about you becoming your own good parent. Yes, it's possible and actually very necessary if you weren't born to the parents you deserved. You will learn how to reparent yourself with kinder messages and actions and how to look to yourself, instead of your critical parents, for support.

Soon after is a crucial chapter: "The Temptation to Go Back to Him When You Are Broke or Feel Lonely and Scared." Yes, you will probably feel this temptation at some point, and you need to know in advance how you can deal with it rationally and remain in control of your thoughts and actions. You will encounter many times of anxiety and wondering if you did the right thing, but your friends may not want to hear about it. They've listened to you complain about him for a long time and were gratified that you finally made a choice about him. Now, they have to listen to these fears? What you may end up doing is squashing those feelings down again due to shame and fear, so let's just get that big ol' elephant out of the center of the living room, and deal with him!

Lastly, I'd like to spend a few minutes talking with you about a subject no one ever deals with openly: self-abuse. I have found that in the aftermath of most long-term abusive relationships, or when there's been a pattern of abusive relationships, women tend to be unkind to themselves in little—or maybe even big—ways. They eat too much or too little, have unhealthy rebound relationships, spend themselves into debt, make rash and impulsive decisions that they regret, or even hurt themselves physically. I don't want that to be you. I don't want you to do all the hard work necessary to remove yourself from all your former relationships only to go on and abuse yourself, just because that is what you are used to. That wouldn't be loving behavior to yourself, now would it?

As you can see, we have a lot to do in this section of our work together. Let's get started!

19

Who Are You Really, and What Do You Want? Getting to Know Yourself Again

I was with my boyfriend Benjie for eight years. We never married, but beginning in year two, we began talking about it a lot. He didn't know if he could be that committed to anyone forever and ever. I guess I should have gotten out then, because marriage was my goal for a relationship.

I was thirty-one when we met, and I knew I wanted at least two children. That had been my dream and expectation for my entire life: marriage and two or three kids. When he told me about the commitment thing, I was devastated. I'd already spent two years with him, and things were great. I couldn't understand why marriage wouldn't be the next logical step, and then children after that. He was great with my nieces and nephews and our friends' kids. He'd even give me a little smile when he played with them; sort of a, "This will be us someday" look.

But, foolishly, I stuck around, because I was convinced that he was the marrying kind. I was patient and didn't bring up the question, knowing it might freak him out. He was handsome, very smart, and had his life and career together, so he was perfect in every other way. I knew we'd make beautiful children together and be able to provide a nice life for them. It would be great. Well, that was my idea, anyway.

Years four and five were a bit turbulent because I began getting impatient with him. I'd ask him if he was happy with our relationship, and he'd tell me he was. Then I'd ask him why we couldn't get married. He'd tell me the same thing he always did: that he didn't know if he could be that committed forever and ever. He asked me why we couldn't just keep it as it was, and when I told him I wanted children and didn't want them to be born into a nonfamily, he'd just laugh and tell me how provincial and politically correct I was. We were living together anyway, so what was the big deal, he'd want to know. I told him about my marriage-and-family dream many times. He thought I sounded like a Stepford wife.

This went on and on, with my wanting marriage and his not. I couldn't understand why he got his way and I didn't, since we both wanted our own way. But, to be honest, he almost always got his own way on anything else, so why should I have expected differently? I told him that if he really loved me, he'd marry me since it was so important to me. He told me if I really loved *him*, I'd drop it. We were at a stalemate. I went to a therapist, and she asked me if I wanted the relationship more than the marriage or the possibility of marriage more than the relationship with Benjie. Apparently, I couldn't have both, but if I stayed with Benjie, he was sort of telling me that I could have the children part. Did I want to get out of the relationship with the man I loved and risk the possibility of not getting married or having children, or stay with him and have children but no marriage?

It seemed logical but unfair to me. Why did he get to win? What if I stayed with him and he never approved children? I talked to him about it, and he told me about the commitment part again. He said if I wanted to have children with the knowledge that he might not be around forever, we could do that. That was just weird to me! If he had children, how could he not be committed? Was he telling me that I'd have to raise them alone? What was so wrong with me, anyway, that he was already anticipating leaving me someday?

I became very depressed and anxious. I asked God for help, as well as my friends. I couldn't talk to my family members, because by this time they hated Benjie for what he was doing to me, plus my parents wanted grandchildren—since I was so kid-focused all my life, they had been sure they'd have them by now.

I decided not to think about it anymore and just enjoy what I had with Benjie, hoping, of course, that he'd come to the "right" conclusion. This went on another couple of years with no mention of marriage or family from him. He told me often how much he loved me and how lucky he was.

Then, the twin bombs hit: last year I found out that he had been having an affair for the previous eight or nine months, and she was four months pregnant. He told me that he was planning on marrying her. You can imagine how completely shredded I was. And then, as I was packing to leave our condo, I got a call from my gynecologist's office telling me that the pap smear I'd had a week earlier came back from the lab, and they needed to do another one. She said it was "suspicious." To make a long story short, the subsequent tests indicated that I had ovarian cancer. It was not too far advanced, and I got all the treatment, but I can never have biological children.

Now I'm thirty-nine years old, I'm in cancer recovery, and my boyfriend of eight years is married with a child … and he seems to be ecstatic. He's offered support and friendship to me. Can you believe that? Almost every day, I have to keep my father and male friends from going to his home or office; they want to kill him.

I can't tell you what happened to my life. Most of the time, I fight with a lot of bitterness toward him and life in general. I'm also grateful to be alive, and I hope that there will be marriage in my future and children in my life in

some way. But that may be stretching it. I feel like I wasted the best years of my life with Benjie and with a dream that he was always telling me he would not fulfill. I don't know what to do from this point on.
—**Eva, age thirty-nine**

That is a sad story, isn't it? What happened to Eva and her lifelong dreams of marriage and family? What about who she was and what she had always wanted? She took an unwise gamble and lost in a very tragic way.

I truly believe this to be true: *when a man presents himself to you as a creep, believe him!* Don't try to change him, fix him, or help him understand what you think he really wants. Just believe him. He's a creep, but at least he's being an honest creep! He's telling you the truth. Don't fall in love with his "potential."

During the first several years of his relationship with Eva, Benjie was perfectly honest with her. He told her that he didn't want to get married then or ever. He told her he didn't think he could make the type of commitment she needed. He told her that if she wanted children, he would provide the sperm, but he didn't think he'd be the father she wanted for her children. He told her all that again and again. He gave her an out. She just didn't want to believe him, because he was so "perfect in every other way."

What does that mean? If your dream or priority is marriage and family, it doesn't matter how perfect your guy is in other areas. He's not perfect for you. He's perfect for a woman who wants neither marriage nor children. Get off the dime, and go find what you deserve elsewhere.

Eva lost herself in the relationship with Benjie and lost sight of what she wanted in the process. Don't let this be your life story, as well.

When you've been in an abusive relationship, you're told who you are, what you want, and what you shouldn't want. You're told how to act, what to say, and how to feel. Along the way, you forget who you are.

It's now time to get back your sense of power … or find it for the first time. It's time to decide who you are, what you want, and how you can get it!

When I was a girl, I loved watching the movie *The King and I*. I loved the costumes, the magical land, the love story, and most of all, I loved the song "Getting to Know You." Have you heard the song? These are partial lyrics:

> *Getting to know you,*
> *Getting to know all about you.*
> *Getting to like you,*
> *Getting to hope you like me.*

What would happen if that song were sung by you *to* you? How great would it feel to really get to know and like yourself? To feel free and easy, bright and breezy for the first time in a long time? To say and feel what you wanted? And what if all of these wonderful feelings were because of the beautiful and new things you were learning about yourself? Does that seem impossible? Well, it isn't anymore. You now have the opportunity to get to know and like yourself again and to create whatever type of life *you* would like.

PERSONAL POWER IS YOURS!

The difference between what we do, and what we are capable of doing, would suffice to solve most of the world's problems.
—Mahatma Ghandi

How long did you give your abusers power over your life and feelings? Now your life and feelings are yours to do with what you like. You have free will, and no one is calling the shots but you. There's good news and bad news with this picture, however. Having personal power means that from now on, you are completely responsible for your life. In the past you gave this power to others, but now you've taken it back. The good news is that whatever wonderful accomplishments you have, however you succeed, will be through your own efforts. That's great and will be very rewarding. The bad news is that if you fail—whatever that means to you—you can't blame your abusers any longer. It's all up to you. That's the free will part of the equation.

Albert Einstein once said, "We are what we think about ourselves every day." He was a pretty smart guy. In your life, you will create exactly what you think you deserve. Therefore, according to Mr. Einstein, if you want a different and positive life, you will need to give yourself positive messages of encouragement to support your changes.

You have free will in the messages you give yourself and the ways in which you think about yourself, as well. How do you choose to think about yourself? Are you

- strong;

- frightened;

- frail;

- weak;

- confident;

- unlovable;

- powerful;

- stupid;

- a failure;

- angry;

- not good enough;

- thoughtful;

- loving;

- generous;

- successful;

- a quitter;

- magnificent;

- resilient?

At this point, you may relate more closely to the negative comments than the positive ones. That's all right; it's normal. Don't start giving yourself negative messages for it! Remember that the negative voices in your head are those of your abusers. You can decide whether to listen to the voices and how you respond. Who says that you have to agree with them or that they are true? Now you have the opportunity to chuck them out in the recycle bin and listen to your own clear and powerful voice.

CHOOSING TO LIVE ACTIVELY RATHER THAN REACTIVELY

Now you have personal power, free will, and choices. When you are living in an abusive relationship, you generally live reactively to your partner's moods and decisions. In my book *Destructive Relationships*, I describe what living actively versus reactively looks like. When you are living actively, you

- pursue your own interests;

- speak up when things don't feel right;

- think about your own goals and go after them;

- make a personal plan about how to succeed at your goals.

  On the other hand, when you live reactively, you

- adjust your moods and plans to your abuser's moods and plans;

- defer what you want in life until "the time is right";

- keep quiet when you should stand up for yourself.

Which group did you fit into? Don't be ashamed if it was the reactive group. That would be logical in an abusive relationship. Your abuser's needs and wants are so powerful and time-consuming that yours just seem to fade into the background. Maybe you've been told that it would be selfish of you to think about yourself and define your own dreams. What consequence would you have had to pay if you stood up to your abusers? You see, this is why it's logical, and almost necessary, to live reactively when you are in an abusive relationship. That doesn't mean doing so was good for you, however.

Now it's time to decide what you want and go after it! How do you do that when you've been the helpmate and the unselfish, martyred woman for so many years? Here's a little activity that can help.

WHAT HAS IT COST YOU?
GETTING TO KNOW YOU, GETTING TO KNOW ALL ABOUT YOU

It's time to get out your journal again and write the following questions down. Then, do quite a bit of thinking about your answers. You may not have them right away. As a matter of fact, I would encourage you to write down what you think right now. Then, after you've finished reading the book, come back to them and decide whether you'd like to revise. You always have the right to change your mind.

- What do I want from my life?

- Who do I want to become?

- When I have the answer to #2, how will I act? How will I feel? What will my life look like?

- What obstacles will I have to overcome in order to have what I want?

Have you ever asked yourself these questions? If so, how long has it been? Do you feel guilty or embarrassed by asking yourself these questions? The focus is on you, rather than on others, so this activity may seem uncomfortable.

I've been talking a lot about personal power in this chapter, but it may be a foreign concept to you. If you can take a few moments right now to think about what it is, this concept will help you define your goals—what you want to achieve for yourself—more clearly.

Look at the list below and place a checkmark next to each criterion that fits for you. Think about these carefully and honestly, remembering that no one is looking at your answers or judging you. Feel free to mark more than one response.

Personal power is about

- money;

- a nice house;

- freedom from fear;

- education;

- knowing your kids are OK;

- a good job;

- contentment;

- self-reliance/not having to depend on others;

- self-confidence;

- spirituality;

- self-knowledge.

What pattern did your responses reveal to you? If you checked external items—ones you can see—such as money, job, house, and education, that's perfectly fine. Now you understand that you must make an immediate life plan that includes steps to achieve concrete necessities in your life. If you chose intrinsic—inward, not easily seen—ideas, that's fine, too. You will need to do more emotional work on yourself to achieve this goal. Who's to say you can't have all of them now that you're in charge?

Another important factor to consider and prepare for is that, while you may be happy—as well as a bit anxious—that you are out of your abusive relationship, not everyone else in your life may feel the same way. After all, they've gotten what they wanted from you in the past. Now you are giving them a very clear message that this will no longer be the case. They are not in control of your life; you are. You may be shocked to find that some people are resentful or will entice you to return to the old you: the one who could be easily persuaded and gave selflessly to others without considering her own well-being. They know and like that passive woman who never asks for anything and allows others to walk all over her. It works for them, for your passivity gives them enormous payoffs.

I learned this lesson in a few difficult ways. When I separated from my children's father, I lost almost every single person in my life: my parents, my brothers, their wives and children, almost every one of my so-called friends, my aunts and uncles and cousins. All the people I was closest to in my life left in one fell swoop. Poof, they were gone. As I said previously, rumors were swirling around me. What could possibly possess me to leave such a prince? But no one asked me anything directly. It was more than devastating; it changed everything I had ever believed about these people and my life. I was angry—actually, I was extremely sad, very frightened, and frustrated beyond belief. How could they think these things about me? The me they had known for almost forty years? The person who had been there for them, helped them, listened to them, put up with them?

The other time I learned the lesson that others may not like the new and powerful me was just before my first book, *But I Love Him,* was released in 2000. My mentor and friend, Dr. Paul Fick—a brilliant therapist, author, and human being—told me, "Your friends may be happy for your success; they just may not be *that* happy." I thought it was a funny comment and hoped it wouldn't prove to be true. By that time, I had carefully acquired new, nontoxic friends who appreciated who I was, because I appreciated who I was. Writing and publishing that book was an amazing accomplishment; I never would have even considered this undertaking had I remained with my first husband. At the time of publication, I was newly married to my adorable and supremely supportive current husband, Frank. His love and encouragement, as well as that of my new friends, were what kept me going when I was writing the book. What if these new and seemingly lovely people weren't happy, but instead were resentful of the book and what I just knew would be certain success?

Well, the happily-ever-after part is that they were completely happy and thrilled for me! The difficult part was that the toxic, destructive people in my former life started to contact me and wanted to come back into the fold, which of course I did not allow. I did not embrace the former friends who treated me like dirt when I needed them most and had completely deserted me. You see, I was in control of my life by then, and I decided not to entertain their calls and wishes of congratulations. Instead, I decided to look upon their sudden change of heart as a study in unhealthy human behavior and leave it at that. Just because these people whistled, it didn't mean I had to jump anymore. Now I knew I was finally healthy and in control of my life—and it felt great!

WHAT HAS IT COST YOU?
WHAT WOULD YOU DO IF ...

Let me ask you a couple more questions so that you can begin to crystallize who you are and what you want.

- If you knew that you had three months of health left, how would you want to spend that time?

- On your deathbed, what would you be sad that you had never accomplished? What passion had you denied yourself?

Let me caution you about these questions: they are solely about you. In other words, your answer to question one cannot be that you would want to go back to your abusive mate and he would give you the most loving and supportive three months of your life. Likewise, the answer to question two cannot be that you wished you had lived the rest of your life in a happy relationship with your mate. Those types of answers mandate that your abuser change. That didn't happen, and you haven't any control of that situation, so while these questions appear to be fantasy, actually they aren't. One day, we will all be in the positions posed in those questions, and I would certainly prefer that you didn't have regrets about your life and situations you could have changed; where you held the power but did not use it.

Do you remember Eva at the beginning of this chapter? How do you think she would answer these questions if she were to focus totally on herself? She certainly has some regrets, doesn't she?

IS IT LUCK OR GOOD PLANNING?

Now that you've had some thoughts about who you are, what you like, and what you want, it's time to start acting on this information.

Many people have said to me "You're so lucky!" which I believe to be poppycock. They consider me lucky—and people in your life will consider you lucky as well once you start really living your life—because I have achieved the life I planned. Notice that I said "planned," because none of what I have or who I've become came to me on a silver platter. As you may have guessed, I have achieved my current life through a long, arduous process. Books don't fall out of the sky with my name on them. I don't have patients in my therapy practice because they just happen to trip into my office while they were on their way to buy a gallon of milk. And I don't have the lovely relationships I have in my life because all those people had nothing better to do on any given day but seek me out. No, I prefer to think of luck as Oprah Winfrey—who told me that I should write my first book—explains it: "Luck is when preparation meets opportunity."

Think about that simple but masterful idea for a moment. What we want to do together is make you so prepared for success that opportunity will just have no other choice but to make an appearance!

Dr. Phil McGraw's first book, *Life Strategies*, talks about what it takes to be a success. It is composed of three simple words: *be, do, have.* That is, *be* committed to a goal; *do* whatever it takes to achieve that goal; and then you will *have* what you want.

Sounds easy, doesn't it? Unfortunately, most people fail in their attempts, because they skip the second step! Of course, *do* is the most difficult one. Let's look at what you will have to *do* to achieve the goals you set for yourself. Will you have to

- go back to school;

- get more training;

- request information brochures;

- work late;

- make child care arrangements;

- deal with your own fears and guilt;

- make a lengthy apprenticeship with a mentor who does the job you would like;

- work with a spiritual adviser;

- examine the difficulties and patterns in your life that have not worked for you thus far?

Being honest with yourself and holding yourself accountable are crucial steps in this process. Remember, it's all up to you at this point. No one can keep you down except you and your attitude. In *Life Strategies* Dr. Phil discusses a seven-step process for achieving goals that I believe to be incredibly wise. My version of his points are as follows:

1. Describe your goal in terms of a specific event or behavior (not a feeling you'd like to have).

2. Create a measurable goal (like losing ten pounds).

3. You must create a timeline (it can't be "someday").

4. You—and only you—must be in charge of the outcome (not changing your abusive mate).

5. You must have a real plan to help you reach your goal (looking at the previous list will help you).

6. Create small steps to your goal (making a daily to-do list is wise).

7. Make yourself accountable to someone else (tell someone about it and check in with her regarding your progress on a weekly basis).

Now, let's be honest, ladies; that's a lot of work. Are you willing to take those seven steps? No one is listening, so you can answer truthfully. If you can realistically say that this is not the perfect time for you to accomplish these tasks, that's completely fine. Maybe taking baby steps at this highly emotional juncture is enough. That's perfectly OK. You have had to make huge life decisions and larger leaps of faith. Remember, you are responsible for your life now, so be honest with yourself. Maybe this isn't the right time for you. Maybe when your kids are a little older, it would be a better time. Or maybe when you lose five pounds, or several months from now. Maybe any of those times would be the perfect moment for you to begin your life with passion and commitment.

Just remember that life will continue day to day, no matter what you decide. It will not wait for you to catch up or for your perfect moment to magically occur … because you make the magic. Unless you do something differently, all of your tomorrows will be identical to your yesterday and today. If that's good enough for you, that's more than good enough for me. After all, only you can take action in your own life.

Remember my favorite quote: most people prefer the certainty of misery to the misery of uncertainty. You've certainly known misery on a first-name basis. What would happen if you stuck your toe out just a little and began planning and acting as if you cared about yourself and your life? Do you recall the worst-case scenario? What is the worst thing that can happen in your life? Will that happen if you begin making plans and acting on them in small ways? No, so you are already ahead of the game!

WHAT HAS IT COST YOU?
WHAT WILL YOUR NEW LIFE LOOK LIKE?

One good way of trying on a different life—while planning for it at the same time—is to create a crystal clear picture of your goals. Take out your journal and write down the following questions, think about them very closely, and then write down your answers. Really get into this activity. It's not only instructional, but a lot of fun, as well.

If you woke up tomorrow and your life was exactly the way you planned it, how would you explain what it looked like and what you were doing? Remember to be realistic and consistent with your goals.

- Where would you be living?

- What kind of job would you have?

- What would you look like in terms of weight, hair color and style, dress, and so on?

- What would your atmosphere smell like?

- What would you eat for dinner that night?

- Are you happy?

• Who are the people in your life?

Were you able to see yourself in your goal? Before we end, let me explain goals to you as I regularly explain them to my patients. Imagine for a few moments that you are in my office, sitting or lying on my cream-colored couch. Get comfortable, close your eyes for a moment, and then read this text out loud:

> Imagine that you are at the beginning of a long, straight country road. There are beautiful, large trees creating an archway over the road, and at the end of this road is your goal. Do you see it clearly? Good. This is a long road, as many country roads tend to be. There may be a few potholes on the road and gravel that you'll have to watch out for so that you don't fall. Now, visualize little country lanes intersecting your long road. On each one of those lanes are enticing stores: antique shops, fresh produce stands, a charming little country cafe, and maybe even a group of local art galleries. If you want to get to your goal, you will have to be disciplined enough not to go down each of those lanes, or at least to not dawdle too long. If you take each of the little roads—as you are entitled to do—you may still reach your goal, but it will take far longer to get there than if you denied yourself some of these lovely distractions and trudged on to the end of the street. If you decide to peruse the galleries, you will first have to walk down the side street, spend time in the shop, walk back to the main street, and then begin down that road again. You can certainly do that. Life is dull without any distractions and rewards. You can decide how many distractions and rewards you want and how quickly you want to reach your goal. Your life will be full of distractions and detractors. Some of them may be your own fears. Each time this happens, ask yourself, "How will taking this side street get me closer to my goal at the end of the road? Does it actually take me farther away? Will I have to backtrack and lose ground in order to move forward?"

Well, my dear, you have visualized your goals and learned how to take the steps to prepare to meet opportunity. You have nothing to fear, as success is the only logical end to your road.

Shortly, we will discuss your relationship patterns and the ways you can change those, as well. Remember, you're in charge!

20

Changing Your Abusive Relationship Patterns

When I started really taking an honest look at my life, I found that almost every one of my relationships was abusive. Actually, if you leave out one friend, all of my relationships were horrid. I had just accepted the abuse as normal all my life, since I was raised to accept and be grateful for whatever someone gave you. If they gave you abuse, you were just supposed to shut up and take it—and be happy about it!

All the boyfriends I've had have cheated on me, lied to me, and generally treated me like a slave and nonperson. Of course, I forgave every one of them and tried to fix them and help them. All the bosses I've ever worked for—whether men or women—have been total creeps who used and abused me, making me work late every night, not caring if I was sick, verbally abusing and harassing me. My own brother and sister have always been mean to me. I'm the youngest, and I always thought that I should have been babied and treated nicely, but it was actually just the opposite. They are seven and nine years older than I am, and they always stuck together and left me out, treating me like a parasite and an unwelcome guest in the house. I couldn't seem to please my parents, even if I got straight As at school, and my friends have just been obnoxious and catty. I can't trust any of them.

Here I am, breaking up once again with an abuser and wondering what's wrong with me. How do I attract all these people in my life? Am I destined to have this kind of life, or is there some hope that I can have decent, trustworthy, kind people around me? Right now, I'm very discouraged and don't think I'd know a good person if they appeared like a vision from God.
—**Trisha, age twenty-one**

HOW DO YOU BREAK AN ABUSIVE RELATIONSHIP PATTERN?

I've met so many women who, like Trisha, have been involved in primarily abusive relationships all their lives. They can count on one hand the number of kind and nurturing relationships they've had. When you've experienced only unhealthy mates and friends, you begin to lose confidence in your abilities to judge others and develop great distrust in everyone, including yourself. A life of inevitable pain seems to be a life not worth living, doesn't it?

But you've worked too hard and come too far to go back to that kind of life! From now on, you can make a pledge to yourself that you will allow into your life only emotionally healthy people who can enrich you. It is actually very easy to do that, and once you begin to replace toxic relationships with healthy relationships, your life becomes so simple in every way. I can tell you that from personal experience. For the last eight years, I have not allowed one toxic person to infiltrate my relationship universe. In the rest of this book, I am going to relay to you the skills that are responsible for that. Then you too will be able to judge an abuser at fifty paces … just as abusers were formerly able to judge you as a person who was willing to be abused.

You will need to change several patterns so that you can simplify your relationship life:

- Stop using denial and delusion as coping mechanisms

- Learn to stand up for yourself

- Decide what you need and deserve rather than letting others dictate what you need and deserve

- Set healthy boundaries

- Stifle your instinct to be a helper/rescuer to everyone (whether they deserve your help or not)

When you master these skills, and learn to let go of your emotional fears discussed earlier, you will be emotionally smarter than anyone you know!

DENIAL

Denial is a nifty, little coping mechanism. It prevents you from seeing a person or situation as it really is until you are ready and able to deal with it. It is a basic defensive skills that is meant to protect us. When the mind feels threatened, it ignores useful information that would enable us to see a situation clearly so that it doesn't have to deal with the harmful situation at the time.

Overall, the main reason why you may have remained in an abusive relationship so long is that you weren't looking clearly at the entirety of the abuse. If you were, you would have had difficulty justifying your abuser's behavior, and you would have had to make a decision. I have counseled women who have said the following phrases, which illustrate denial in action:

- He only cheats on me when he's drunk. It's not his fault. He hangs out with crummy friends and only drinks when he's with them.

- Most of the time, our relationship is so nice. He pushes and shoves me around when he's stressed, but it's not like he's ever hit me or anything.

- Other people say he's got a bad temper. I don't see it that way. I think he's a really nice guy a majority of the time. He had a horrible childhood and can't help the way he is. He bangs his fist and puts it through walls and stuff, but it's because of his parents. He's never had love, and I can provide that for him.

- He'll walk out on me sometimes, and it hurts my feelings. He calls me names and makes me feel real bad. But he always comes back, so that must say something about the way he feels about me, don't you think?

- When things settle down for him at work, I know our home life will be better. He's had four jobs in the last year, and none of them have worked out. His bosses don't seem to appreciate the skills he brings to the companies. That's a lot of transition, so I just have to be patient, and I know things will get better.

- My boyfriend told me he knows he has a problem and wants to be different. He's going to start working on his problems. He's promised me that he's going to change, because he said I'm the best thing that's ever happened to him, and he doesn't want to lose me. He's going to read some relationship books I got him. How could I leave him now when he's going to change? I've got to give him another chance.

- Yes, he does yell at me, but most of the time I deserve it. He tries to teach me things and make me a better person. He graduated college and is really smart. I barely got out of high school. He knows a lot more than me, so when he tells me I'm stupid, I think he's probably right a lot of the time. But he's never laid a hand on me. If he did that, I'd definitely throw him out.

- He's mean to me, it's true, but he's such a good father. When he's acting out with me, it's when the kids are asleep, and they don't know anything about it.

I could really go on and on with the denial and excuses, but you get the idea. None of these women are looking at their situation clearly or in a way that's emotionally healthy for them.

What if one of those women said to you, "Well, yes he yells at me, calls me names, cheats on me, can't hold a job, drinks, treats me like I'm an idiot, gets physically angry, and my kids see all of it even when I think they don't ... but I'm choosing to stay with him, and we're spending the rest of our lives together, because he's the very best I can do!"

Do you see how ridiculous that would be? That's the reason why denial is so handy. Until you are prepared to move on from that abusive relationship, you have to protect yourself emotionally by living in denial. Your mind cannot think of you as that foolish!

Here is an easy way to remember what denial really is:

Don't

Even

KNow

It's

A

Lie

Denial usually begins as a very good survival tool in childhood. If you lived in an abusive home, you know this to be true. When you were a little girl, you didn't have any choice or control over what was happening in your home or to you personally. You were dependent on your parents to fill your needs, even if they did a crummy job doing just that. What could you do? You couldn't leave, so what good would it do you to look squarely at the horrible situation in which you were living? The way you protected yourself was by pretending the abuse didn't exist or that it didn't affect you. That may be a brilliant thing to do when you're eight; but when you're thirty-eight and do have power and control—should you decide to exercise it—denial is not useful at all. However, because denial was so useful as a child—and so familiar—you unknowingly call upon it once again, only to discover that you are increasingly unhappy without knowing why.

DELUSION

Delusion is an even more serious way of protecting your mind against hurtful thoughts and difficult decisions. As you've just seen, when you are in denial, you want to believe that a situation is not occurring. Deluded people, even when presented with absolute proof of a situation, continue to believe what they'd like.

Women in domestic-violence situations do this quite often in a variety of instances; however, the most common and serious usually concern their children. They believe that because their children were not physically abused by their fathers, but "only" heard their parents' heated battles or "only" saw their mother cry after daddy said something unkind to her, the children were not adversely affected and certainly were not abused. Even when presented with reams of evidence demonstrating that merely living in this type of household is highly damaging to children, a woman may delude herself into believing the evidence is incorrect or that, while it may apply to other children, it doesn't apply to hers, because her kids are doing well in school. This denial gives her another compelling reason to stay in her abusive situation, because—according to her—the children are not being damaged, therefore it must be best for them to remain in a two-parent household.

Delusion grows out of shame and guilt. In the example I just gave, I'm sure you can see that if a woman were to confront her delusion about abuse not damaging children, she would have to confront her own shame and guilt at subjecting her kids to this type of life. Then she would have to make a difficult decision not only about leaving, but also about the upset she has directly caused her children thus far.

LEARNING TO SAY NO

Speaking up and standing up for yourself is a crucial part of changing your abusive relationship patterns, as is learning to ask for what you want and declining what you don't want. This may sound scary to you. After all, you've been the good girl, the accommodating, selfless girl. What will people think if you begin standing up for yourself now? Will they hate you? Will they think you're a bitch? Maybe. But they will also respect you more and won't try to mess with you.

Learning to ask for what you want and also to say no to what you don't want is a process—you shouldn't expect to learn these things overnight. Your biggest emotional fears will give you clues about why that may be true. If one of your biggest fears is being alone—as is the case with almost everyone—then you may fear that if you say no or don't go along with what others demand of you, they will leave you—emotionally and/or physically. Yikes! What could possibly be worse than being alone? To answer that, go back to your worst-case scenario. Will that occur if you stand up for yourself? No. Then let's go on.

As I mentioned earlier in the book, your abuser has pressured you to agree to things through emotional blackmail: FOG—fear, obligation, and guilt. You have been trained since you were a child to be agreeable and to go along, and now it is difficult to rock that boat, because you've been that woman for so long. In the process, you've taught others how to treat you: like dirt. Because you haven't stood up for yourself, others have the opinion that what they say to you and what they ask of you is fine. You have not told them differently.

Don't expect anyone to read your mind. As we discussed earlier, when we were talking about irrational beliefs, mind-reading doesn't work. Unless everyone in your life works on a psychic hotline, you're in trouble.

In my last book, *Destructive Relationships*, I gave an example of a time when I stood up for myself and changed the entire dynamic of my relationship with my brothers.

I have three brothers—two older and one younger—and their idea of "boy bonding" used to include making fun of or upsetting me. It's strange enough to think about young kids doing this, but we're talking about people in their twenties and thirties! They'd come to my home and make jokes about me and items I collect—primarily teapots and other tea items—and occasionally they would even break one. I'd express my displeasure in a jokey kind of way (not wanting to look too aggressive, mind you), then I'd excuse myself and go into my room for some reason. In privacy, I'd call them all sorts of nasty names and vow that I'd never invite those mean boys to my home ever again! Of course, when it was time for them to leave—after they'd eaten my food and enjoyed my high-tech toys—we'd make plans for them to return. Yes, it was sick, I'll give you that one.

Anyway, one day I must have been PMS-ing, because when my brother Barry made a snide comment, instead of laughing nervously along with the rest of the boys, I looked him in the eyes and said (very innocently and with great curiosity), "Wow, that was a cruel comment. I'm wondering why you felt like you needed to say that to me."

Well, my gal pal, you could have heard a pin drop! Barry looked at me and said, "What?" I repeated my question and just continued to look at him. At this point, my other two brothers were fading away left and right. Barry looked nervous—his posse was disappearing, and I was challenging him. He asked, "Where's the TV remote? The game's going to start soon."

At this point, I was actually enjoying this exchange, and I replied, again very nicely, "I'll get it for you in a minute, as soon as you answer my question."

He was getting more uncomfortable by the minute, but I didn't let him off the hook. He asked, "Umm, what was your question?"

"I said that you made a cruel comment to me, and I'm just wondering why you felt like you needed to do that," I answered.

He stared at his feet for a minute, and with my other brothers listening—from across the room—he said very quietly, "I really don't know why I said it."

Now was my moment! I could have lambasted him or really stuck it to him, but I was the bigger person. I just wanted to make the point that I have feelings and he couldn't continue to use and abuse me. I was going to make him account-able for his actions, so I said, "That was an honest answer. I appreciate that. Just don't do it anymore, OK?"

He was still staring at his feet and quickly mumbled, "OK."

"No, Barry, I really mean it. None of you can treat me that way anymore. It's mean, and I don't deserve it."

After a pause to let it sink in, I gave him the remote and told all of them to have fun. Then I slipped away into my room to let out the shaking I didn't want any of them to see, mop up the perspiration from under my arms, and congratu-late myself!

That was the turning point in my relationship not only with my broth-ers—with whom I now have a completely respectful relationship—but with myself. From that day forward, I didn't allow anyone else to abuse me again.

What I said to my brothers was so simple yet so powerful. All I did was hold them accountable for what they said to me. What was wrong with that?

Here is the grand point of this long story: your right not to be verbally or emotionally battered is more important than another's desire to verbally and emotionally batter you! Doesn't that make simple sense?

Here are two nice-girl ways of saying no that are very easy:

1. If you are a reflexive yesser—by that I mean you say "yes" to anything any-one asks you to do right away and then either resent yourself or them later—you can say this: "Let me think about that and get back to you." Easy, huh? All you've done is request the right to think about it. What's so wrong with that? If you are being asked by an unusually abusive person, he might say, "Well, when will that be?" to which your sweet reply could simply be, "After I've thought about it. Then I'll get back to you." This response usu-ally so unnerves abusers that they just say OK and then go ask someone they know who will say yes reflexively.

2. The second nice-girl way of saying no when you really do mean it is this: "Thanks for thinking of me, but I won't be able to do it this time." How about that one? You've actually thanked them, you sweet thing! You're still not going to do what they've asked, because you don't want to, but you've been so nice about saying no that they are a little flustered. The keys here are

to say it nicely and not to be apologetic. Notice that I didn't begin the sentence with "I'm sorry but ..." What do you have to be sorry about? You have every right to refuse the request.

Remember, if you are truly fearful that the person making the request will dump you as a friend or think ill of you just because you exercised your reasonable right to refuse a request, you will need to do some thinking about two things: your friend's character and your own desperation.

You have a perfect right to stand up for yourself and to hold others accountable for their cruel actions against you or your children. Why are their rights to abuse you more important than your self-respect? If they would ditch you for that, you will need to look at the quality of their true character. That may be a painful exercise in seeing how much they actually disrespect you and how narcissistic they are.

You will also want to look at how desperate you are to have people in your life ... any people. If your friends treat you this way, then perhaps you are one of the millions in this world who believe that it is more important to have the illusion of friends—even though they treat you like slime—than dump them and risk being "friendless" for fifteen minutes while you regroup and cultivate true and caring friends. As I mentioned earlier, the term *abusive friend* is an oxymoron. Family members who treat you like this are doing so because they are following your example of the way you treat yourself. If you treat yourself so carelessly and with such disregard, why shouldn't they? Once you stand up for yourself—in a loving and caring way—you are showing them a different and healthy way to treat you. They will respect you so much more than they ever have.

TO THE RESCUE!

Let's look at your rescuing/helping tendencies realistically for a moment. If you stopped helping and enabling all the abusers in your life, what would happen? You may be thinking that I'm asking what would happen to them? Nope; I mean, what would happen to you? You see, I already know what would happen to them: they would be perfectly fine. I'm wondering what your life would be like if you weren't the good little helper to everyone in it. What would you do? How would you fill your time? How would you have evidence that you were a good person? Would they continue to value you and want you in their lives if you didn't do everything for them and rescue them from all the terrible and ridiculous mistakes they make?

This sounds pretty harsh, I know. But let's look at your altruistic tendencies another way: you're a narcissist. Ouch! You are actually using all this help for your own good. It allows you to feel superior to those people for the time being—after all, they need you and would be such failures without your expertise—and it's a handy way of distracting you from your own feelings of helplessness and inadequacy. Yes, yes, I know that the other person feeling better is a nice side benefit, but it is not the true source of the desire to caretake.

Think of the feeling of power and control you get when you help another person. I'm not saying that all helping behaviors are bad and insidious, just that there is a payoff for you, as well. Your action is not completely altruistic.

Enabling and rescuing are actually very damaging, not only to you but also to those you feel you must help. You do not teach personal responsibility, empowerment, or consequences for behavior when you rescue people. You are not allowing them to do things on their own, which leaves them feeling inadequate, defective, and dependent. You are not allowing them to grow as people, which oftentimes come at a price. Sometimes, that price is that the people in your life mess up, have to take responsibility, and receive consequences for their behavior. In effect, you are stealing from them and inhibiting them from learning lessons involving about how to go into the world successfully. Now, why would you want to do that?

You may be helping and rescuing to cover feelings of shame and guilt—which is the most common unconscious reason—and therefore no one can see you as you really feel you are: shamed, defective, and flawed. It is far more important for you to get a handle on those personal feelings than to continue to rescue others, which is essentially trying to control the three things that are out of your control.

WHAT HAS IT COST YOU?
WHAT WOULD HAPPEN IF YOU STOPPED RESCUING?

You know now that acting as a rescuer is unhealthy for both you and the person you are attempting to rescue. Not only that, but when you rescue someone once or twice, you essentially set yourself up for a full-time job helping that person out of the many scrapes they seem to become involved in. You make yourself indispensable and are people-pleasing at the same time. What a powerful one-two punch!

I'd like for you to think about people or situations in your life in which you feel compelled to help—often to the detriment of your own time, energy, and feelings. I will give you some examples and then some questions to answer:

- If I don't run the church bake sale, it won't get done. The pastor has asked me, and they are really in a bind!

- My son left his lunch at home again today. He does this at least once a week, but I'm his mother, and it's part of my responsibility. I couldn't bear the guilt if I knew he went hungry today.

- My husband came home from a night of poker with the boys and was so drunk that he has a hangover this morning. I'd better call his boss and tell him he's sick … again.

- My mother is such a drama queen! Once again, she made a horrible scene at the department store when she tried to return some shoes that she'd worn for three months. They wouldn't take them back, and now she's asked me to do it for her. If I don't, I'll have to hear about this for the next year.

- My daughter and her girlfriends constantly have little tiffs and a weird on-again/off-again relationship. Today one of the other girls hurt her feelings, and I think I should call the girl's mother and talk to her. She's thirteen years old. Will this ever end?

Here are the questions:

- In which instances am I most likely to overextend myself?

- What sort of things do others ask me for?

- What feelings do these requests bring up for me?

- What will happen I don't comply with these requests?

- How would I feel if I didn't help this time?

- Would the person I usually help desert or insult me if I didn't help?

- If so, what would that say about the quality of our relationship?

Try to answer these questions as honestly and logically as possible. I understand that this is difficult, given your emotional investment in this topic. Remember, there is nothing wrong with being helpful, as long as it's for the right reasons, you are not constantly rescuing the same person, and they are equally helpful to you in times of true need.

RELATIONSHIPS WITHOUT BOUNDARIES

Boundaries are crucial to emotional well-being. When I see patients for the first time, one of the items I assess right off the bat is their ability to set and maintain healthy boundaries. When women are in unhealthy relationships, I find that, almost without fail, their boundaries are unclear or mushy. They may try to set them but allow others to infiltrate and destroy them.

When you decide to become emotionally healthier, one of the most important steps is to set boundaries with all those around you. A boundary is an invisible line that you do not allow others to cross. It separates you from them. If you are having some difficulty with this idea, let me elaborate by giving you examples of what it looks like when you give up your own boundaries in a relationship. You

- are unclear about your own preferences;

- alter your behavior, plans, or opinions to fit the current moods or circumstances of another (i.e., you live reactively to another person);

- do not notice your own unhappiness, since pleasing is your main concern;

- do more and more for less and less;

- are satisfied if you are coping and surviving;

- take as truth the most recent opinion you have heard;

- are manipulated by flattery so that you lose objectivity;

- make exceptions for behaviors you would normally not tolerate;

- try to create intimacy with a narcissist;

- act out of compliance and compromise;

- see the other person as causing your happiness or excitement;

- feel hurt and victimized but not angry with the other person;

- do things you really don't want to—you cannot say no;

- frequently become involved in dramas that are beyond your control or don't involve you personally;

- don't have a bottom line;

- often feel afraid and confused;

- commit yourself for as long as the other person needs you to be committed.

When you allow others to violate your boundaries, you are not only being unkind to yourself, you are teaching others to disrespect you. Every woman should have a line that cannot be crossed emotionally and physically.

You may have seen yourself in many of the examples listed above. It is time to ask yourself what would happen if you established boundaries with those you care about and help them—and yourself—become accountable for sticking to those boundaries.

I constantly set and model boundaries for my patients. For example, on my office voice mail I have an outgoing message stating that I may not return patients' calls received after seven thirty in the evening on weekdays, and at any time on weekends, until the next business day; so if they are having an extreme emergency, they should hang up and call 911. Why do I do this? Firstly, because I am entitled to a personal home and family life. After seven thirty, my time is devoted to my family and to myself. We all deserve this. On the weekends, the same holds true. Secondly, I am teaching my patients to control their desire to depend on me all the time. I strongly believe in my patients' own abilities to be resourceful and make good decisions for themselves. If I didn't, I wouldn't be a good therapist. Thirdly, not every little problem requires my immediate help, although the patients may think differently. I would rather they either sit with the discomfort of their problem for an evening and see that they will survive, or use that time to come to their own conclusions. I believe I am demonstrating the very methods I am trying to teach them in their own lives. Do all my patients like this policy? No, not at all, and many initially rail against it. I do not make exceptions for them. I give them the same reasons I just gave you, and based on that information, they can decide to seek therapy elsewhere or not. Either way, my boundary is clear, and I do not allow them to infiltrate and destroy it. I think I am showing good therapeutic and life skills by not being at their beck and call twenty-four hours each day. Hopefully, they take this example and use it in their own lives.

I encourage you to think about the ideas we talked about in this chapter. I know it was a lot to grasp at once. Take your time, reread the chapter, and practice these concepts slowly. You will quickly find that while they are initially difficult, uncomfortable, and frightening, they will soon become second nature.

When that occurs, either all of your relationships will become healthier or you will make a decision that they aren't worth keeping as they are. You will also develop new relationships deserving of the new you! Either way, you will have taken an important step: you will have broken your abusive relationship pattern.

21

Becoming Your Own Good Parent

I don't remember the exact moment it hit me; I know it was two years ago, but I can't recall why it happened when it did. I just remember thinking to myself, "My mother is never going to be the mother I wanted or needed. I have to stop pretending that it will happen."

I was in the middle of a nasty divorce and was feeling lousy, just because anyone who has a heart feels lousy when they are going through a divorce, no matter what the circumstances are. It's still sad that you had to do it, you know? So, I was telling my mother how bad I was feeling—mistakenly hoping once again that she would understand and offer some support—when she stopped me cold in my tracks and said, "Oh for God's sake, stop whining. What do you want? You're the one who wanted that divorce, not him. He would have done anything to keep you. He was a good man, and I told you that time and time again. But, as usual, you didn't listen to me. I told you good men were hard to find, especially for women your age and with your looks. And now look what you've done. You regret it; too bad—you should have listened to me. He'll find a woman who appreciates him."

Can you believe a mother would say that to a daughter who was feeling horrible? Not only didn't she offer her support, not only did she blame me, but she also defended him. She doesn't even know the real guy, only what he shows her. She never believed anything I told her about him during the marriage when I was once again looking for her support. She didn't care or believe that he was cheating on me. Yes, he found lots of other women who appreciated him, that's for sure. He was killing my soul, humiliating me, lying to me about everything. Oh, I could go on and on. He was a beast.

But, in spite of everything, I still wish that he could have changed and appreciated what he had and that we could have had a good marriage. He didn't want to do any of that, so we're getting divorced, and now he's trying to screw me!

So, now that I think about it, I guess the moment I realized my mother wasn't ever going to be my mommy was when I got rid of my abusive husband. I decided it would be pointless to kick him out and then allow my mother to continue to abuse me. I wasn't going to rely on her to be my mother anymore, just as I wasn't going to rely on him to be my husband. Does that make sense? He was my most important relationship, and I was letting the dream of him go; why not my dream of having a mother, as well?

Since then, I've continued to speak to her. I just don't give her any information. With Dr. Murray's help, I've learned how to reparent myself—and be a good parent at that. I was always afraid to have kids, because I was afraid I'd be a mother like my mother was to me. How else would I know how to mother? Well, I've found out that I can be a pretty good mom to myself, and maybe there will be a future for me that includes a child.

My life is much more peaceful. I draw boundaries with my mother, and when she violates them, I hang up or leave. I don't let her cross my lines. I still wish that I could have had a good mother. I think I deserved one, but I can't change the past. I can only move forward.

—Nancy, age thirty-five

Do you share Nancy's story? Many of us have been scarred by uncaring, inept, selfish, narcissistic, neglectful, substance-abusing, or critical parents. Maybe they didn't know how to parent because they weren't shown a good model, either. In our parents' day, you had kids because that's what you did when you got married. There was really no decision about it. So what did you do if you didn't know how to parent or you really never wanted to in the first place? You could read Dr. Spock books, but there were no television shows teaching parenting, no mass quantity of parenting books, no Internet support groups, no mommy-and-me classes, or anything else of the sort. You just did it.

As you've seen in the previous chapters of this book, the images you grew up with were critically important to the woman you've become. Since self-esteem is such a big part of an abusive relationship, the fact that you may not have been given the opportunity to develop a positive regard for yourself as a child and younger woman directly relates back to your parents and what they owed you.

You can't do anything about that now. You cannot change who your parents were or who they continue to be. You don't have control over that aspect of your life. You do have perfect control, however, over the way you choose to think, act, and react to this knowledge today.

You may not have been parented in the way you deserved. We know for sure that Nancy was, and continues to be, parented in a cruel manner. You are still parented by your mother and father. It doesn't matter if you are seventy years old. If your parents are still on this Earth, they continue to parent you in some form or another, if only by virtue of the fact that they are your parents.

I recall a truly sweet story that my mother told me about twenty years ago. She and her father went to a movie. At the time, he was in his late eighties, and my mother was in her early sixties. He went to the ticket office and said, "One adult and one child, please" and handed the ticket person the appropriate amount of money for two such tickets. The employee looked around for a small child and, not seeing one, asked where the child was. My grandfather pointed to my mother, whereupon the ticket person began chuckling and said, "Sir, that woman is an adult. You'll have to buy an adult ticket for her." In all sincerity, my grandfather protested, "But she's *my* child." It's difficult to argue with that logic, and they saw the movie as adult and child.

If you didn't receive the parenting you deserved or required for good emotional health, you can correct that now. You cannot correct the unhealthy parenting you received, but you can reparent yourself in a healthy way, so that you feel loved and nurtured by yourself.

WHERE ARE THE EMOTIONAL HOLES IN YOUR CHILDHOOD?

When you think about your childhood, what seems to be missing for you? What do you resent, regret, or hold onto that you didn't receive? What are the missing elements that you believe would have left you feeling whole? Maybe some of the following apply to you:

- Feeling accepted for who I was

- Feeling known

- Not being compared to my brothers, sisters, cousins, or other children

- Being listened to

- Not feeling like a bother

- Feeling special

- Feeling cared about

- Not being humiliated or yelled at

- Feeling loved

- Being respected even though I was a kid

- Not feeling stupid

- Not being labeled

- Being physically taken care of

- Not being neglected

- Feeling like my parents cared I was alive

- Not feeling lonely

- Not being given more responsibility than I could handle at my age

- Not being my mother or father's confidante

- Not having to choose sides

- Not having to worry if they were OK

- Not feeling scared all the time

- Not having to pretend I was someone else

- Not being able to be vulnerable and share with them

- Feeling supported

- Not having to feel bad for who I was

- Not feeling that everything I did was wrong

This is just a partial list of the way you may feel. I'm sure you have your own unique wishes for the parenting you didn't receive.

What can you do about that now? You can take the items on your list and show them to yourself. By this I mean that if you didn't feel accepted for the person you were as a child, you may continue to be unaccepting of yourself. How can you change that by being your own good parent?

- You can stop complaining about the size of your hips. Now you're the one berating you.

- You can look at yourself in the mirror and say, "Those hips are wider because I'm a woman, not a little boy," or, "Those hips grew wider because I was performing the greatest feat of mankind: I was growing a child," or, "Those are the magnificent hips that I carried my babies on," and so on.

- You can look at new pants in lovely, slinky fabrics that glide sensuously over those hips.

Do you see what I'm saying? If you felt unaccepted by your parents, or if they told you that you weren't good enough exactly the way you were, you don't need to continue to feed that process. You felt dishonored then and resent it now, so why would you continue to be unaccepting of yourself? You can reparent yourself. You can tell yourself in a hundred different ways what's great about you.

If you felt that you weren't listened to as a child, or that no one cared how you felt or what you said, you may have just given up. Now is your opportunity to speak up. You can write letters to your congressperson and state your opinion. You can look in the mirror and pretend to tell anyone you want exactly how you feel. You can write your thoughts down in your journal. You can write letters to the editor of your local newspaper or a national magazine about an article that either inspired or enraged you. You can talk until you're blue in the face. Lots of people care about your opinion.

A word of caution: those people may not be the people you wish cared about your opinion. The people who care the most may be complete strangers. Can you deal with that? Remember, you don't have the ability to control others, so if they didn't care when you were a child, and they didn't care when you were seventeen, and they didn't care when you were twenty-eight, and they still didn't care yesterday, it doesn't look very likely that they will care today. Why do you need to pin all your hopes and dreams and especially your opinion about yourself on them? Lots of other people care! Instead of looking at those who cannot or will not care and forming your life around them, look to others—even if they are strangers—instead.

And, while we're at it, why not look inside? What do *you* think of yourself? Are you worth being listened to? Are you worth being cared about and loved? Should you neglect or label yourself? Do you have to feel scared? Do you have to feel that you're not enough just as you are? Of course not. You have a choice now. You're the parent!

You've probably heard children tell other children, "You're not the boss of me!" Hey, guess what? They're right. No one is the boss of you except you! Your abusive mate is not the boss of you. Your parents are not the boss of you. Your friends and kids are not the boss of you. Your boss is not even the boss of you! You are.

You can begin giving yourself different messages about who you are and who you'd like to become. You can celebrate your specialness and the things that make you the most fabulous woman—bar none—on this planet.

I'm sorry your parents didn't do this for you. It helped mess up a good portion of your life, especially your relationship life. But you're the mommy now. Your little child is a newborn. She's just beginning her life and needs your guidance. What are you going to tell her about who she is?

ACTIVITY
AFFIRMING YOURSELF

In her book *Verbal Abuse Survivors Speak Out On Relationship and Recovery,* Patricia Evans discusses the importance of affirmations. These are sentences and ideas that you can repeat to yourself during the day until they become part of your consciousness and help you believe in yourself. Repeating these affirmations is a way of reparenting yourself. I've extracted several that I think may apply to you below:

• I can do something special for myself today.

• The Creative Force supports me in discovering new things about myself.

• What others say and do has nothing to do with me.

• I remember to say "Stop it" to all abuse.

• The moment I hear anything hurtful, I speak up quickly and very firmly.

• I am growing more and more able to say no and yes to what I don't want and what I do want.

• When I act in accordance with what is true, the universe, which is always true, supports me.

• I do not let fear and doubt stop or dissuade me.

• I protect myself from dangerous and toxic people and situations by avoiding them.

• I listen carefully to my gut feelings, my intuition, and my consciousness, which tells me who and what to trust and not to trust.

- I am more and more aware of myself.

- I bring like-minded people around me.

- I make better and better choices every day.

- I have the courage and strength to actualize my intentions.

- No matter how badly I feel, I can act to improve my situation.

- Today I let go of the past and focus my thoughts on a creative project or uplifting idea.

- Watered by tears and fed with truth, my spirit revives.

- My good choices in the present make my "good luck" in the future.

- I am more valuable than diamonds or gold, so I protect myself accordingly.

- I do not have to explain myself to anyone.

- Wherever I have missed the mark, I forgive myself.

- I do more each day to meet my own goals.

- I know that I can ask for assistance.

- I refuse to let self-doubt stop me.

- I face the unknown with confidence.

- I know that I can live with uncertainty, because change is the constant of the universe.

- I am choosing for my happiness and tranquility.

- I feel a warm and protective blanket wrapped entirely around my heart.

- I have great respect for myself and the work of my soul.

- I surround myself with people who radiate positive energy and are secure, calm, and strong.

After reading these affirmations, select seven of them that relate to reparenting yourself with love and nurturance. Each day in the coming week, choose one of the seven, and repeat it aloud several times. You should do this exercise with as much peace as possible, at a time when you and your home are quiet. It may be in the shower or bath, while you are brushing your hair or teeth, or when you get into or out of bed. Try to quiet all outside noise and personal thoughts, and concentrate on what the affirmation means to you that day. What feelings does it bring up? How can the wisdom of the affirmation help guide you in your day's journey? What can you do differently that day to respect and honor the affirmation?

When you have taken in that affirmation for the entire day, choose another one the next day, and repeat the exercise. It is a very powerful exercise in becoming your own good parent, because your intention is choosing your feelings and your path.

In a short time, you will find that you have not only become the woman you want to be but also the parent you deserve to have.

22

The Temptation to Go Back to Him If You Are Broke or Feel Lonely and Scared

I felt so proud of myself that I left. It was such a hard decision, and it took six years to make it. But I saw that things were just getting worse and worse, and the kids were old enough to know what was going on. I felt so guilty about that. I have to be honest: if I didn't have the kids, I might have toughed it out with Randy and hoped for him to get the awakening I'd been hoping for. I could have made a separate life for myself while being married to him. It wouldn't have been the best marriage, but I don't know; maybe I could have made it work.

Anyway, I was proud that I was able to make the right decision for myself and my kids and get away from Randy's cruelty. For the first couple of weeks, it was really painful. I mean, like physical pain. My body ached a lot. Maybe it was the residue of stress leaving my body. It felt almost like having the flu. The kids cried a lot and said they wanted their daddy. Since he'd never been physically abusive with them, we agreed to share legal custody, but they lived with me and visited him every other weekend and saw him for dinner once or twice a week. Randy travels a lot, so his schedule is unpredictable. It seemed best this way for all of us.

However, in spite of that, it felt good to come home to a house where I knew I wasn't going to be yelled at or checked up on, and all the other garbage he used to do. We had agreed that I could stay in the house with the kids until the divorce was final and we sold the house, so I knew I had at least six months to get my act together, which felt good. I was lucky.

The next few months were really difficult. The newness of the separation wore off, and the finality of my marriage really being over started to hit. Randy began being very punitive with money. He docked child support for little things and wouldn't pay for doctor's visits and camp. He was arguing over alimony and paying me late on purpose. I was strapped for money most of the time and had to deny the kids small things that we used to do, like going for a slice of pizza and renting videos. They would tell me that they wanted to live with daddy, because when they were with him, they got to do fun things.

Randy also started dating a lot and seemed to especially like one woman in particular. That really hurt. I knew we were divorcing, and this was going to happen sooner or later, but truthfully, I thought it would be a lot later. I knew he was having sex with all of them—he'd let me know in little, snide ways—and that just about killed me. It was like he was cheating on me, but he wasn't, you know? I had decided to wait at least until the divorce was final before I started casually seeing men and couldn't even imagine doing that, to be honest. I thought the longer I waited, the better it would be for the kids. I didn't want them to feel like my time or attention was divided or that I took my marriage to their father lightly. I just didn't think dating would be right. To my horror, they liked the woman Randy was seeing more seriously. They liked her a lot, and I heard them ask him over the phone if she could come along when they saw him on a weekend visit. That crushed me.

I started feeling lonely, thinking that maybe I had made a bad decision. Then I realized that I had made the right decision but that my ego was hurt because he was going on with his life as if I had never been in it.

Joey, my son, started acting up and getting mouthy with me. He was angry with me, I know. Haley, my daughter, stopped talking to me and told me that I didn't know anything about how she was feeling. They acted perfectly nicely with their dad, so I know it was about me; they blamed me for the divorce. My friends told me that they took their feelings out on me instead of Randy because they felt safer with me. I understood that, but it still felt bad.

I gained twelve pounds in the first six months we were apart, while Randy looked better than ever. That wasn't fair. The kids would tell me about how nice he was to the other women, and that just leveled me. I figured that he was right all along: there was something wrong with me, not him. After all, if he could be nice to them but not me, there must have been something wrong with me.

I felt lonely, scared, bitter, and broken, and I didn't know what I was going to do with my life. That lasted about nine months, until the kids told me Randy was going to buy a new, big house with the proceeds of the sale of our old house, and they could come live with him if they wanted … and they wanted! They told me that they thought they'd be doing me a favor since I was always so upset. It would make my life easier. Wow, that was a shocker.

I had to get in gear. I had no idea my life had sunk so low that my own kids could see the pain and wanted to get away from it.

I hadn't really worked, except small, part-time jobs, in the last four years. I had to get back into the job place, so I consulted a career counselor, who tested me for all sorts of jobs and sent me off for training. Now I was going to school two nights a week, which is when the kids were either with their dad or at friends' homes. It was hard to go back to school, but it also felt good. Suddenly, I had a purpose and a reason to get my mind to work. I also developed a little social network. A group of us would go out for coffee afterward, and believe me, I could barely afford that, so I'd just sit and nurse my coffee and chat for an hour. They were mostly women like me who were going back to work after a breakup, and we had a lot in common.

One of the women had a large house she couldn't afford to keep up on her own, so we decided that the kids and I would move in with her and share expenses. It worked out beautifully. She had a son who was two years older than Joey and another one who was two years younger than Haley, and actually they all got along well. She only lived six miles from my old home, so the kids were able to stay in their old school and be near their father. We shared child care, and it was like having a sister. I never would have imagined myself in this type of housing situation before, but I love it.

Some of her friends became my friends. We both agreed to go on a diet-and-exercise program together and corralled two other women to do it with us, so that was actually fun.

Today, it's been a little over a year since the separation. I still miss being married, but I don't miss being married to Randy. I haven't started dating yet. It still doesn't feel right, but I do have male friends and enjoy that. The kids are still adjusting to this new life. They went to a few sessions of counseling, and that seems to have helped them cope better. I started a part-time job, which is fine. I don't feel confident enough yet in my skills to do much more than I'm doing, but I know I'll get there.

I have faith and patience that my life will work out the way it should. At least I have a peaceful home now, which I never had. I've lost most of my weight and am feeling better about myself. I never thought I'd be a single working mom with two kids, but here I am. I'm doing the best I can.

—**Valerie, age thirty-nine**

Women sometimes ask me how long it will take for them to feel better after a breakup. My answer is "As long as it takes." I wish I had a better reply, but the truth is that there is no magic formula. A breakup is excruciatingly painful, but I think it's supposed to be. If you spent a certain number of years with a man, shared your soul, your spirit, your body, and your dreams, made memories, and maybe had children with him, you'd be cold and heartless if you could leave it all behind you with a Queen Elizabeth wave of your hand. Ta-ta to all that!

My very good friend and "sister," Myra Gordon—who was formerly a therapist—listened to me whine and whimper all the way through my divorce and told me, "At the five-year mark, you'll write him a thank-you letter." I found that unbelievable. Five years later I would actually be thankful for my marriage to my first husband and also thankful for the divorce? As always, she was right. But let me tell you, many days of those five years were no picnic.

Almost without exception, women who have escaped abusive relationships feel lonely and scared after they leave, many for quite some time. If your abuser is financially punitive—as almost every single one is—you may also find yourself in a pickle money-wise. That adds to the fear and doubt—and sheer panic—that you may already be feeling.

When you have lived in a constant state of emotional crisis and are riding the abuse roller coaster, you get used to drama and trauma. Your stress and adrenaline levels are almost always elevated. On any given day, there is always something you must do immediately. Your life is chaotic, but that's how you are used to living day to day.

When you are able to escape this chaos, you may think that because your life is now your own, it will run smoothly and peacefully. Maybe it does and will. However, almost immediately these negative feelings may—and probably will—surface.

What're you to do with these inevitable feelings? Prepare for them so that you are not shocked when they appear and will know how to get through these hard times with the understanding that you will survive.

COPING WITH LONELINESS

When you are in an abusive relationship, oftentimes you actually feel exquisitely lonely but may not realize that's what you are feeling. Although you may have a man in your home, the pervasive feeling of being alone and lonely is crushing. You may even mistrust your own feelings. "How can I feel alone when he is here? I must be crazy!" Feeling alone when you are in a romantic relationship is perhaps the loneliest place on Earth. You may have been so caught up in daily chaos that you haven't noticed how alone you are.

You've been alone for a long time; you've just been alone with someone else in the room. Does that make sense to you? Many women understand this intellectually, but there is still some amount of comfort knowing that they are not alone in their home, or that they are not alone with their children.

You will need to take stock of your own messages. As I previously stated, are you really telling yourself that a body—any body, no matter how badly that body is treating you—is preferable to no body at all? Osama bin Laden could be sitting in that La-Z Boy, and that would be better than an empty recliner? Do you hear how that sounds? OK then, let's get the idea out of your head that your abuser in your home would make you feel less lonely than you do now. The fact is, your man was a terrorist. He mistreated you and stole from you. His presence in your home is not preferable to that of your own heart and soul. The chaos and heartbreak he creates with his presence is not better than peace and quiet—even if it's too much quiet—in your home.

But you are lonely; I do understand that completely. Weekends can be especially difficult. Evenings can be hard. Going to bed and being the only one in it can be painful.

Let's make a plan for what you can do when you feel lonely, or better yet, in advance of your feeling lonely. If you are an introspective sort, you can look forward to quiet time to think about your life and make positive plans for your future. You can do this while eating your meals alone, or if you have children, you can look forward to doing this in a warm bath after they go to bed. Make sure that you don't drown in introspection and trying to find to the reasons why your relationship fell apart. Do not ruminate and marinate in "what did I do wrong" questions. The fact is that he is an abuser and he refused to change, which made it impossible for you to be with him any longer. That's the whole story.

Can you make plans with friends for the times when you know you will feel most lonely? Can you talk with at least two people per day who are healthy and who make you feel better—rather than worse—about your decision? These would be people who don't ask too many questions about your relationship, who respect your privacy, who aren't interested in gossip, and who have good boundaries. While it may initially make you feel better to verbally slam your former mate at every opportunity, it may end up backfiring on you later. You may be known as the gal who's a mental case and can't move on or stop talking about her guy. Or, for people who don't understand the dynamics of abuse, you may be known as the woman who was being treated so vilely but refused to leave. Others don't have a right to the details of your life, and I don't recommend sharing them with everyone you meet, either.

Make sure that you initiate plans for yourself several times per week, whether they are spending time with others or tackling home projects that give you a feeling of accomplishment. Maybe you always wanted to plant an herb garden, but with all the chaos he caused you, there was never a good time. Now there is. Or perhaps there is a closet you've wanted to organize, or you've decided to paint your bedroom a girly color now that you don't have to share it with a man. You can spend a whole weekend making or shopping for new pillow shams!

If your loneliness seems to be causing you to change your eating and sleeping habits, please pay attention to this. After your breakup, you may not feel very hungry, or you may find that you can't get a good night's sleep. This is normal for a week or so, but if you have the following symptoms every day for two weeks or more, please consult your doctor, as these are signs of depression:

• A change in eating habits (either poor appetite or overeating)

- No pleasure in activities you used to enjoy or no pleasure in anything at all (also known as *anhedonia*)

- A change in sleeping habits (either sleeping too much or not enough)

- A feeling of agitation or listlessness

- A feeling of constant fatigue or loss of energy

- Not being able to think clearly or concentrate and focus

- Feelings of worthlessness or hopelessness

- Recurrent thoughts of suicide without a specific plan

It is normal to feel depressed after such a significant loss, but if these symptoms do not clear up, and you feel this way every day, I encourage you to seek help. Many times, loneliness and depression go hand in hand. The more depressed you become, the more you isolate yourself from others. Conversely, loneliness and isolation are very depressing, so this is a vicious circle that only you can break.

This period of loneliness can be very scary for many women who do not see any light at the end of the tunnel. They may think that there is no hope of breaking out of this feeling, that they are destined to be alone and miserable, or that they made a terrible mistake by leaving. Again, these feelings are normal; if you are able to understand that and make small, positive actions for yourself, you will immediately feel somewhat better. The more often you do them, the better you will feel.

WHAT TO DO WITH THE MONEY FEAR

When I was in the process of considering divorce, I told my therapist about my enormous fear of being a bag lady. I saw myself living under a bridge with my children in an empty refrigerator box, wearing gloves without fingers (which would be highly unlikely since we live in southern California and you can't buy gloves to save your life, even in the winter). I was paralyzed by the fear of being without money. My former husband was an attorney, and we had a fairly comfortable lifestyle. I *had* to stay! This wise woman told me in a very quiet and calm voice, "You'll make your own money." What? Where did she get her shrink degree? The woman had to be crazy! I was married to a lawyer, I hadn't really worked too much outside the home for years, and she was telling me that I was going to be fine financially, because somehow—in a parallel universe—I'm going to make enough money to quell my fears of living with fingerless gloves. Uh, no ...

She ended up reassuring me of this fact several times with the calm of someone who had already seen the future, and this was it. While I still didn't believe her, I did end up ending the marriage. I lowered my lifestyle, went to graduate school, got my degree, studied for and received my therapy license, opened a practice, wrote some books, started giving presentations around the globe and appearing on television and radio shows. Huh? Wait, how did all that happen? All of a sudden, I was making my own money, just as she had said. But I'd never taken sole care of myself before. What happened?

I believed in myself.

Yes, it really was that simple. I'd like to tell you that it was some secret recipe, but it wasn't. I just decided to believe 100 percent in myself and the abilities I was sure would soon become apparent if I looked hard enough. I decided that I'd make a really outrageous plan for myself, fake it till I made it, work really hard at the plan, not allow for the possibility of failure, and just see what happened. I was my own science experiment, if you want to know the truth.

I remember telling my then friend—now husband—Frank just after my divorce, "I plan to graduate from school, get my license, have a private practice, publish books and articles, and give presentations." I actually said it with quite a bit of conviction. He didn't know me well, and anyone would have to say that those proclamations were a little far-fetched, so he asked, "What do you plan on writing books on, and what are you going to talk about in these presentations?" A reasonable question, I suppose. I answered him, "I haven't figured that much out yet. I just know I'm going to do it."

Believing strongly in yourself and making a plan go a long, long way in this world. Well, that and being just crazy enough to think you can pull it off, it seems.

For all of us who have been financially supported most of our lives, the idea of being responsible for ourselves is absolutely frightening. Not just a little scary, but *Nightmare on Elm Street* frightening. How will we do this? Will we get by? How will we feed ourselves and our children? Where will we stay? Oh my gosh, what have we done? Time to shop for fingerless gloves and search out an empty Amana box!

If you have retained legal counsel to help you, do not settle for anything less than what you and your children deserve financially. Abusers routinely punish their women with money. They make financial threats and so on, so do not entertain his ideas or listen to him ramble on about how you will be financially devastated. Turn everything over to your legal counsel. That is what they are hired to do. If he's had children with you, he will have to help provide for them. That is the law. If you were married to him and he makes significantly more money than you, he will most likely have to pay you some sort of alimony or financial settlement. It doesn't matter what he tells you or how much he threatens you. That is why I highly recommend that you not listen to him and just turn the matter over to whomever is helping you. Do not try to strike a financial deal with him on your own without your legal counsel looking at it first. Abusers are great at trying out this scam on their women. You can try to work out the financial part with him, if you need to save money on lawyer's fees, but make sure that someone else goes over the agreement with a fine-toothed comb before you sign it, no matter how much he pressures you for a quick signature. He is just manipulating you again and only has his own interests at heart. Remember, once you sign the document, you may have signed up for little to no money; and there may be no way to fight it once it's done.

Now it's time for you to take action on your own behalf and make a financial plan for yourself. Do not assume that he will support you and the children indefinitely or that he will be on time with all of his support checks. Many single mothers—and women in general—find themselves dealing with creditors, stressing about money, and living paycheck to paycheck because a former mate is absent or constantly late with support checks. If you cannot cover his shortfall on your own, you are putting yourself in great financial jeopardy. Think of his checks as a great backup, but learn to rely on yourself and your own abilities for financial security.

As we discussed in previous chapters, you will need to make a list of everything you must accomplish to either find a job, find a better job, get a promotion at your current job, or make sure you remain at your current job. Do you need training or career counseling? Should you polish up your resume? What about talking with your boss about promotion possibilities and what you would need to do in order for that to happen?

Maybe—if you are not currently working or want to make a career change—you must first find your passion. Think of what you most enjoy doing, and then get creative in your thinking about how you could possibly make that a career. Many women have begun handmade jewelry, T-shirt, cookie, fudge, and gift basket careers from their kitchen tables. Start small, and then grow your thinking. You would be surprised what creativity, ingenuity, and hard work can do for you!

There are many books on the shelves now about home-based businesses, which are wonderful for women with small children, older women who feel they can't compete in a young job market, or any woman who would like to be her own boss. I encourage you to check these out, as well.

The point is to have a plan, a goal, and a timeline for yourself. "Someday" doesn't cut it when you have rent or a mortgage to pay. Credit card companies aren't swell about you sending them an IOU with a promise to pay your balance someday. Get very clear and concise with your dreams and goals, and work at them every day. I can assure you—despite your money fears and feelings that you must return to your abuser for that reason—you, too, will make your own money.

WHAT HAS IT COST YOU?
WHAT YOU CAN DO ABOUT YOUR FEARS OF LONELINESS AND LACK OF MONEY?

As you've just read, taking concrete steps to help yourself is the best medicine there is for loneliness and fears of money loss. Taking action is one of the best cures for depression and anxiety. Get your journal out, and let's begin brainstorming.

Let's tackle loneliness first. Write down these two column headings side by side: *what I usually do when I'm lonely* and *what I can do differently when I'm lonely.*

What do you usually do now when you are feeling alone and lonely? Do you eat? Cry? Sit and ruminate over where you went wrong? Sleep? Watch *Terms of Endearment* over and over? Write everything down so that you can see your self-destructive patterns.

Now, think about what you can do differently when you are feeling blue. How about calling a friend? Praying? Reading an inspirational biography or a very engrossing book? Journaling? Taking a warm, scented bath? Exercising? Playing with your pet or your kids? Finding volunteer activities? Watching *The Shawshank Redemption* (one of my all-time favorites, with an uplifting message)? Think of all the positive things you can do that will help you out of your funk and take your spirit to a higher place. Keep this list someplace handy, and then do one of the action items each time you feel lonely. How might that make you feel?

Now, the financial piece of the project. Write down two more columns in your journal: *my biggest financial concerns* and *steps I can take to alleviate my concerns.*

Some of your biggest concerns may be things like "can't pay the rent," "can't buy clothes for the kids," "won't ever be able to go to another movie or out to lunch with my friends," "may have to accept welfare," "will be constantly worried about paying bills." Those are legitimate concerns. Let's look at what you can do about these.

Let's just say that you couldn't pay your rent. What would be the worst thing that could happen? You may have to live with someone else or in a shelter, right? Actually, neither of those is so horrible, and you won't be sporting fingerless gloves and living in an empty Amana box. What would it mean for you to live with a girlfriend or relative for two or three months until you were on your feet? Humiliating? Get over it. You are going through a difficult transition, and you're doing the best you can. Living in a shelter for a month or so certainly wouldn't be optimal, but you also wouldn't be on the street under the bridge I was saving for myself. You can deal with your pride, if you have to.

If you have to accept welfare for a few months while you train for a job, you'll need to understand that this is what you've paid taxes for all your adult life; now you are collecting on a small portion of it for a minute amount of time. You are allowed to ask for short-term assistance while you learn new skills. It's not for the rest of your life, and if you feel too proud, no one else has to know about it. Making sure that you and your children have food is more important than your pride. It's not your worst-case scenario, right? Once again, you are ahead of the game.

Again, I strongly encourage you to make a financial plan for yourself and be very specific about it. *Be, do, have*—do you remember the equation?

Be committed to a goal, do whatever is necessary to reach it, and then you'll have what you want.

It's a very simple plan that requires some direction on your part. Do remember that if you are depressed and anxious, you will need to be kinder to yourself while you make these plans, because your focus and concentration may not be sharp. Work on your plan a little bit every day. Do not overtax yourself or pressure yourself to find every answer in one day. This is a process, but not a long process. Give yourself a short time limit—perhaps two weeks—to finalize your plans. Even if you are not feeling up to snuff, you can accomplish this. Keep telling yourself that when you have completed it, you will feel much more empowered and that your hopelessness will be greatly diminished.

You can do this. It will be difficult, but I believe in you.

23

Are You Self-Abusive?

I really thought I was doing pretty well after the divorce. I had a job that I liked and had already gotten a small promotion. I found a nice place for myself and my daughter and was handling the bills and her schedule. It was hectic, but I was managing. Some days I was very tired, but I figured that was par for the course and a small price to pay for my freedom.

I don't know how it started. I think the stress started piling up, and Paul missed a couple of child-support checks. Now I was trying to make ends meet and had these horrible tension headaches most of the day. The baby had the flu, and I needed to stay home with her. I couldn't bring her to daycare when she was sick, and my mother wasn't any help. She was still mad at me for breaking up with Paul. I hadn't worked at my job long enough to accumulate sick days, so I was missing three days of pay that I couldn't afford to lose. My boss was calling, asking when I was coming back to work. It was a mess.

At first, I'd forget to eat. Later, I wasn't really hungry, so I didn't eat. I starting having a glass of wine in the evening after the baby went to sleep, and then I started having another one when she took her afternoon nap. It just sort of took the edge off the stress. Combining the alcohol with not eating wasn't good. I felt lightheaded and weak, so a friend of mine gave me these pills she uses when she doesn't have enough energy. They helped me. But then I couldn't sleep, so I was taking an over-the-counter sleep medicine. I was caught in this cycle for about eight months, and it seemed like it would never end.

I kept on having stress on top of stress. I realize now that I was creating a lot of the stress myself and getting involved with people and situations I should have kept clear of. I had this whole new group of friends from work that were younger and hipper than I was, and they created so much melo-drama. I hadn't had drama in my life since Paul left, so I just jumped onto theirs and started going to bars after work. All that junk girls in their early twenties do. The boyfriend dramas, the work dramas, the drug-and-alcohol dramas, the diet dramas: I was involved in all of it.

Eight months later, my world came crashing down when my daughter came crashing out of her high chair—because I wasn't watching her; I was having a glass of wine and talking on the phone with one of the work drama queens—and hit her head on the corner of a step. Blood was gushing everywhere, and at first she was screaming, but then she stopped. I rushed over to her but couldn't keep my own bearings, and I fainted. I don't think I'd eaten anything that day and had been doing a little drinking and had popped an upper for energy. There we both were, passed out on the floor.

Fortunately, Paul came over to pick the baby up for their visit and found us. We'd probably be dead if he hadn't. He rushed us both to the hospital emergency room, and the rest is a pretty nasty story.

She was taken away from me for almost a year while I went to drug-and-alcohol classes along with personal therapy. Happily, Paul was able to take her; otherwise she would have been in foster care, which I wouldn't have been able to handle. I could only see her under supervision; I wasn't allowed to be alone with my own child. I can understand the reasons now, but I was really crushed then.

I'm better now and have moved forward with my life. It was so scary for me to see how horrible that whole time was and what I was capable of doing to myself and my child. It was definitely worse than anything Paul had done to me while we were married.

—Jesse, age thirty

As I've mentioned before, almost without exception, the women I've seen in my therapy practice who have been in abusive relationships become self-abusive in some way once they are free of the abuse by their partner.

It seems difficult to imagine that this could occur. They've worked so hard to leave the relationship and do better for themselves only to become abusers themselves? To themselves? Haven't they already suffered enough abuse?

I want to share a very important concept with you that I've come to understand almost as a universal truth: sometimes, the most abusive relationship we have is with ourselves.

Drama and trauma as a way of life can become addictive. There is always something to take care of, someone to save, a tragedy to manage. What do you do with all the peace and quiet? Who is going to abuse you now? When there is no one left in your life who can abuse you, I guess the only one left is yourself.

I typically see several types of self-abuse in women who have left abusive relationships:

- Substance use—drugs and alcohol

- Self-injury—self-mutilation (e.g., cutting); hair-pulling (eyebrows, eyelashes, pubic hair, hair on the head, etc.)

- Eating disorders—too much or too little or bulimia; and compulsive behaviors—shopping, sex, gambling

- Neglect of health

- Creation of chaos and drama

Let's look at these problems briefly, one by one, so that you can be well aware of the dangers they present in your life.

SUBSTANCE USE

When a woman is engaged in an abusive relationship, she quickly learns what "works" for her; that is, the way she can survive the abuse and function in her daily life. One of those coping mechanisms may be to use drugs and/or alcohol to numb her reality and her feelings.

She may have seen her mate use substances to cope—or even her parents when she was a child. Even though she may have detested the idea of them using, she may now use substances to relieve her stress and anxiety. It is not a far leap to find it useful when she's feeling lonely, the kids are acting up, a project is late at work, her ex is still abusing her from afar, and the transition from partner to ex-partner is proving difficult.

The trouble is that using drugs or alcohol as a way of escaping your life works so well and you feel so much better while you're doing it, you may decide that you have the right to feel that mellow all the time. Why shouldn't you feel good? You've been through a lot, and really, no one understands how difficult your life still is, do they? And if a drink, a pill or two, or a joint works, are you hurting anyone? Just a little bit every once in a while is OK. It's not like you're an addict, right? Then a little bit every couple of days is fine. Then, just once a day is really swell, and it still doesn't mean that you're an addict, just that you've learned to control your stress and anxiety. Too bad everyone can't be as together as you. You actually think you function better at work and as a mom, since you're so relaxed. The little things that used to bug you don't seem to have as much of an effect. Worries? Problems? Stress? Bad thoughts and feelings? That's for other people. You've got your own little secret to peace.

Aside from the obvious flaws in these arguments, substance use prevents you from seeing the reality of your life. That may seem like a great idea to you at the moment, but here's the rub: you will never do any better in life or develop more loving relationships than right now. Your emotional growth is stunted or stopped altogether, and your children suffer horrendously. As with Jesse in the story above, you may do something really stupid while under the influence and have your children taken away from you. And, if you grew up in a substance-using family, you should be a whole lot smarter than to inflict the same life you had on your own kids. You have complete control of that one.

SELF-INJURY

We hear stories about teenage girls cutting themselves. I've seen many of them in my private practice. They use knives, razor blades, paper clips, and sharp edges of anything, really. The idea behind self-injury is that the psychological pain you are feeling is greatly diminished when you cut yourself. The physical pain is much easier to bear than the pain in your soul. For some, it works for that brief moment, and they experience a feeling of calm. But then—because this type of pain is a vicious taskmaster—the feelings come back, and the overwhelming impulse to cut again arises. The blood and scars are physical manifestations of the pain that cannot be seen.

Self-injury is a serious anxiety disorder and can sometimes be indicative of even deeper, hidden trauma that has never come out, such as childhood sexual abuse. It is very compulsive and quite difficult to control on one's own. Therapy, and possibly medication, is needed to address this issue.

If you are self-injurious—whether this involves cutting yourself, pulling out your hair, or burning yourself—please get to the bottom of this serious problem. You must locate the core of your deeper anxiety, and you must learn coping and calming skills for the times when you feel the need to harm yourself. This is a problem that will not go away on its own or through willing it away. While you may stop cutting yourself or hair pulling temporarily, as with substance use, the underlying problems will still be there. Without help, you will then pick up another type of self-abusive behavior.

EATING AND OTHER COMPULSIVE BEHAVIORS

There are three types of eating compulsions: undereating, also known as anorexia, overeating, and bulimia, which is bingeing and purging. All are harmful to your mental and physical health.

Compulsive overeating is mindless and "stuffs" unpleasant feelings down. This is not to be confused with hormonal cravings for specific kinds of foods or occasionally eating half of a chocolate soufflé (did I just give away my secret?). When you use food as a coping mechanism, you feel soothed and anesthetized at the time that you are eating. You decide that you will deal with the guilt later.

You don't get to the feelings underneath the food, and you use the weight you accumulate as a shield of protection against unwelcome thoughts.

An anorexic initially uses food as a weapon of control for various reasons: to rebel against her parents' need to over-control her or their desire for perfection, to show herself that she is in charge of herself years after sexual molestation, and to quell her own self-doubts. These are just a few of the many reasons a girl or woman becomes anorexic. The paradox is that even though anorexics may be incredibly hungry, they feel proud that they can choose not to eat. Many anorexics enjoy preparing large, elaborate, gourmet meals for their families and friends without ever taking a single bite, but instead pushing their food around the plate so that it appears that they're eating. Anorexics may also exercise compulsively or use laxatives to control their weight. What began as a way of controlling their world now becomes the monster that controls them. As with singer Karen Carpenter, anorexia can lead to serious health complications and even death.

A bulimic woman eats compulsively and mindlessly, almost in a trancelike state, and then purges through throwing up or using laxatives. Again, this disorder begins as a tool of self-control to a bulimic. It seems like the perfect plan: she can eat whatever she likes and then just get rid of it soon afterward. A "good" bulimic learns to purge very quickly, quietly, and efficiently.

But bulimics don't enjoy or even taste the food they eat; they use it as a means of coping and calming themselves and defending against unpleasant feelings, such as an abusive relationship. While the woman is bingeing, she feels the illusion of calm and numbness; immediately following this, however, she feels anxious, frightened, and guilty. Bulimia is a very dangerous practice, as it severely harms the body's chemical balance and can also lead to death.

There are many compulsive behaviors that numb feelings: shopping, gambling, and sex seem to top the list with women who have been in abusive relationships. All three are designed to reduce anxiety and give you momentary excitement or the illusion of self-control when a person actually feels that she has none.

Compulsive shopping is accepted as a normal way for a woman to relieve tension and anger. If you feel lonely or bored, go to the mall. Need a little lift? Buy a couple pairs of shoes, and why not a purse to match? Did your son act up at school today? A quick trip to the Lancôme counter can work wonders. Did you just find out that your ex has a hot, new girlfriend? Why not reassure yourself that you've still got "it" at the Victoria's Secret store? These scenes of advertising dollars in action are in themselves somewhat humorous; but when shopping becomes a way out of dealing with your feelings, it's a problem.

Compulsive shoppers get a high out of buying anything and everything. They may shop aimlessly and unconsciously and may not even have a place to put all their loot. If you look at the compulsive shoppers' purchases a year later, you may find unworn shoes, tags still on clothes, and bags of unused accessories. They are ashamed of their compulsion and keep it a secret from their friends and family. They usually put themselves in financial peril, which causes even more anxiety and more shopping or other self-abusive behaviors.

Sexual acting-out is common, as well. Many women who have been in abusive relationships—especially if they were not honored sexually—may become serial daters, having sexual relationships with many men in a short amount of time. Some women have defended their actions to me by saying that they are "dating like men." While I don't believe that all men date in that manner, I would have to say that a man who has sexual relationships with, say, twenty women in a month has the same problem.

I'm not necessarily talking about someone who has a sexual addiction/compulsion here, although that is certainly possible. What I am discussing is a woman who—now out of her abusive relationship—seeks out men to reassure herself of her attractiveness and worth. The fact that they want to be sexual with her on the first date may make her feel slightly bad, but may also prove to her that they have an animal attraction to her; she's irresistible. Her ex was all wrong about her. Plenty of men want her! Having sex indiscriminately, of course, is a dangerous practice, both emotionally and physically.

Although we think of gambling as a man's compulsion, women are the new up-and-comers. With Indian gaming casinos popping up all around many states, more and more women are becoming addicted to the idea of a quick buck. Many states also have weekly lotteries, which can be a huge enticement to a woman who finds herself in financial straits. Women may be more likely than men to begin gambling as a way out of financial difficulty. The lure of winning a small amount of money quickly becomes an enticement to gamble more and more. Of course, gambling is, almost without exception, ruinous to your finances. If you never start, you won't have to slowly and painfully dig your way out of ruin. The excitement of winning a few dollars cannot match the pain and guilt of losing your children's lunch money. Understand gambling for what it is: it can be a fun way to spend a few dollars while on vacation (if you have a strict limit of how much you're willing to lose), but if you use it as a way of creating false excitement in your life to avoid looking at your problems—or if you think you can use gambling to solve financial debt—you are putting yourself in real danger.

NOT TAKING CARE OF YOURSELF

When you have been in a long-term, abusive relationship or a series of abusive relationships, your self-worth and confidence may be at an all-time low. Your partner may have told you that you are fat, ugly, stupid, lazy, and that no one would ever want you. Who cares about you?

You may have started to ignore your physical symptoms that require a doctor's attention, even though you take your children to the physician at the first sign of a sneeze.

You may not eat well, eating whatever your baby leaves on the tray of the high chair or grazing on junk food all day. You may not sleep enough and feel exhausted much of the time. You might have stopped any form of exercise and watch old movies instead. Understand that many of these behaviors are signs of depression, but when they are ongoing, they can become self-abusive as well.

If you don't feel that you are worthy of being treated kindly by yourself, keep in mind that these are your abuser's words in your head; they are patently untrue. You deserve better treatment from yourself. Remember, when you nurture yourself, you aid in your own recovery.

CREATION OF CHAOS AND DRAMA

Most women formerly in abusive relationships have difficulty in this area. Because they're used to the daily drama of abuse and the urgency it creates, it's difficult to adjust to a new, peaceful way of life. While adrenaline surges are tough on the nervous system, the body adjusts. Coming off that high, however, can be a source of difficulty.

It's not that these women consciously create chaos; it is just a way of life. It seems that there is always someone who needs rescuing. Women in abusive relationships seek out others who need their help and then overly involve themselves and feel responsible for others' well-being. They are on the inside of the office dramas and their parents' squabbles, they are their friends' confidantes and then are ordered to take sides, they find new friends who have a bushelful of problems that need constant solving, and so on.

Creating drama and chaos is unhealthy and takes you away from the state that I hope you can become accustomed to, which is quiet and calm. When you become involved in others' melodramas, you tend to forget your own problems. It's very similar to watching soap operas, except you actually have the opportunity to participate!

Involving yourself in chaos will not move you forward in your own process of healing and resolve. You will remain stuck in this spot as long as you desire drama.

WHAT HAS IT COST YOU?
HOW ARE YOU SELF-ABUSIVE?

You may have found yourself in any one or several of the self-abusive categories in this chapter. Don't worry; it's normal and natural to use self-abusive tactics in this difficult transition period. That doesn't mean that it's healthy or useful, however. Self-abuse is not something you want to continue. You want to be the champion of your own nurturance and recovery so that you don't have to suffer in any other abusive relationships again … especially with yourself.

Get out your trusty journal, and let's do some thinking about the ideas in this chapter. On one sheet of paper, write *my self-abusive behaviors*. On another sheet of paper, write *what I'm trying to hide/cover*, and on a third sheet of paper, write *what I can do instead*. You will want the ideas you put down on each sheet to line up and match.

What self-abusive behaviors did you find fit with your life, and can you figure out what you are trying to avoid feeling by engaging in those behaviors? Here are some ideas to get you started:

My self-abusive behaviors:

- Overeating

- Compulsive shopping

- Creating chaos

- Drinking too much

- Not getting enough sleep

    What I'm trying to hide/cover:

- Stuffing my hurt feelings over my ex

- Trying to get back at him

- Wanting to feel worthwhile, because I feel worthless

- Trying to forget what he did to me
- Feeling lonely and scared

  What I can do instead:

- Journal my thoughts when I feel like eating and I'm not hungry
- Call a friend when I want to shop
- Tell myself that I'm not Mother Theresa, and maintain boundaries
- Exercise when I feel like numbing myself with alcohol
- Take a warm bath and massage my feet and scalp until I drift off to sleep
- Do a good deed for a stranger

PART VI

MOVING FORWARD HOW TO BUILD NEW RELATIONSHIPS IN YOUR NEW LIFE

It's been almost six months since I broke up with Casey. Well, that's not completely accurate. It's been that long since my parents made me break up with him. I'd probably still be with him if they didn't break it off, which is now pretty scary to me. In the beginning, I hated them, and Casey and I were trying to figure out ways to sneak off together and run away. It was all pretty weird and crazy at the time. I couldn't understand why they made me break up. They were so scared for my well-being, they told me, which I thought was absolutely nuts. HE NEVER HIT ME, and I'm pretty sure they knew that, so I couldn't figure it all out. I thought they were being overly dramatic and just wanted to control me.

Now that I'm out of the relationship, and I can clearly see all the stuff he actually did do to me, it's almost harder than when I was in it. I can't believe I put up with all the obnoxious stuff he did. He made me feel like dirt a lot of the time. I didn't have many friends left and never did anything with anyone except Casey. I was always saying I was sorry, and I can't even remember why. I just wanted our relationship to be OK, and when I apologized, it made it OK again. I cried a lot. I could go on forever now, but I didn't see any of it then. I was willing to give up my family and everything I had to be with him. The relationship made me nuts; I can see that now but couldn't then.

It's still hard every day, but at least I have my friends back and my family's support. He has a new girlfriend, and that's tough to see every day at school. I don't want to date yet, because I don't want the drama and don't trust myself yet. I just want to hang out with my girlfriends again and be a teenager.
—**Becca, age sixteen**

Well, here we are at the final section of our work together. Now that you've done so much inner work, the payoff—remember, we all do whatever we do for a payoff!—is that you can now understand your inner patterns, how you began your abusive relationships, and why you've chosen to keep them in your life, and what they've cost you. You've learned how to be the captain of your own life ship, you've changed your abusive relationship patterns, you've acknowledged that separation from your male abuser—if you have decided to leave him—will be difficult but doable and ultimately rewarding, and you've also learned to reparent yourself in a kind and loving manner.

At some point, you may want to try out new and healthy relationships with both men and women. I hope that a nurturing, romantic relationship is in your future, and I'm confident that with all the difficult work you've done, it most certainly will cross your path. But first, you need to prepare yourself for that meeting of the souls.

In this section, I will want you to look at one more unpleasant idea: how to avoid becoming an abusive parent. Do you remember the last chapter, in which we talked about self-abuse? We discussed the idea that when women are used to abuse as a way of life, they often become self-abusive when there is no one around to abuse them. The same can be said of abusing children or taking out your fear and frustrations on your children. While it is not intentional, it is not outside the realm of possibility.

Then we will discuss what to look for in new and healthy relationships with both men and women, and we will teach you how to get used to these nurturing relationships. Once again, when your only relationship reference point is abuse, you may not have a clear idea what a healthy relationship looks like. When you find one, it may seem uncomfortable to you at first.

Let's face it: unless you are able to ship your ex to Siberia, you may have him in your life for some time to come. If you have children with him, you will not only need to see him, but you must also negotiate with him on many different issues concerning the kids. Because he is an abuser, he will most definitely use these occasions as opportunities to abuse you. You must learn to set boundaries and keep them, which—as you know—is very difficult with an abusive man who continues to desire power and control over you. We will talk about good strategies to make sure you are emotionally and physically safe in your encounters with him.

Finally, I'd like to send you off into your lovely, new, nonabusive life with a few thoughts and good wishes.

But first, I'd like to clue you in on a little trick I've played in my writings. You may have wondered about the interesting title of this book—as well as my first book, *But I Love Him*—both of which begin with the word *but*. The reason is this: but is an eraser word. It erases everything you said before the word but. A common example is when I explain to a woman that she's in an abusive relationship. I talk about emotional, verbal, psychological, financial, and spiritual abuse. She may contemplate all of this information and agree that all of it has happened. She will reply, "You're right; he's done so many of those things to me for years and years, BUT HE NEVER HIT ME." In effect, she has tried to erase the part of the thought in which she's agreed and acknowledged that her partner has multiply abused her and gone straight to the part in which she tells me that he's never hit her. Do you see what I mean here?

But is also a word of resistance and denial. The but in the sentence means that you are not willing to look at your situation clearly and would rather deny its true existence.

Up until this point, I can understand how you might feel a lot of resistance to my ideas and even deny the abuse to some extent. At the end of our process together, I hope that you will see your life clearly and embrace the stage of the grief-and-loss process known as acceptance a little more often than you were at the beginning.

Off you go, my friend, into this final section of our work together. I know that with these final thoughts and suggestions, you are destined for a wonderful life.

24

Are You an Abusive Parent?

I was so completely degraded by my parents when I was a child that I couldn't imagine becoming a mother myself. I didn't know how else to be a parent except the way I was parented. That scared me to death. I had told every man I dated early on in the relationship that I didn't want to have children. I didn't want there to be any misunderstanding.

I guess you can imagine my surprise and horror when I found out I was pregnant at age forty-one. I didn't think that would ever happen to me. I sort of saw it as a sign, though. I had avoided becoming pregnant throughout my fairly promiscuous teens and young adulthood and then had several long-term relationships after that. I thought that this was someone's idea of a lesson for me—that I was supposed to have kids now that I had spent almost twenty years in therapy working out my parent stuff. This was sort of a last gasp at motherhood.

I had a little girl, Mandy, and I have to admit that having a boy probably would have been easier on my psyche. From day one, I swore that I would do everything for Mandy that was 180 degrees different from the way my parents treated me. It was almost a mantra, and I was conscious of it all the time.

I think I was lucky, because by the time I was forty, I had been so successful in the technology field and had accumulated so much in savings that I could essentially retire—at least for several years—and stay home with her, at least until she began going to school all day.

If she cried, I went right to her crib and comforted her. I anticipated when she would be wet and when she'd be hungry. I sang and talked to her all the time. I carried her in my arms or on my chest most of the day. It was just the two of us, since her father thought I'd gone back on my word that I never wanted children in order to trap him, so he left when I told him I was pregnant. That was fine; I didn't need him, and if that was his true character, I didn't need him influencing my child.

When Mandy got a little older and became more demanding in a toddler sort of way, I really tried my best to meet those needs. I found her exhausting. She seemed very needy to me, and most days, I was just completely worn down by her demands. She followed me everywhere, and I couldn't even shut the door to the bathroom. She wanted to sleep with me, and I started finding her constant presence very intrusive. I tried to understand her needs and felt badly that she didn't have a father, so I'm sure I overcompensated by trying to be both mom and dad to her.

She'd have what I called hissy fits that seemed out of the ordinary to me, even for a three-year-old. She'd throw herself on the floor and have a real tantrum until I gave in. I know it was wrong of me to give in to her demands so much, but I was usually so tired and worn-out that it was just easier.

I began resenting her and then feeling horrible guilt for feeling that way. I tried to hire sitters so that I could go out in the evening and spend some time with a friend, but she'd get so hysterical, I didn't think it was fair to the poor sitter. I felt trapped with her. I began having all sorts of horrible thoughts about her, which made me feel even worse.

No one ever told me that while you always love your kids, you might not always like them, and that it was normal to feel that way. Also, because I didn't have any good parenting models, I didn't know that in trying to be the opposite of my parents, I had actually created a little monster.

I found myself saying things to her that I never thought I would, like, "You're such a brat," "You don't really feel that way," "I told you to be quiet; you're making me crazy," and a lot of other unfair things. It shocked me every time I'd hear myself say those things, but I kept doing it. The worst thing in the world had happened, and she was only four years old: I had turned into my mother.

Finally, I went to some parenting classes and learned how to become a better parent. I read parenting books and learned to confront my fear of becoming my mother. I was parenting Mandy from that point of view instead of doing what I internally knew was right for her. It took a few months and a lot of suffering with her, but we finally got through it, and now she's a better child—because I'm a better mother. Wow, being a mother is hard work, and not just of the physical type! Nobody warns you how much of your own personal stuff is going to be challenged when you become a mom. I'd say it's a daily struggle, but the difference is that now I think I'm winning my own battle.

—Maureen, age forty-six

I've counseled court-mandated offenders, regular moms and dads who feel confused and overwhelmed by their children, and parents who just want new and different parenting skills. Among those thousands of parents, I've never met any who deliberately wanted or tried to abuse their children. They all loved their kids and wanted what they felt was best for them—or better than they had themselves. None of them woke up in the morning with the intention of physically or emotionally wounding their children. If you were treated unfairly as a child, I'm certain your parents felt the same way about you.

However, child abuse occurs on many levels, and it's often just as insidious as adult domestic violence. Remember that all abuse is about power and control. You certainly have almost total power and control over your children, and the younger they are, the more easily you can exert that power and control. Doing so is always devastating and leaves a lifelong impression on them.

No one teaches us how to parent. It is often remarked upon that you need a license to catch fish, but you don't need one to have a child. If you've had poor parenting models, how would you know how to love and nourish your child in a healthy way? There is a lot of societal pressure to be the "perfect mom," although no one ever tells us what the perfect mom is. Is it June Cleaver on *Leave it to Beaver*? Is it Claire Huxtable on *The Cosby Show*? Maybe Marge Simpson on *The Simpsons*? Who knows?

Women who were abused as children—whether it was emotionally, verbally, sexually, or physically—are often horrified when they find themselves mistreating their own children in the same manner. Although they grew up giving themselves the mantra "I'll never be like my mom (or dad) when I have a child," they may unconsciously hurt their children in the same ways they were damaged. They know of no other way to cope during stressful times.

Many times, a parent violates a child and is not only unaware of the abuse, but justifies it. I'll always remember the parenting classes I held for court-mandated child abuse offenders. These were moms and dads whose children were taken away from them because they abused the little ones, and now a judge had prescribed a year of parenting courses as part of their probation. Whenever I got to the section on spanking a child, sparks flew. They'd defend their right to spank their child with a lot of energy. I'd reply that spanking is another word for hitting, and that parents only spank in anger—when they are frustrated and out of control—so it is difficult to control themselves and make better parenting decisions about other ways to discipline the child. I always had several parents tell me that they were spanked when they were kids and didn't see anything wrong with it.

"You don't?" I'd ask. "You just told me that you were spanked as a child, and you're saying that it was OK with you? How did you feel about the parents who spanked you? Were you afraid of them?"

"Well, yeah, I was afraid of them. But they gave me a whipping when I was bad, and I turned out all right."

"I'd have to disagree with you on that front. A judge sentenced you as a child abuser and mandated you to a year on my couch listening to me drone. Therefore, I'd have to say you're completely wrong about your being OK and about the whole spanking/hitting issue." Usually they were quiet after that ...

If you were verbally abused as a child, you may be tortured to hear yourself being critical and demeaning to your own child now. "You're the laziest kid I've ever seen," "You're stupid," "You'll never amount to anything," "Who's gonna want you the way you act?" "You don't feel that way," "Only a crazy person would think like that"—comments like these may have flown out of your mouth in frustration at one time or another.

Girls who were physically abused may find themselves "spanking" their children with a belt or slapping their little faces. They may also grab their children's shoulders and shake them violently or grab their arms too tightly to restrain them unnecessarily.

A child who is sexually abused may grow up to be a mom who feels uncomfortable with physical touch, even with her children. She feels awkward hugging them or holding them close to her. She may see their wanting to be close to her as a violation of her personal space. Though consciously she may not relive her abuses, deep inside her she feels the same fear and tension she once had when she was being molested.

ACCEPTANCE AND RESPECT

Sometimes, I think that the word *acceptance* is the hardest word in our language to really understand. Do you have to accept a person's behavior to accept him as a person? Does acceptance mean that you don't care anymore? Can you dislike a behavior but accept it nonetheless? Very often, accepting something really means that we are willing to compromise, to abandon the idea of getting what we really want. Acceptance is a very complicated idea.

When you become a parent, you want the very best for your little person. You want him to live a happy, carefree life. You want him to have good childhood memories. You want to raise him with a feeling of self-confidence, joy, and knowledge that he can be anything he wants. You want him to feel that he's the most wonderful creature on Earth. Then reality sets in. Maybe your child is very different from you, and it's difficult to relate. Maybe he's too much like you, and you relate a little too much, projecting your thoughts and feelings onto him. Maybe you had hoped for a very academically intelligent child but got a C student who has to work very hard even to get that grade. Maybe you hoped for an athlete or ballerina but got a child with two left feet. Maybe you were disappointed to find that your child is handicapped in some way, so all of your dreams and fantasies about his life have to be revised.

Understand that it is emotionally abusive to your children when you don't accept them for who they are. They feel ashamed of who they are; they feel defective as a person. You may remember that feeling. In order for children to develop a wonderful self-concept, it is vital that they feel accepted as they are by the only people who may do that all their lives. They need to perform in one way or another for every other person they now know or will ever know. Why should you make them feel that they need to be someone else in order for you to accept them? I know that this is a very difficult concept at times, and I have been as guilty as the next person of not accepting my children at various times. Now that they are adults, they remember those times and have told me how they felt when they were younger and felt unaccepted. It is painful for me to hear.

Allowing your children to be who they are, and not subjecting them to comparisons, is one of the greatest gifts you can give them. It allows them to grow up with a freedom that is worth more than any material item you can give them.

Respect is another important idea as it relates to your children. As adults, we often think that children should respect us, but we don't turn it around to realize that we also need to respect them. In a family, there needs to be equal respect for all members. That means, if you expect your children to respect you, you will also need to show them respect, as well. Do not take this comment to indicate that you and your children are equals on every level. No; you are far higher on the family food chain, and one of your jobs is to instill this knowledge in your kids.

One of the pervasive problems I see as a therapist is that parents want to be their children's pals, rather than their parents. While it's true that you want to have a friendly relationship with them—which includes listening to them in such a way that they can talk with you, watching television and movies with them, playing games with them, and so on—you are their parents, not their friends. I am still alarmed when I think of the woman I counseled several years ago who was having problems with her four-year-old son. In the first session, she proudly told me, "I said to him, 'Why would you want to say that to me? We're best friends!' He really hurt my feelings, and I told him so. Don't you think that was a good idea? He needs to know that I'm a person, too."

I am rarely speechless, but I paused a moment to collect my thoughts and then asked her, "Why would a four-year-old be your best friend? You're thirty-eight years old. I'm a little afraid to ask what you have in common with a preschooler. And while I'm asking, why would you want your four-year-old to have a best friend who's thirty-eight? Wouldn't another four-year-old make more sense?"

She was a bit stymied by the question and hardly knew what to say. We then began working on learning to set boundaries, knowing who is in charge in her household, and becoming a parent rather than a pal.

While it was important for this woman to respect her son at a four-year-old level, he was not equal to her in terms of privileges, duty, and so on. I hear little children telling their parents that they need to go to sleep at eight o'clock if the kids are, so the adults lie in their own beds pretending to sleep until the children are in dreamland. They should tell them, "No, we are adults. We can go to bed later than you. When you're older, you'll earn the privilege to go to sleep later, too." Why are children telling their parents what to do … and why are parents accepting these directives?

In a word, the answer is respect, but not the type we've been discussing—respect for yourself. When you don't have respect for yourself, you transmit that knowledge to your children. They subconsciously think, "She doesn't respect herself, so why should I respect her?" They've also seen you allowing disrespect from your male partner and perhaps your parents, friends, and so on. This just cements the idea in their minds that they needn't respect you.

Children need to feel respect for their mom. You are the most important woman—and probably the most important person, period—in their lives. You can imagine what it does to a little person's psyche when his own mother doesn't respect herself or expect respect from others, when she lowers herself to becoming a "best friend" to a toddler, is so desperate to be liked that she dismisses what she knows is in the best interest of her children in order to look like the "cool mom," and doesn't set and keep rules and boundaries. This is very confusing and damaging to children, who require rules and boundaries in order to feel a sense of security. They don't need cool and hip; they have MTV for that, heaven forbid.

Especially in the aftermath of a breakup, children need to know that you are going to be OK, which gives them a feeling that they might be OK, as well. Children of all ages are narcissistic; it's all about them. This doesn't make them bad people or mean that you've done a bad job as a mom. It's just who they are. During a breakup, they worry about what will become of them, and it's up to you to show them that, while this is a very difficult and heartbreaking time, you—and therefore they—will be all right.

HOW CAN THEY LOVE MY ABUSER?

Respecting them also means that they are allowed to have their own feelings that are separate from yours, especially about your partner. Yes, he was abusive to you and may have been abusive to them, as well. However, they have confused feelings about him and may love him even if they are terrified of him. They may be relieved that the fighting is over but still miss him and wish he were home. Much like you, they never wanted the relationship to end; they just wanted the fighting to end. They wanted it to be different, not over. They wished for change as much as you did.

However, unlike you, they don't have any control over the situation. No one consulted them, and they didn't have a vote. They may cry and whine. When they are angry with you, they may tell you that they want to go live with their daddy. They may tell you it's all your fault that he left. They are sad and confused, and you are the safest person to take these feelings out on.

This is where moms are liable to abuse their children.

The kids may begin to make the same comments as the abuser. "If you cooked dinners Daddy liked, he'd still be here." "Why didn't you try harder to make him happy?" "Why did you make him leave? Why didn't you ask us?" "Daddy was crying the last time we saw him, and he said it's because you told him he had to leave us. He's so sad that he can't live with us anymore." Quick, what is your first temptation? To tell them everything that happened or to say that daddy's lying and always tries to act like the good guy, right? That would be abusive to your children.

Your kids are allowed to have their devastated feelings. Their reaction may be uncomfortable for you on a number of fronts. It may mirror feelings of despair in you as well as bring up a sense of guilt, failure, and total responsibility for the end of the relationship without looking at the true causes.

When your children make comments such as the ones above, without agreeing with them, you can tell them, "It must hurt you to see your dad like this. I know how much you love him," "I can see that you are very sad. Do you want to talk more about it?" "Since I'm not your daddy, I don't know what he's thinking. That sounds like a good question to ask him," and so on. Do you see that you are honoring their feelings without slamming your ex, and also giving them ways to cope and a caring ear that will listen to them? This is nonabusive behavior, and it is truly being the kind of "friend" they need.

LIMITS, BOUNDARIES, AND PROFESSIONAL HELP

You may be depressed and worn out in the aftermath of your breakup. There is a lot to deal with emotionally and practically. It may be tempting to overcompensate for your children's hurt feelings and your guilt by allowing them to do almost anything they want. This may seem kind to them at this difficult time, or it may just be easier, but it is not good parenting. More than at any other time in their lives to date, they need to see that despite your sadness, you are still strong enough to go on and lead them through the darkness that they feel. Their world has been turned upside down, and while you may feel relieved, angry, vengeful, and a whole host of other feelings, the primary emotions your children feel are intense grief, anger, and despair.

You can understand your children's feelings and still be a parent. This means that you keep the household rules in effect, which will give them comfort and a sense of continuity. In the direct aftermath of my breakup with my children's dad, I told them, "The situation is changing, but the mom remains the same." While I didn't know if that would be helpful to them at the time, it was the truth. Only recently have they told me that this statement made them feel less scared about what was going to happen. At least they felt that one thing in their life was going to remain consistent. Don't think it wasn't difficult for me to act as if I was the same, though. It was just something I felt that I owed them.

Keep an eye open for signs of depression in your children. These would include more than several days of

- difficulty sleeping;

- appetite change;

- nightmares;

- regressive behaviors, such as thumb-sucking and bed-wetting;

- crying;

- talk of "not being here anymore";

- acting-out behaviors, such as hitting, pushing, yelling, or name-calling;

- loss of interest in playing with other children or doing pleasurable activities.

If you notice any of these behaviors, it may be time to seek professional help for the child and the family together. Often, a therapist can teach children how to cope with their feelings and the inevitable changes they are about to face. She can also teach you how to deal with your child's feelings and questions while also coping with your own pain. There is help available at every price range and on a sliding-scale basis. Your insurance provider or primary care physician may have suggestions. Check the mental health section of your telephone help pages, as well as the Internet.

WHAT HAS IT COST YOU?
WHAT CAN YOU DO WHEN YOU ARE FRUSTRATED WITH YOUR CHILD?

As you've seen in your own abusive situation, abuse stems from many sources, but the important concept to remember is that you didn't deserve it, no matter what you did. The same holds true for your children. As we discussed, you may have been abused as a child, and, when you're frustrated to the max, you may lash out at your own kids. This is not acceptable, so let's brainstorm about what you can do instead. Take out your trusty journal and write down these ideas: *what s/ he did or said; how it made me feel; what I did or said; how I felt afterward; what I can do instead.*

Now, write down a few instances of something your child did that upset you, such as being whiney, pleading for daddy, calling you names, blaming you, etc. What came up in you in response? Feelings of anger, rage, guilt, shame, regret, despair? Did you have similar feelings to the ones you had when you were a child? Did it bring up your own abuse—either as an adult, with your partner, or as a child? What did you do or say to your child when he acted in this way? Did you slap him, give him a time out, tell him to shut up, push him aside, or tell him that his dad was an abusive jerk? How did you feel after you did this? Ashamed? Embarrassed? Relieved? Justified? Guilty? Afraid?

Now, let's think about what you could have done instead. Could you have told your child that you are too upset to discuss this with him at the time but will speak with him in a few moments, and then taken a time-out yourself? How about listening to the feelings behind the anger or whining and inviting him to open up to you? Could you have affirmed his feelings while letting him know that you will not tolerate his behavior towards you, and that the next time, there will be consequences (and spell them out)? Could you have put your arms around his little shoulders and said either "You look like you could use a hug" or "I know how difficult this is for you. I'm here, and I love you"?

These are important questions to look at. You love your children—even if you don't always like them—and want what is best for them. If you've been a martyred partner and mother, it will be difficult for you to separate your pain from your children's. It will be hard for you to see them suffering without feeling that it is all your fault. Remember, it was your partner's idea to abuse you; however, it was your idea to allow the abuse.

Have your children been damaged? I'd like to tell you that the abusive relationship didn't affect them at all, but that would be a lie. There has been damage.

That doesn't mean that you need to take total responsibility for that damage or that they will never heal, but it will take time. One of the most important decisions you've made is the one to take them out of this environment and show them a model of a woman who now respects herself and will not tolerate abuse in any situation. She is also strong enough to be a good mother and enforce rules and boundaries. This is good and nonabusive mothering.

25

Looking for Nonabusive Men ... and Women

I recently took stock of my relationships and discovered that almost all of them were abusive in some way. It shocked me, but I saw that all of the people in my life were using me, were narcissistic and only out for themselves, and used me like a doormat. They didn't really consider my feelings or opinions.

I thought that when I ended my most recent relationship with an abusive boyfriend, I would be done with unhealthy relationships. That felt freeing. But then I looked at all these other bad relationships and realized that I was going to have to give up virtually everyone in my life, if I was going to be truly free. That scared me to death, but not as much as the idea that I would have to suffer with these feelings for the rest of my life.

—**Tammy, age twenty-six**

WHAT ARE HEALTHY RELATIONSHIPS, ANYWAY?

At this point, you may think that there is no such thing as a healthy relationship. After all, healthy relationships may have been few and far between in your life. Doesn't everyone have some baggage they're carrying around? That's a fair question, and the answer would be yes, everyone carries a few Samsonites through their lives. The test would have to be this: how many suitcases do they have, how many do they want you to carry for them, what happens when a suitcase opens and all their dirty undergarments get thrown around and examined, and how do they react to that?

We can lug that baggage with us. When you are in a healthy relationship, you don't ask others to deal with it, and you also try to throw out whatever articles you don't need in order to lighten the load.

Do you remember our discussion of boundaries earlier in the book? Developing healthy boundaries in a relationship is crucial and makes it very simple to negotiate any situation. Here are some guidelines on developing healthy relationship boundaries (taken from *Destructive Relationships*). When you have good boundaries in a relationship, you

- have clear preferences and act upon them;

- know when you are happy or unhappy;

- live actively rather than reactively;

- create your own reality rather than letting another person tell you what reality is;

- extend yourself to others only when they are appreciative;

- trust your own intuition;

- are encouraged by sincere, ongoing change in others (rather than promises of change);

- have your own interests and hobbies that excite you;

- have a personal standard of conduct that applies to everyone and demands accountability;

- know the difference between well-intentioned feedback and manipulation or control;

- relate to others only when they show respect for your feelings and opinions;

- look at another person's behavior, rather than your feelings;

- don't need another person to make you feel "complete";

- insist that others' boundaries are as safe as yours are … and respect them;

- feel secure, focused, and clear-headed most of the time;

- are always aware of your choices;

- understand that you create your own future and don't depend on others to do so for you;

- decide how, to what extent, and for what length of time you will be committed in a romantic relationship;

- know that you have a right to privacy, and protect it;

- don't use denial as a coping mechanism, but see things as they are even if they are painful.

I know that appears to be a long list, but if you look at the items closely, they are actually common-sense approaches to living a healthy life.

When you've been in a long-term, romantic relationship with a man—or a series of them—you may forget that women can be extremely abusive, as well. Not only can women show abusive behaviors to their men, but to other women. You may have certainly experienced your share of abusive women in your mother, sisters, female boss and coworkers, and perhaps female friends. The ideas that we are going to discuss in this chapter about choosing healthy relationships apply to women as well as men.

Understand that just acknowledging your involvement in abusive relationships has been a powerful turning point in your quest for better emotional and physical health. It also bodes well for new and improved future relationships. You're done with unkind, no-win people in your life. At this point, it may seem unlikely that you may someday find a new romantic partner, but I hope a new relationship will find you when you are emotionally ready. Companionship is a good thing; you don't need to fear it if you choose wisely. Love is lovely when it is nurturing and you are an equal and respected partner. Just because you may not have experienced such a relationship in your life doesn't mean it's not out there.

ARE WE DESTINED TO CHOOSE THE SAME PERSON OVER AND OVER UNTIL WE GET IT RIGHT?

Well, that would be a scary thought, wouldn't it? Unfortunately, the answer is a conditional "yes." Now wait; before you close this book with shrieks of "I've been duped! She had me read all the way to the end of the book and then tells me that I'm going to repeat this all over again? After I've stayed up nights reading and doing these crazy activities?" Hold on there, horsey. If you've worked on the activities and examined your life thus far, you've done the necessary work to insure that you won't have to repeat your past relationships.

Let me explain how this works. According to famed relationship expert, Dr. Harville Hendrix, we choose the mates we do based on the idea of *Imago*. This is a Latin term for image, and it is a composite picture of all the people in your early life who influenced you most, both in positive and negative traits that were similar to your parents. Dr. Hendrix's belief is that "you unconsciously choose a partner, an Imago match. This partner has the potential to help you heal unresolved pain from childhood, can help you understand the hidden reason you picked your partner and show you how to heal your relationship and yourself."

What does this mean for you and the prospect of future healthy relationships? Let me give you a couple of examples. I've met many women whose abusive mate is an alcoholic. It is frustrating to them that not only do they lack the power to keep him from drinking, but when he drinks, he is especially abusive. Not shockingly, I very often find that the women had an alcoholic parent. These women may not consciously think, *I couldn't fix my parent, but I can fix this guy. That is my job, and I'm sticking with it, no matter what.* In other cases, a woman may have grown up with critical, unkind parents who did not honor her as a separate person. She goes on to become involved with men and women to whom she grovels for a crumb of approval or recognition to no avail.

In the Imago theory, whether your partner is kind or abusive, he has the ability to help you heal and resolve this childhood pain you've carried for so long. Love is a great healing tonic, and that is the preferred method of resolving your childhood issues. However, as you've seen through this book, understanding the role your childhood abusers played in your adult relationships has healing properties, as well. When you've resolved the trauma and unfairness of your childhood, you can also let go of your current abuser and go on to live a life free of future abuse. You understand that you cannot change the past and what was done to you. You can choose to either let go of those people who have hurt you or build strong boundaries around the relationship now. You don't have control of these folks, but you do have complete control over how you think about them, how you behave around them, and how you react to them.

"I WOULDN'T KNOW A HEALTHY PERSON IF HE WERE THE LAST HUMAN ON EARTH"

A former patient of mine said that to me after she'd gotten out of her twelve-year, abusive marriage, which was preceded by several other destructive relationships. In fact, most of her relationships—with everyone in her life—were unhealthy, and she felt destined to continue that cycle. You may feel the same way: nervous, frightened, and untrusting of others and even of your own judgment.

Why don't we go over the warning signs of toxic people so that you can be 100 percent certain you'll know them, even if they are the last human on Earth:

- *Everything is your fault:* This person blames you for everything and anything that goes wrong in his life. If he loses his job, it's because you didn't make him hot oatmeal the morning of his important presentation. If he forgets his cell phone at home, it's because you didn't think to ask him before he left if he had it. He doesn't take responsibility for his mistakes or for the problems he's created, and you—not he—suffer the consequences.

- *He ignores your boundaries:* Do you recall the list of healthy boundaries in the last chapter? He ignores them. He doesn't understand where he ends and you begin, and he prefers that you don't, either. He blurs the line of separation between the two of you.

- *He's a control hound:* He wants to tell you how you should dress, how much makeup looks good on you, and who your friends should be. He's always making little "suggestions for your benefit." You understand: it's just to help you out and make you a better person! He decides where you go for dinner, even though he starts off making you believe you have total choice. Funny how you end up going where he wanted to anyway and ordering what he wants so you can share. He makes all major decisions, even when he pretends you have a hand in them.

- *He thinks in black and white:* We discussed this idea earlier as it applied to you, but in thinking of unhealthy relationships with others, try to imagine a partner who is so wedded to his beliefs that he can't be wrong, even when he's so obviously wrong. He thinks in terms of right/wrong, good/bad, yes/no. He is so one way or the other that there is no room for options, differing opinions, or you!

- *He has addictions:* When you are involved with an addicted person, his relationship is with the addiction, not with you. Given a choice, he will always choose the addiction over you. If he is addicted—don't minimize his addiction now; you know if he has one—he has many emotional problems he doesn't want to address, and he merely covers them with his addiction of choice. Get out, and don't make the same mistake again.

- *He engages in criminal behaviors:* You'd think this one would be a no-brainer, but I'm constantly shocked by the intelligent women who become involved with a guy who's had previous experience with the law: theft, drug possession ("it wasn't his; he was holding it for a friend"), drug dealing, weapons, or previous domestic violence ("it wasn't true; his ex was crazy and made the whole thing up to get him in trouble"). OK, so maybe—as you'd like to think—that was when he was young and stupid, and everyone's entitled to a mistake, right? Sure, but is this guy with the background really the only man on Earth you could establish a relationship with? Remember: the best predictor of future behavior is past behavior. Your future should be looking a whole lot better than this by now.

- *He's a cheater, cheater, pumpkin eater:* What about the guy who has a history of cheating on his past girlfriends or wives? Maybe he likes to view a little Internet porn once in a while. Or perhaps he fudges his time card at work once a week. That's all cheating, and don't think that he wouldn't cheat on you either. Cheaters are cheaters. If he's cheated on an ex or his boss, or he's cheated in other ways and gotten away with it—or not—why would you expect him to suddenly act straight-up with you? Come on now—is this really the best you can do?

- *Yeah, but——:* Do you recall when we talked about but as an eraser word? It erases everything that was said before the but. When you're having a conversation with him, and it sounds like he's agreeing with you, listen for the but. He's just discounted everything you've said. It's quite similar, actually, to my counseling women that—based on their descriptions of their man's behaviors—they are in an abusive relationship. They seem to be listening intently and then say, "Yeah, but he's never hit me …"

- *Liar, liar, pants on fire:* If you strike up a new relationship with someone, and you notice him telling little, white lies when it would be of no consequence to tell the truth, that's your clue to exit—quickly. How can you trust him or believe anything he tells you? What this behavior tells you is that your guy has a difficult time facing problems and taking responsibility for his actions. While it may have begun as a childhood coping tool in an abusive family, it is now a habit and pattern. You don't need to try and rescue him and think that by showing him love and unconditional acceptance, you can break him of this flaw in his character. You just need to get out and not look back.

(The list above was adapted from *Destructive Relationships* and also from the book *How to Recognize Emotional Unavailability and Make Healthier Relationship Choices* by Dr. Bryn Collins.)

Now you have two lists regarding boundaries with which to gauge your and your potential partner's emotional health before you decide to become involved. As I've mentioned, boundaries are key to a good and healthy relationship. Without boundaries, anything goes, and no one—except an abuser—is happy. Make sure that you establish and maintain good boundaries, not only with a romantic partner, but with everyone in your life. You will find that your life becomes very simple.

GETTING USED TO HEALTHY RELATIONSHIPS

A woman I counseled at the domestic violence shelter once told me, "I've been in so many abusive relationships, that's all I know. I don't know if I could be in a good relationship. I think I have this abuse stuff in my veins."

She has a good point. Many women who have experienced a series of destructive relationships don't think they could tolerate something different, something quiet. Many teenage girls have told me that, though they didn't like their boyfriends' mistreatment, it felt comfortable, and in a way they missed it when they broke up with him. They had constant cravings to go back to their abusive boyfriend and felt tremendous societal pressure to stay away, even though they didn't want to.

"I miss him," they tell me. "He wasn't bad to me all the time, and when he was nice, it was so good that it was worth putting up with the bad times."

Many women who have been in abusive relationships find normal relationships boring and lacking in energy. They can't imagine a lifetime with a man who doesn't cause trouble and excitement. This is understandable but unhealthy. It's a self-esteem issue as well as an addiction issue. Yes, you read correctly. An abusive relationship is highly addictive, and that addiction can be every bit as strong as a drug. Let's look at what a healthy versus unhealthy romantic relationship looks like in stages, so that you can better understand men who cross your path.

STAGES IN A ROMANTIC RELATIONSHIP

First, let me debunk a popular and romantic myth: there is no such thing as love at first sight. There is lust at first sight, and lust is great. Just don't mistake it for love. Chemistry is not the same as deep and lasting commitment, and you can't know anything about the deep and lasting part of a guy across a crowded room.

Love is not an out-of-control feeling; it's a choice. Love takes time to create and grow. To know if someone is really worth your love and time, you want to see him in all sorts of different situations, especially difficult and disappointing situations. When life doesn't go the way he'd like, does he rant and rage? Does he blame it on others? Does he use substances or compulsions to cope? Does he intellectualize to avoid dealing with his feelings? How does he treat his mother, grandmother, sisters, and women in general? How does he cope with unpleasant anniversaries, such as his old wedding anniversary, the anniversary of a parent's death, etc.? Has he been fired from jobs because his bosses disliked him? Is he a victim in many of his stories of woe? We've discussed the victim mentality, and hopefully at this point you agree with me that you aren't a victim when you are an adult. These are all-important considerations before you decide to give of yourself to another person.

There are three distinct stages of love. We all go through the first one—infatuation—to some degree, no matter how old we are. Then, if the relationship is to last in a loving and nurturing manner, it progresses into mature love as two separate but equal partners. However, if you are incomplete—if you have not completed yourself—you will advance into an addictive love cycle, which is what you have experienced in your abusive relationship. Let's look at these stages more closely.

SIGNS OF INFATUATION

- Usually occurs at the beginning of a relationship

- Physical and sexual attraction are central

- Characterized by urgency, intensity, sexual desire, and anxiety

- Driven by the excitement of being involved with a person whose character is not fully known

- Involves nagging doubts and unanswered questions; the partner remains unexamined so as not to spoil the dream

- Based on a fantasy

- Is consuming and often exhausting

- Relationship is not enduring, because it lacks a firm foundation

SIGNS OF MATURE LOVE

- Develops gradually through learning about each other

- Sexual attraction is present, but warm affection/friendship is central

- Characterized by calm, peacefulness, empathy, support, trust, confidence, and tolerance of each other; no feelings of being threatened

- Driven by deep attachment based on extensive knowledge of both positive and negative qualities in the other person and mature acceptance of imperfections

- Partners want to be together but are not obsessed with the relationship

- Based on empathy

- Energizing in a healthy way

- Partners have high self-esteem; each has a sense of self-worth and feels complete even without the relationship

- Individuality is accepted

- Each brings out the best in the other; relationship is nurturing

- Partners feel no need to rush the events of the relationship; a sense of security and no fear of losing the partner

- Each encourages the other's growth

- Relationship is enduring and sustaining, because it is based on a strong foundation of friendship

QUALITIES OF AN ADDICTIVE LOVE RELATIONSHIP

- A feeling of not being able to live without the partner

- Insecurity, distrust, lack of confidence, feeling threatened

- Low self-esteem; looking to partner for validation and affirmation of self-worth

- Fewer happy times together; more time spent on apologies, fear, guilt, and broken promises

- Needing the other in order to feel complete

- Feeling worse about oneself as the relationship progresses

- Loss of self-control

- Making fewer decisions or plans; waiting for the partner to tell you what to do

- Discomfort with individual differences

- Tearing down or criticizing the other

- Feeling as though one is killing time until with the partner again

- Rushing things, like sex or marriage, so as not to lose the partner

- Breaking promises to oneself or others because of the relationship

- Being threatened by the other partner's growth

- Constant insecurity and jealousy

- Using drugs or alcohol as coping mechanisms

- Friends or family report that the person is different from the way she used to be

Did you see yourself and your previous relationships on these lists? They are good guidelines for you to consult when you decide to become involved in a future relationship. Remember, it is normal and natural to go through the infatuation phase for a short time and then, if the relationship is a healthy one, proceed into the mature love phase. It doesn't mean that the relationship has dulled or lost its spark and chemistry. I believe that when many women are beginning to enter this calmer period of a relationship, they think something is drastically wrong and that this spells the beginning of the end of the affair. In fearing this, they begin to stir up chaos and drama to keep the excitement high. Calm and contentment is a preferred way of sustaining a good relationship. I can't tell you how many men I speak with who are fed up with drama and just desire some peace.

NEGOTIATION & FAIRNESS
Partners seek mutually satisfying resolutions to conflict, can accept change and are willing to compromise

RESPONSIBLE PARENTING
Partners share parental responsibilities and are positive non-violent role models for children

SHARED RESPONSIBILITY
Partners reach mutual agreements on fair distribution of work and make family decisions together

ECONOMIC PARTNERSHIP
Partners make financial decisions together ensuring that both parners benefit from financial arrangementts

EQUALITY

HONESTY & ACCOUNTIBILITY
Partners accept responsibility for themselves, acknowlege past behavior, can admit being wrong, and communicate openly and truthfully

NON-THREATENING BEHAVIOR
Partners speak and act in ways that cultivate and support a safe and comfortable environment in which they can express themselves and make decisions

RESPECT
Partners listen non-judgementally, are understanding, emotionally affirming and value their partner's opinion

TRUST & SUPPORT
Partners support each others' goals and respect each others' feelings, friends, activities, contributions and opinions

This wheel is the definitive blueprint of a healthy, loving relationship of any kind. All of the behaviors on this graphic are respectful, loving, kind, and friendly. This means that you should be giving and receiving every one of the items on this wheel—not just some of them—in each of your relationships. If you think this is too much for you to handle, then understand that as a sign that you're not ready to try your hand at a new relationship. Likewise, if you believe that those are too many behaviors for a man to give you, take it as a sign that your self-esteem still needs significant work. After all, which of these behaviors do you think you are unworthy of: Honesty? Respect? Open communication? Non-threatening behavior? Trust and support? Fairness? All of these ideas work together in harmony to create they type of relationships you deserve.

INVOLVING YOUR CHILDREN IN A NEW ROMANTIC RELATIONSHIP

Ah yes, the inevitable question: when should you introduce a new mate to your children? Fourth date? Two months? When you are really serious?

Well, first of all, let's not get ahead of ourselves. There is no law I'm aware of that requires each and every woman to have a mate. As women, we are programmed since childhood to believe that we should get married and that staying single is undesirable. Society whispers behind the backs of unmarried women who are in their late thirties and forties: old maids, must be a lesbian, man haters, too much baggage, probably has too many nasty habits, and so on. This creates a kind of desperation and hysteria about becoming attached to a man—any man—almost at any cost. As a young or fully grown, adult woman, you are now free to choose how you want to live. You're strong. You get to choose what is right for your life.

Now, as to the children question: remember, you are the only role model your children have for the relationships they can expect for themselves in the future. Well, not exactly the only role model. You can let them watch MTV or reality dating shows for guidance and role modeling (picture my tongue firmly in my cheek as I advise this). If they see your unhealthy relationships, you can certainly expect that they will have a similar relationship when they are teens or adults. Why wouldn't they? If it were enough for you, why wouldn't it be enough for them?

If you decide that you would like to become involved in a romantic relationship, think long and hard about the lists above before you proceed, and certainly before you introduce your children to a new partner, one who they will inevitably see as a replacement for their dad. When a series of men wanders in and out of their lives, children become very insecure and view relationships as purely temporary. Therefore, I suggest that you wait until you are very certain about your new relationship before involving your kids in any way. Remember, mature love means that you don't need to rush a situation. You will know if your potential mate enjoys and longs for children well before he meets yours. Don't rush to create the illusion of a new family for yourself so that you feel more secure and comfortable. Allow yourself some time and separateness without the urge to merge. This is when the greatest relationship growth occurs.

Love is wonderful and grand. It's one of the greatest feelings on Earth when it's healthy and nurturing. Allow yourself the luxury of time and space for love to grow and develop. Remember, it doesn't occur overnight, and immediate and strong physical attraction doesn't always bode well for a lasting relationship.

WHAT HAS IT COST YOU?
WHAT CHARACTERISTICS ARE YOU SEEKING IN A MATE?

Dr. Phil McGraw states that "you can't claim it till you name it," and I believe that's absolutely true. In this activity you have the opportunity to make a list of every character and personality trait you would like in a new friendship or romantic relationship. Remember, you get to choose!

Take out your journal, and make a long list of every single trait you would like in this new person who will enter your life. This can include both the significant and the insignificant. No one is going to read this but you, so if you want a man who earns a good salary (you get to choose the number), who has blond, curly hair and blue eyes, who has never married, and who weighs in at around 175, put all those on your list. Heck, I don't care!

When you've finished with your long list—which may take several days to complete—take a hard look at it. Go through and choose ten items on the list that you will not negotiate on. This means you can not do without these. If you are thinking of a romantic relationship, and a man in question possesses only nine of your nonnegotiable items, he's not good enough for you.

Be cautious about what you place on your Top Ten list. If a six-figure salary is most important to you, by all means put it down. However, understand that if you place honesty or dependability at a lower level than income, you may end up with a man who is a captain of industry but who is also a lot like your former mate in other areas. You may or may not wish to reconsider. You are essentially drawing up a composite of the man you'd like in your life.

Many women consider this approach very unromantic and formula driven. They want to be swept away by love. To them, I ask: if you were about to buy a new car, would you have a list of features you require? What brand of car are you looking for? Do you know what color you want? If it should have automatic windows? A stereo system? Manual or automatic transmission? Station wagon, SUV, sedan, or sports car? Now, if you have a list of requirements about something you trade in every few years, why would it be unreasonable to have a list for the person you plan to spend a lifetime with? Someone with whom you will share your mind, body, and soul?

Here comes the kicker: take another good look at your Top Ten list. Are *you* everything on that list? Yes, you read that correctly. Before you ask another person to fill all of the requirements on your list, you need to first make sure you are all of those items yourself. In other words, you need to be your own best companion before you ask someone else to join you in that process. As women, we often have incomplete areas of our hearts and minds that we expect a man to fill. Men do the same. What you then end up with is two incomplete people joining together in a desperate attempt to feel complete. That is always a mistake. You must be a complete entity yourself before you begin to look for another.

Now, look at the list. If you want someone who makes a large salary, you should be making some significant money, even though you don't necessarily need to earn as much as you want him to. In relationships, money often equals power. You may have already seen that in a previous relationship. What you would essentially be telling a potential mate is, "I'm without any money and am expecting you to provide for me." That is not a good place to begin. You may be easily taken advantage of or quickly resented. If you want someone who is honest and trustworthy, you must first look at your own life and ask yourself very honestly if you are honest and trustworthy.

Your work, then, is to become the person on your list. This may be an exhaustive process. You have done some of this work already by completing the activities in this book, but it may require further reading and/or therapy. You are worth the effort and time it will take. Remember, don't rush. This isn't a race, and the journey is more important than the destination.

26

Dealing with Your "Ex" in Your New Life

I naively thought I was done with him when I filed for divorce. I thought he'd cooperate—as he promised he would—when it came to the children. He had told me, "I hate it that you won't give me another chance, but I'm still Becky and Justin's father, so we need to remember that we have to be civil for them." He didn't need to tell me that, but it seems like he didn't hear what he was saying. He's been a nightmare over the kids, and now it's spread to everything else around them. He fights me over everything and anything; it doesn't matter how small, he makes a huge deal of it.

Here's a good example: I wanted to take the kids to my parents' house for the weekend before Thanksgiving. He had them for that day and was technically supposed to have them the weekend before, but I told him he could take them the following weekend and the Friday after Thanksgiving, so that if he wanted to visit his folks with the kids, he could. They live three hours away, and I just thought it would be nice for all of them. My parents told me they would have their Thanksgiving the weekend before, if I could get the kids. They also live a fair distance away, so I thought the kids could have Thanksgiving with each set of grandparents. I was willing to trade weekends with him so we could accommodate this for the benefit of the kids and make it a nice holiday for him. I thought it was reasonable.

Anyway, he started screaming at me and calling me a selfish, manipulative bitch, always trying to change the rules and get what I want for myself. I was stunned, to tell you the truth. I couldn't believe what I was hearing. I said, "OK, we'll keep it as-is, and you just have them for Thanksgiving Day, return them that night, and I'll take off for my parents' house the next day through the weekend. They said they'd have Thanksgiving either weekend for the kids. I was just trying to do you a favor." He became livid again and told me I never do anything for anyone but myself, so there must be some guy that I'm meeting up there the weekend before, which was so ridiculous I couldn't even begin to entertain the argument.

I told my parents the new arrangement, and they said it was fine, they'd have Thanksgiving the weekend afterward. Two days before Thanksgiving, my ex calls me and tells me that he's taking me up on my offer and will have the kids the day after Thanksgiving and all that weekend. I started to cry and was so upset, because, as always, he just expects me to jump now and go along with his plan. Mind you, it was after the original weekend I had suggested, so I couldn't take the kids to my parents now the weekend before, and I had already made plans with them to do Thanksgiving the weekend afterward, so I would also be messing up their plans. I told him that, and you know what his answer was? "That's right, put your parents before me just like you always did when we were married. Of course their feelings are more important than mine are. Well, I don't have to take that crap from you anymore, so I'll have the kids when I said. And, oh by the way, my girlfriend will be coming with us."

Stunned? I guess that would be a good word. First of all, this was our first Thanksgiving apart, and he already had a girlfriend and was bringing her into my kids' lives—and at a family holiday, no less. Now they wouldn't be able to have any Thanksgiving with their other grandparents—which they were looking forward to—and they were going to meet dad's girlfriend at a family occasion. I couldn't stand it. I called my mother to tell her that we wouldn't be there, and she told me to get a spine and stand up for myself already. She told me to call my lawyer and get his advice about what to do.

This goes on all the time. He just lives to sabotage me and make my life miserable. He'll call under the pretense of asking something about the kids, and then it disintegrates into his insulting me and being hostile and obnoxious, which always leaves me shaking.

Maybe it would have been easier to stay married to him …
—**Ruby, age thirty-six**

Whether or not you've had children with your abuser, the chances are that you will not cease all contact with him when you dissolve your relationship. Why? Because, as we've discussed, all abuse is about power and control, and your abuser still wants total power over you. That desire for power stems from his own feelings of shame and powerlessness, although he doesn't understand that, of course. He just knows that he wants you to feel badly about yourself. He didn't want to play fair when you were in a romantic relationship, but now you are his sworn enemy, so all gloves are off. He's always enjoyed making you feel small, frightened, and insecure, and if he can maintain this control over you from afar, so much the better.

You can decide whether or not you want to allow him to maintain this control over you. It's strictly your decision. What? It doesn't seem that way? Well, my friend, let me let you in on a little secret: you actually have all the power and control in the relationship; you just aren't using it wisely. What you are dealing with is a little boy who wants what he wants and throws a temper tantrum when he doesn't get it. In this case, what he wants is control. Too bad; he can't have it anymore. It's not about you, per se; it's about his feeling like a frustrated toddler who can't get what he wants. If you can bear this in mind, you can keep some emotional distance, especially when he starts his tirade of insults against you. He's yelling and making unfair and untrue accusations because he can't get what he wants: power and control. When you stop believing what your abuser says about you, and you also stop reacting to it (because you have 100 percent control of your own thoughts, behavior, and reactions), you can begin making better decisions about your relationship with him.

Now, I grant you, if you have children with your ex-abuser, you're joined at the parenthood hip until the kids are at least eighteen years old. Just because he isn't *in* your life doesn't mean he's out of it, either. However, you can still take charge of this relationship.

One behavior I often find in women who've been in abusive relationships—and who have to maintain some sort of relationship for the children—is that they revert back to the woman they were when they were together. Ruby's story at the beginning of this chapter is a common one. Another one is that it's dad's turn to pick up the kids at soccer practice on a Wednesday night and then take them to dinner. Mom makes plans with her gal pals—or a new guy pal—for her own evening of relaxation, only to have her ex call her at the very last moment (like the moment he's supposed to be picking up the kids) and tell her he won't be able to pick them up because he has to stay late at work and won't be able to have dinner with them, either. What is she supposed to do now? Should she say, "Hey, buddy that's not my problem. I have plans now, and you'll just have to tell your boss you have to leave and get your kids"? Sure, she can say that, but she knows he's not trustworthy, so she can't be sure he won't leave her children waiting on a sidewalk for the next four hours.

He knows the children are the button he can push with her. It's interesting to see how often he pushes it, especially when he gets wind of a new man in her life! She wouldn't be able to live with herself if she didn't cancel her plans to pick up the kids and spend the evening with them. She knows they will be disappointed that they won't be having dinner with daddy (yet again). If she tells him that she already has plans, he could accuse her of only thinking about her own pleasure, when—in the meantime—her kids will be sitting in the dark because of *her*. Do you notice how he's now twisted it all around to shirk his responsibility and make the whole problem about her, when actually she had nothing to do with it? However, when he decides he wants to see the kids on an off day, he expects her to drop anything she has planned with them and comply.

Here are some clues that you are continuing to allow your abuser to have unwarranted power and control over you in your new life:

- Are you constantly whirling around in your partner's tornado?

- Do you have to adjust your and your children's schedules to meet his last-minute wants and needs?

- Are you afraid not to do so, because otherwise he might think you're not nice or cooperative?

- Might he throw a fit and call you names, just as he did when you were with him?

- Is it just easier to comply with his demands?

- Do you use a meek, little voice when he is around?

- Do these types of situations cause you extreme stress?

If you answered yes to any of the questions above, you are reverting back to the woman you were when you were in a romantic relationship with your partner. You are accepting the behaviors that caused you to break up with him. Does this make sense to you?

You left him for many good reasons and have done a tremendous amount of work. Do you recall what those reasons were? Did he call you names? Did he threaten you? Did he humiliate you? Did he try to make you feel like a bad person or a bad mother? Did he dishonor your feelings and opinions? Did he lie and cheat? Did he try to make you feel crazy? These are all fine and acceptable reasons to leave a relationship, if the abuser will not change his behavior. Since you made the correct determination that he would not change, why would you go through all that angst only to allow him to continue to treat you this way?

Please understand and be very clear about an important abuse dynamic: when a partner is abusive to you, he doesn't become an angel when you leave. You can expect the identical behaviors from him now that you did when you were together ... except now they will be ramped up to the fifth power! I am still stunned when women tell me that they are shocked to find their ex behaving in such a flagrantly horrifying manner after the breakup. "I can't believe he's doing this to me," they cry. I can't imagine why not. Don't expect him to have learned his lesson by your leaving. No, he's still the same person, and he hasn't taken responsibility for the breakup. If anyone asks him why the two of you aren't together, don't expect him to say, "Because I was an abusive son-of-a-gun and treated her horribly. I didn't value her opinions and made her feel like dirt all the time. I was mean and made threats to her, humiliated her, degraded her, lied all the time, fought with her over stupid stuff that really belonged to me. I projected the shame I felt about myself onto her, and, God bless her, she took it for far longer than she should have."

Unless it benefits you as well, it is important to stick with the visitation schedule the courts have laid out and not bend to his desire to change the schedule at his every whim. First of all, it's not good for your children. Kids like to know where they are going to be and with whom. They thrive on routine, which makes them feel secure. They have had enough upheaval in their little lives, and sticking to a schedule helps them feel more in control of themselves. Secondly, if they are of school age, they deserve to play after-school sports and make play dates with their friends, knowing where they will be. It's very unkind, selfish, and intrusive to expect them to change their plans. They have only been along on this relationship ride with you; they didn't choose any of it. Thirdly, constantly giving in gives your ex the wrong impression about you. It tells him that you are still the same woman he can manipulate and connive. Then what happens? All of the empowerment you've worked so hard for is out the window, and you are right back under his thumb as he laughs at his success.

These scenarios are one of the prime reasons why women who have been in abusive relationships feel they haven't made any progress in their lives two or three years after the breakup. Sometimes, they feel that they've made three steps forward and four steps backward. When they look at their feelings, they can almost always trace them back to contact with their ex.

I suggest to women that they keep their contact and discussions with their ex extremely limited, on a business level, and on a need-to-know basis: nothing personal or chatty, no matter how tempting it might be:

• I called an appraiser to look at the house, and he'll be here next Tuesday.

• Jamie went to the dentist, and he said she needs to have a tooth filled, so I just wanted you to know when your insurance claim comes in.

• I haven't gotten your support check this month, and the child care bill is due next week, so I'll be looking for it in the mail this week.

- Janet has a ballet recital next Wednesday at seven o'clock in the school auditorium.

In other words, don't give him the opportunity to begin a no-win discussion with you and break your spirit.

Many times, exes use these necessary talks as chances to throw a quick jab or two at their partner. "You know, the last time I picked up the kids, it looked as if you had gained at least ten pounds since the week before," "I'm so much happier without you. I never realized what a bitch you were until I left," "All my friends tell me how much better I look since the breakup," or "Wow, I thought I had missed the sexual revolution. Good thing I was wrong!"

If just the very sound of his voice feels like nails on a chalkboard, and you feel terrible after you speak with him, it's perfectly all right to communicate only through fax or e-mail. Just let him know that you are keeping copies of all the communiqués. That way, he won't write anything inappropriate, and you don't have to put up with any nonsense. I have found this plan very helpful, and it leads to a much quicker recovery.

Remember: you are in charge of your life now; he isn't. You are allowed to put a stop to any undesirable behavior on his part. Eleanor Roosevelt once said, "No one can intimidate you unless you allow them to," and she was absolutely correct.

WHAT CAN YOU GAIN?
HOW CAN YOU REACT DIFFERENTLY?

Situations that demand contact with your ex will inevitably come up. They can be difficult and draining, at best. It takes a long time to get over the hurt and betrayal of a failed relationship, especially when it was abusive. He may be in your life for a long time to come; that's a fact. You can minimize the pain by establishing and maintaining control of yourself and of the interaction. Get out your journal, and let's figure out how you can accomplish this for yourself.

Write down all the difficult situations you have been in with him. Next to them, write down your reaction. Now, here's your chance for a do-over. Write down what you would say and do the next time the situation comes up. Here are a few examples to get you started:

- You had plans to stay with a girlfriend for a weekend your ex had the kids. You decided to give yourselves facials and pedicures and chose the perfect chick flick from Blockbuster. The kids are packed and ready to go. Two hours before his expected arrival, your ex calls and says that his buddy invited him to go fishing, it's the only weekend he can go, and as a matter of fact, he is in the car with him right now. He says to tell the kids he's sorry, tell them he loves them, and he'll see them next week.

What you did: You begged and pleaded with him (all the time sensing the rising enjoyment in his voice), telling him you have a life, too. He told you to stop acting like a hysterical ninny ... you can see your girlfriend anytime you want.

What you can do next time: Tell him this is completely unacceptable and that you will (1) expect a higher support check to reflect the additional time you had, (2) this won't be tolerated any longer, and (3) you are making a note of this and sending it to your attorney along with all the other times he's done this so you can examine a renegotiation of support.

- He calls under the pretense of confirming the time of the next settlement conference and then proceeds to tell you about his swinging bachelor life.

What you did: Listened with tears in your eyes and told him that it sounds like he's living a very exciting life. Then you got off the phone and bawled your eyes out.

What you can do next time: Calmly tell him the conversation is over and hang up immediately. Then, say out loud, "Oh yeah, now I remember the reason why I broke up with him. Thanks so much for the clarification, moron!"

Do you see where I'm going with this activity? Those situations are unfair and hurtful, but you can still maintain some amount of control within them. One of the keys is to remain as calm as possible—even if it's fake—and be civil, even though he isn't. Don't try to stoop to his level of insults and childish behavior. It may make you feel great in the moment, but it's not the woman you want to become. He will eventually see that he can no longer goad you into hysterics and screaming matches with lines such as, "Well, if that's what you think, then you must be an idiot," "Same to you, buddy, but more of it," and other second grade playground taunts. Just because he's acting like a creep doesn't mean that you have to stoop to his creepy level. You're so much better than that now.

27

Off You Go!

I never thought I would be the person in my group of friends who split from her boyfriend. We had been going together for seven years. I was sure we were going to get married and be together for the rest of our lives. All our friends called us an old, married couple, because that's how we acted.

I thought I did all the right things: I didn't have sex with him for several months until I felt very committed to him and knew that he felt the same way and wasn't just using me. I never moved in with him, even when he wanted me to, because I wanted to maintain my own place and some separateness and individuality. My grandmother always told me, "Why buy the cow when you can get the milk for free?" I believed that and thought that if we moved in together, there wouldn't be any incentive for him to propose marriage. We were having sex, though, so he probably thought he had the milk anyway. Who knows?

I was a good girlfriend, and he pretty much had whatever he wanted. I'm not a high-maintenance girl and don't need much. I don't want my own way all the time, and I went a whole lot more than halfway to meet him. I think he took advantage of my easygoing nature and ended up wanting more and more while I got less and less. Maybe that's typical for a lot of women.

He started being sort of controlling and slamming his fist to make a point or shutting me out when he was mad. He wouldn't talk to me for days. It just got worse and worse; he got very mean and nasty. I struggled with him and his behavior for about five years, to be honest. I had thought it was only the last year, but when I look at it, he began this stuff several years before that; I just didn't want to see it. I tried being nicer, playing by his rules, doing even more things he wanted. He started wanting sex in a way I wasn't comfortable with, but eventually I went along with it, which I regret now. It finally got to the point where my parents couldn't even talk to me, because they were so heartbroken about the way I was. I had to leave.

I'll spare you the details of how horrible it was for a long time. It took me more than a year to start coming out of my fog and depression. I was functioning, but barely. My friends were stunned. I guess we were pretty good actors, and they never knew anything was wrong. They think I'm crazy to have left him. I feel like I gave him the best years of my life and never thought I'd recover from the hurt and disappointment.

Slowly but surely, I began feeling more and more like myself. I began treating myself better by being with healthy people, eating more healthfully, exercising, trying a new sport, and giving myself daily affirmations and a chance to succeed. Now, two years after the breakup, I feel really free and happy. Sure, I still wish it could have worked out with my former boyfriend; that would have been nice. But I just started seeing someone I like a lot. I'm being very cautious and understand better what I want and what to look for. It took two years to heal and be clear on that. I know I won't wait another seven years for someone. I want children and won't give anyone more than a couple of months to see if we are compatible—it's worth that extra time to make sure.

I have to say that I truly like who I am now. I like how I am. I'm very optimistic for the future, which I never would have believed a couple of years ago. Things are looking good!

—Shelby, age twenty-nine

Well, here we are together at the end of this very long journey. How have you fared? I know that if you have carefully read the chapters in this book and performed the exercises, you may feel both emotionally spent and exhilarated at the same time. You may feel a pressing fear mixed with anticipation. This is very natural. No one feels good in learning about her abusive relationships. It may feel good to have your feelings validated, but it's certainly not the best possible news. You may have thought this was going to be a book designed to help you fix your abuser or your relationship, instead of a book that helped to fix your way of thinking.

I'd like to leave you with a few thoughts—some by me and more by others whose work I admire—to help you along in your new life. The first one concerns treating yourself well and in a healthful manner. When you have done the type of emotional and life work you have just completed, it is important that you treat your body and mind in a respectful way that shows gratitude for what they have given you. Your body and your mind are the only two things you truly own for your entire life. As you've seen throughout this book, you may have given both away to your abuser rather cheaply. Now that you have them back in your possession, I'd like you to think about treating them well.

Here are seven suggestions from Janet Luhrs, author of *The Simple Living Guide*, to achieve and maintain good and natural health:

- *Sunlight:* Expose yourself to sunlight for fifteen minutes per day. Not only does the sun—even through a lightbox, if you live in a dark climate—boost your mood, it gives you four hundred units of vitamin D, which gives you strong bones.

- *Fresh air:* Getting outside—rain or shine—every day to breathe in fresh air helps your entire circulatory system. It also allows you to view the miracles of nature and extend your gratitude for what is around you.

- *Temperance:* Don't indulge in any one thing. Temperance is the same as balance and can be practiced in eating, resting, exercising, and playing. Remember, all things in moderation.

- *Rest:* Our lives are quick, quick, quick, but your body and mind need time to rest and recuperate. Get as much rest as your body truly requires each night, and devote one day per week to restful pursuits.

- *Exercise:* Moving your body outside in fresh air removes poisons and toxins from your body. Get up in the morning and stretch, thanking your higher power for this new day. Walk or bike with the kids to school, if possible, or walk the dog around the block. Just walking from a farther parking space to your office or the market will do the trick.

- *Water:* Water is free or inexpensive, depending on what kind you like, so you can use it liberally. Doctors tell us to drink eight glasses a day for optimal health. It's the perfect beverage. You can also use water to take a warm bath or shower at night as part of a quieting bedtime ritual. You'll sleep much better for it.

- *Nutrition:* We are only as healthy as what we put in our bodies. When you are stressed or rushed, the temptation is to drive through a fast food place or eat a frozen meal, or worse, eat leftover from your children's plates. Your body helps you every day and deserves more than that. You can teach your children a lot about respecting yourself and the value of your body by sitting down to a good meal together each evening. I understand the pressures in your life. If you can't allow yourself or your kids thirty minutes in a twenty-four hour period to be kind to your body and soul, there's whole lot more work to be done here!

In addition, here are a few suggestions of my own:

- Only hang out with people who treat you with respect and kindness.

- Don't watch too much television news or reality-type shows. They are not beneficial to your mind or soul and can actually be quite depressing. Watch just enough news—or better yet, read the newspaper—to learn what's going on in the world and your community, and then switch it off. Reality shows are almost always humiliating and degrading, especially to women.

• Read good books. Now is the time to expose your mind to uplifting or classic books. When I started a book club with a friend of mine, my world instantly became better. I look forward to meeting with seven intelligent women and discussing our ideas about something fascinating we all read each month. Of course, the fact that we all contribute to a homemade dinner doesn't hurt, either.

• Find a passion. What did you love to do when you were a kid? Dance? Sing? Draw pictures? Look at birds? Rollerskate? Find a group that does this, and join in. You will be pursuing a lifelong love as well as meeting new people who enjoy the same things you do.

• Believe in yourself. You already have every single thing you've ever needed to make a success of your life, you just haven't believed it. Behind every tragedy is an opportunity, if you choose to see it that way and act on the opportunity portion of it.

Speaking of turning difficult life decisions into creative opportunities, let me share with you a little ditty I have posted on my refrigerator door (I can't have my children's school art there anymore; they've just graduated from college).

Attitude
by Charles Swindol (from *In Balance* magazine)

The longer I live, the more I realize the impact of attitude on life. Attitude, to me, is more important than facts. It is more important than the past, than education, than money, than circumstances, than failures, than successes, than what other people think or say or do. It is more important than appearance, giftedness, or skill. It will make or break a company … a church … a home. The remarkable thing is we have a choice every day regarding the attitude we will embrace for that day. We cannot change our past … we cannot change the fact that people will act in a certain way. We cannot change the inevitable. The only thing we can do is play on the one string that we have, and that is our attitude … I am convinced that life is 10 [percent] what happens to me and 90 [percent] how I react to it. And so it is with you … we are in charge of our attitudes.

There you have it: yet another person telling you that you have 100 percent control of how you think, act, and react. What you have experienced is a real tragedy. I feel horrible that you've had to experience all that you have. Yet, my sorrow for you—and indeed, your sorrow for yourself—will not change the past, any mistakes you have made, and decisions you reached long ago. You can ruminate on them from now until the end of time, and you will still be in exactly the same place you have been, wondering where your life went and when your life is going to begin.

My strong and lovely sister, here is one final thought to consider.

To Achieve Your Dreams Remember Your ABC's
by unknown author

Avoid negative sources, places, things, and habits.
Believe in yourself.
Consider things from every angle.
Don't give up, and don't give in.
Enjoy life today; yesterday is gone, and tomorrow may never come.
Family and friends are hidden treasures. Seek them and enjoy their riches.
Give more than you planned to.
Hang on to your dreams.
Ignore those who try to discourage you.
Just do it.
Keep trying no matter how hard it seems; it will get easier.
Love yourself first and most.
Make it happen.
Never lie, cheat, or steal … always strike a fair deal.
Open your eyes, and see things as they really are.
Practice makes perfect.
Quitters never win, and winners never quit.
Read, study, and learn about everything important in your life.
Stop procrastinating.
Take control of your own destiny.
Understand yourself in order to better understand others.
Visualize it.
Want it more than anything.
Xccelerate your efforts.
You are unique. Of all God's creatures, nothing can replace YOU.
Zero in on your target, and go for it!

Take good care of yourself. I have full confidence in you and your abilities. Your life will be wonderful if you make it so. Off you go!

Resource Guide

You have already accomplished so much in our work together. Now is your opportunity to make additional progress toward your own emotional well-being. This resource guide will help you move forward into new and clearer thinking about yourself and your relationships.

I have included books and Web sites that I have found useful both as a woman and as a therapist. I have referred patients and friends to the sources I list for you. I have not included counseling agencies or individual therapists, because the choice of a therapist is a very personal one based on a relationship you build with that person. However, should you desire counseling, be assured that there are therapeutic services available at every monetary level. If you look in the front of your telephone book under county mental health agencies, you will find useful information to help you begin this process. The best way to find a good individual therapist is to ask a friend or colleague who has used a therapist she trusts and who has helped them.

You may find other good avenues for finding counseling through your house of worship or the YWCA.

Again, my best to you, and I hope you find this resource guide helpful.

ABUSIVE RELATIONSHIPS

BOOKS

Anderson, Vera. *A Woman Like You: The Face of Domestic Violence.* Seattle, WA: Seal Press, 1997.

Betancourt, Marian. *What to Do When Love Turns Violent: A Practical Resource for Women in Abusive Relationships.* NY: HarperPerennial Library, 1997.

Dugan, Meg Kennedy and Roger Hock. *It's My Life Now: Starting Over After An Abusive Relationship or Domestic Violence.* NY: Routledge, 2000.

Elgin, Dr. Suzette Haden. *You Can't Say That to Me!: Stopping the Pain of Verbal Abuse—an Eight-Step Plan.* NY: John Wiley and Sons, Inc.,1995.

Ellis, Dr. Albert and Marcia Grad Powers: *The Secret of Overcoming Verbal Abuse: Getting Off the Emotional Roller Coaster and Regaining Control of Your Life.* Hollywood, CA: Wilshire Book Company, 2000.

Engel, Beverly. *The Emotionally Abused Woman: Overcoming Destructive Patterns and Reclaiming Yourself.* NY: Ballantine Books, 1990.

Evans, Patricia. *Verbal Abuse Survivors Speak Out on Relationship and Recovery.* Holbrook, MA: Bob Adams Inc., 1993.

Forward, Dr. Susan. *Emotional Blackmail: when the People in Your Life Use Fear, Obligation, and Guilt to Manipulate You.* NY: HarperPerennial, 1997.

Greer, Dr. Jane. *How Could You Do This to Me?: Learning to Trust Again after Betrayal.* NY: Doubleday Books, 1997.

Hegstrom, Paul. *Angry Men and the Women Who Love Them: Breaking the Cycle of Physical and Emotional Abuse.* Kansas City, MO: Beacon Hill Press, 1999.

Jones, Ann and Susan Schecter. *When Love Goes Wrong: What to Do When You Can't Do Anything Right.* NY: HarperPerennial, 1992.

Mariani, Cliff and Patricia Sokolich. *Domestic Violence Survival Guide.* Fresh Meadows, NY: Looseleaf Law Publishing Corp., 1996.

McDill, Linda and S. Rutherford McDill. *Dangerous Marriage: Breaking the Cycle of Domestic Violence.* NY: Spire Books, 1998.

Miles, Reverend Al and Catherine Clark Kroeger. *Domestic Violence: What Every Pastor Needs to Know.* NY: Fortress Press, 2000.

Miles, Reverend Al and Marie Fortune. *Violence in Families: What Every Christian Needs to Know.* NY: Ausburg Fortress Publishers, 2002.

Miller, Dr. Mary Susan. *No Visible Wounds: Identifying Nonphysical Abuse of Women by Their Men.* NY: Fawcett Columbine Books, 1995.

Murphy-Milano, Susan. *Defending Our Lives: Getting Away from Domestic Violence and Staying Safe*. NY: Anchor Books, 1996.

Murray, Dr. Jill. *But I Love Him: Protecting Your Teen Daughter from Controlling, Abusive Dating Relationships*. NY: ReganBooks, 2000.

Murray, Dr. Jill. *Destructive Relationships: A Guide to Changing the Unhealthy Relationships in Your Life*. San Diego, CA: Jodere Group, 2002.

Nelson, Noelle. *Dangerous Relationships: How to Stop Domestic Violence Before it Stops You*. Cambridge, MA: Perseus Press, 1997.

NiCarthy, Ginny, M.S.W. *Getting Free: You Can End Abuse and Take Back Your Life*. Seattle, WA: Seal Press, 1997.

O'Leary, Dr. Daniel and Roland D. Mauiro. *Psychological Abuse in Violent Relationships*. NY: Springer Publications, 2001.

Renzetta, Claire and Charles Harvey Miley. *Violence in Gay and Lesbian Domestic Partnerships*. Binghamton, NY: Haworth Press, 1996.

WEB SITES

Keyword: Domestic Violence. There are more than 200,000 sites, so there you will find many links to information, support groups, books, and organizations specializing in domestic violence. You can narrow your search by specifying the area in which you are interested.

www.lizclaiborne.com. This clothing manufacturer has just started a very interesting and helpful Web site.

ORGANIZATIONS

National Domestic Violence Hotline: 800-788-SAFE. This is a twenty-four-hour referral service for domestic violence shelters and therapists specializing in the treatment of abusive relationships.

CHILDHOOD TRAUMA AND ABUSIVE FAMILIES

BOOKS

Bass, Ellen and Laura Davis. *The Courage to Heal: A Guide for Women Survivors of Child Sexual Abuse.* NY: HarperPerennial, 1994.

Bass, Ellen and Louise Thornton. *I Never Told Anyone: Writings by Women Survivors of Child Sexual Abuse.* NY: HarperCollins, 1991.

Farmer, Steven. *Adult Children of Abusive Parents: A Healing Program for Those Who Have Been Physically, Sexually, or Emotionally Abused.* NY: Ballantine Books, 1990.

Forward, Dr. Susan. *Toxic Parents: Overcoming their Hurtful Legacy and Reclaiming Your Life.* NY: Bantam Books, 1990.

Gil, Eliana. *Outgrowing the Pain: A Book for and About Adults Abused as Children.* NY: DTP Books, 1998.

McCarthy, Barry and Emily McCarthy. *Confronting the Victim Role: Healing from an Abusive Childhood.* NY: Carroll and Graff, 1993.

Napier, Nancy. *Getting Through the Day: Strategies for Adults Hurt as Children.* NY: W.W. Norton and Co., 1994.

Neuharth, Dan. *If You Had Controlling Parents: How to Make Peace with Your Past and Take Your Place in the World.* NY: Cliff Street Books, 1999.

Wisechild, Louise. *The Mother I Carry: A Memoir of Healing from Emotional Abuse.* Seattle, WA, 1993.

WEB SITES

Keywords: Childhood abuse, sexual abuse. There are many links to information, support groups, books, and organizations specializing in recovery of childhood abuse of all kinds.

www.ksu.edu/ucs/dysfunc.html. A Web site containing books and support groups dealing with dysfunctional families.

www.boxplanet.com. A Web site dedicated to information about rejecting and neglectful parents.

ORGANIZATIONS

Adults Molested as Children (AMAC). Phone numbers are different for each city. Look in the community services guide in the front of your telephone directory.

SELF-ESTEEM, SHAME AND GUILT, AND EMOTIONAL WELL-BEING

BOOKS

Aron, Elaine. *The Highly Sensitive Person: How to Thrive When the World Overwhelms You.* NY: Broadway Books, 1999.

Bach, George R. And Herb Goldberg. *Creative Aggression: The Art of Assertive Living.* Gretna, LA: Wellness Institute Books, 1974.

Branden, Nathaniel. *Honoring the Self: The Psychology of Confidence and Respect.* NY: Bantam Books, 1985.

Branden, Nathaniel. *The Six Pillars of Self-Esteem.* NY: Bantam Books, 1995.

Branden, Nathaniel. *How to Raise Your Self-Esteem.* NY: Bantam Books, 1988.

Bradshaw, John. *Healing the Shame that Binds You.* Deerfield Beach, FL: Health Communications, Inc., 1988.

Burns, David, M.D. *The Feeling Good Handbook.* NY: Penguin Books, 1990.

Burns, David, M.D. *Ten Days to Self-Esteem.* San Francisco, CA: Quill Books, 1999.

Jampolsky, Gerald M.D. *Forgiveness: The Greatest Healer of All.* Hillsboro, OR: Beyond Words Publishing Co., 1999.

Matthews, Andrew. *Being Happy: A Handbook to Greater Confidence and Security.* NY: Price Stern Sloan, 1990.

Mellody, Pia. *Facing Codependence.* NY: HarperCollins, 1989.

Middleton-Moz, Jane. *Shame and Guilt: Masters of Disguise.* Deerfield Beach, FL: Health Communications Inc., 1990.

Potter, Ronald and Patricia Potter-Efron. *Letting Go of Shame.* Center City, MN: Hazelden Information Education, 1996.

Sanford, Linda and Mary Ellen Donovan. *Women and Self-Esteem.* NY: Viking Press, 1995.

Steinem, Gloria. *Revolution from Within: A Book of Self-Esteem.* NY: Little, Brown, and Co., 1993.

Vanzant, Iyanla. *Faith in the Valley: Lessons for Women on the Journey Toward Peace.* NY: Simon and Schuster, 1996.

WEB SITES

www.theselfesteeminstitute.com. A Web site dealing with issues of self-esteem.

www.breakingthechain.com. This Web site is dedicated to issues of self-esteem, social anxiety, and anger.

www.aolwomen.com. This Web site has many good articles and resources dealing with all aspects of women's emotional and physical health and well-being.

www.ivillage.com. A Web site dealing with most aspects of women's emotional health and well-being, as well as physical health articles, support groups, and chat rooms. Something for everyone.

PERSONAL EMPOWERMENT

BOOKS

Capacchione, Lucia. *Visioning: Ten Steps to Designing the Life of Your Dreams.* NY: JP Tarcher, 2000.

Canfield, Jack et al. *Chicken Soup for the Woman's Soul: 101 Stories to Open the Hearts and Rekindle the Spirits of Women.* Deerfield Beach, FL: Health Communications Inc., 1996.

Cohen, Alan H. *Why Your Life Sucks: ... And What You Can Do About It.* San Diego, CA: Jodere Group, 2002.

Covey, Stephen. *The Seven Habits of Highly Effective People.* NY: Fireside Books, 1990.

Ellis, David. *Creating Your Own Future.* Boston, MA: Houghton Mifflin, 1999.

Jeffers, Susan. *Feel the Fear and Do It Anyway.* NY: Fawcett Books, 1992.

Luhrs, Janet. *The Simple Living Guide.* NY: Broadway Books, 1997.

Markova, Dawna. *I Will Not Die an Unlived Life: Reclaiming Purpose and Passion.* Berkley, CA Conari Press, 2000.

Martin, Katherine. *Women of Courage: Inspiring Stories from the Women Who Lived Them.* Novato, CA: New World Library, 1999.

McGraw, Dr. Phillip. *Life Strategies: Doing What Works, Doing What Matters.* NY: Hyperion, 1999.

McMeekin, Carl. *The Twelve Steps of Highly Creative Women: A Portable Mentor.* Berkeley, CA: Conari Press, 2000.

Nepo, Mark. *The Book of Awakening: Having the Life You Want By Being Present to the Life You Have.* Berkeley, CA: Conari Press, 2000.

Richardson, Cheryl. *Life Makeovers.* NY: Broadway Books, 2000.

Richardson, Cheryl. *Take Time for Your Life: A Personal Coach's Seven-Step Program for Creating the Life You Want.* NY: Broadway Books, 1999.

Robbins, Anthony et al. *Unlimited Power: The New Science of Personal Achievement.* NY: Fireside Books, 1997.

NEW RELATIONSHIPS ... OR NOT

BOOKS

Anders, Dana et al. *Single and Content.* Nashville, TN: W. Publishing, 1999.

Clements, Marcelle. *The Improvised Woman: Single Women Reinventing Single Life.* NY: WWW Norton and Co., 1999.

Collins, Dr. Bryn. *How to Recognize Emotional Unavailability and Make Healthier Relationship Choices.* NY: MFJ Books, 1997.

Cowan, Connell and Melvyn Kinder. *Smart Women/Foolish Choices: Finding the Right Men, Avoiding the Wrong Ones.* NY: New American Library, 1991.

Forward, Dr. Susan and Joan Torres. *Men Who Hate Women and the Women Who Love Them.* NY: Bantam Books, 1987.

Norwood, Robin. *Women Who Love Too Much: Why You Keep Wishing and Hoping He'll Change.* NY: Pocket Books, 1991.

Schlessinger, Dr. Laura. *Ten Stupid Things Women Do to Mess Up Their Lives.* NY: HarperPerennial, 1994.

Widder, Wendy. *Living Whole Without a Better Half.* Grand Rapids, MI: Kregel Publications, 2000.

Zobel, Allia. *The Joy of Being Single.* NY: Workman Publications, 1992.

WEB SITES

www.ivillage.com. Again, this Web site deals with relationship issues and has chat rooms so that women can share stories and experiences while offering each other advice. There are also many Internet matchmaking services. Key in "matchmaking" to find these.

ORGANIZATIONS

A good many organizations that serve as matchmaking services are listed in local magazines or on the Internet, as mentioned above. Parents Without Partners is a national organization that can be found in the community services section of your telephone book.

About the Author

Dr. Jill Murray has become the leading authority on teenage abusive dating relationships both nationally and internationally. She is already familiar to the millions who have seen and heard her on more than 300 television and 250 radio talk shows, including *Oprah* and *Montel, 20/20, Good Morning America, Leeza, John Walsh,* and *Dr. Laura.*

At the suggestion of Oprah Winfrey, Dr. Murray wrote her first book, *But I Love Him—Protecting Your Teen Daughter From Controlling, Abusive Dating Relationships.* which has become the seminal book to parents, teens, and those who work with children on the subject of teen dating abuse. Her second book, *Destructive Relationships—A Guide to Changing the Unhealthy Relationships in Your Life,* has been called "two years of therapy in a book" and has received wide acclaim.

Dr. Murray has taught at the graduate level and is a highly sought-after guest lecturer and keynote presenter at conferences across the country and in Canada. Additionally, she speaks nationally to more than 100,000 teens and their parents each year on the subject of dating relationships. She also lectures on the topics of domestic violence, parenting issues, motivation, and creating healthy adult relationships.

Dr. Murray maintains a private practice in Laguna Niguel, California, as well as a Web site—www.drjillmurray.com—at which she answers several hundred e-mail letters per week. She lives with her husband and two adorable Shelties and is the proud mother of twenty-five-year-old twins.

978-0-595-41139

0-595-41139-8